Qualitative Research Methods in Psychology

Combining Core Approaches

Qualitative Research Methods in Psychology

Combining Core Approaches

Nollaig Frost

Open University Press

Open University Press
McGraw-Hill Education
McGraw-Hill House
Shoppenhangers Road
Maidenhead
Berkshire
England
SL6 2QL

email: enquiries@openup.co.uk
world wide web: www.openup.co.uk

and Two Penn Plaza, New York, NY 10121-2289, USA

First published 2011

A catalogue record of this book is available from the British Library

ISBN-13: 978-0-33-524151-4 (pb) 978-0-33-524150-7 (hb)
ISBN-10: 0-33-524151-4 (pb) 0-33-524150-6 (hb)
eISBN: 978-0-33-524152-1

Library of Congress Cataloging-in-Publication Data
CIP data applied for

Typeset by RefineCatch Limited, Bungay, Suffolk
Printed in the UK by Bell & Bain Ltd, Glasgow

The **McGraw·Hill** Companies

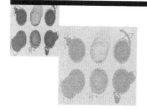

Table of Contents

Contributors

NOLLAIG FROST (Editor) is Senior Lecturer in Psychology at Middlesex University. She has been teaching qualitative research to students at all levels for several years, and uses this approach to pursue her research in motherhood and mental illness. She has led the Pluralism in Qualitative Research (PQR) project since its inception in 2006.

CIGDEM ESIN is Lecturer in Psychosocial Studies at the University of East London. Her research interests are in interactions between individual stories and grand sociocultural narratives, and interconnections between gender, power and politics within historically specific contexts. Her recent research focuses on constructions of sexual narratives among educated young women in modern Turkey.

AMANDA HOLT is Senior Lecturer in Criminal Psychology at the Institute of Criminal Justice Studies at the University of Portsmouth. Her main research interests lie in critical psychology, qualitative methodologies and psychosocial approaches. Current research includes parenting and youth justice, parent abuse and violence in schools.

SEVASTI-MELISSA NOLAS is Lecturer in Psychology at Middlesex University. She studies policy interventions from a social psychological perspective, focusing on conditions that enable or inhibit social change, how people make sense of, respond to or initiate change, and the consequences of both top-down and bottom-up approaches to social change.

PNINA SHINEBOURNE is Senior Lecturer in Psychology at Middlesex University and Lecturer on the Professional Doctorate Programme in Existential Psychotherapy/Counselling Psychology at the New School of Psychotherapy and Counselling. Her research focus is on women's experience of addiction and recovery, with a particular focus on metaphors and images used in participants' verbal accounts and visual materials.

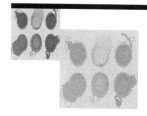

Acknowledgements

Much of the work described in this book has arisen from the research of the Pluralism in Qualitative Research (PQR) team (Nollaig Frost, Belinda Brooks-Gordon, Cigdem Esin, Amanda Holt, Leila Mehdizadeh, Sevasti-Melissa Nolas and Pnina Shinebourne). The study was initially funded by Birkbeck and then by the Qualitative Methods Section of the British Psychological Society. Invaluable assistance and support has come from colleagues. Thanks also to Zainab Ebrahim, Anthony Murphy and Rebekah Griffin. The unswerving support of Monika Lee at Open UP has been greatly appreciated. Special thanks to Nick, Sam and Leona, and Derek and Eleanor, for all their unswerving support.

PART 1
Some Core Approaches

Part Contents

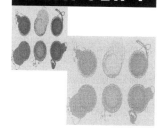

CHAPTER 1

Qualitative Research in Psychology

Nollaig Frost

Introduction: this book

Qualitative research methodology in psychology is now well established. The authors of the *Handbook of Qualitative Methods in Psychology* (2008), Carla Willig and Wendy Stainton Rogers, suggest that this approach has moved from the 'margins to the mainstream in psychology in the UK' (2008: 8), and many other researchers and writers attest to its widespread use elsewhere (e.g. Bryman, 2006; Dicks, Soyinka & Coffey, 2006; Golden-Biddle & Locke, 2007).

In this book we will be describing ways to use qualitative methodology in psychology research. We will outline the single use of four commonly used methods – grounded theory, interpretative phenomenological analysis (IPA), discourse analysis and narrative analysis – and then consider how these can be used in combination. In each chapter we will be providing a history of the method and careful consideration of when and how it might be used. We will look at why we might want to use more than one qualitative method, and what this might tell us about the topic of inquiry and about the research process. By the end of the book you will have insight to the detailed use and application of qualitative research methodology, and an understanding of why and how to select a single method or pluralistic approach to your qualitative research.

Each chapter in the book provides a history of each method, it aims to put into context the way in which the beginnings of a desire by psychology researchers to look beyond objective measurement and rating of causal behaviour led to new ways to elicit 'thick' description (Geertz, 1973) of human experience. The chapters will discuss how each qualitative method can be employed singly to examine data to illuminate meanings and insights not available without considering aspects of the research process such as the role played by the researcher, the context of the data elicitation and the uniqueness of the participant perspective. The book will consider how research questions are developed and how these influence the choice of method. It will focus on the philosophies and assumptions underlying each approach so that as researchers you can make an informed choice about the methodological framework within which you approach your research.

We focus in this book on four of the most commonly used methods, and they demonstrate the many aspects of qualitative data inquiry. They range from ways of examining language use (e.g. discursive psychology, discourse analysis) to looking through data for themes and codes (e.g. IPA, grounded theory) to seeking out stories and their meanings in accounts provided by participants (narrative analysis). What is striking about these methods is that there is always a choice of how to apply them, which models to employ and the reasons for using them in pursuit of meaningful research outcomes. It is this plurality within single methods that led to the development of Part 2 of this book. This looks at plurality across methods in pursuit of a more holistic understanding of the phenomenon under inquiry.

Table 1.1 Methods focused on in this book

Grounded Theory	Asks questions about a range of psychological processes. It asks about what is happening as well as how and why.
Discourse Analysis	Asks questions about how language is used. It investigates what is said as well as why it might be said.
Interpretative Phenomenological Analysis (IPA)	Asks questions about how individuals make sense of their world. It seeks insight to the meanings that events and experiences hold for people.
Narrative Analysis	Asks questions about how individuals make meaning using stories. It seeks understanding of the unique perspective brought by individuals to make sense of their external and internal worlds.

Combining Methods

The combining of different methods of inquiry in psychology is not new. Mixed-method approaches to research have used qualitative and quantitative methods in combination for some time. Mixed-method approaches might be used to enrich or populate data, to find a way to triangulate findings or to conduct a pilot study in order to inform a large-scale quantitatively orientated project (Todd *et al.*, 2004). Mixed-method approaches are commonly found in health psychology and medically related research, and in market research, where funders are often keen to see numbers, objectivity and generalisability, but where researchers want to support the process with rich description of experience from the perspective of the individual patient, client, practitioner or consumer. Several developments in approaches to research have arisen from the application of mixed-method approaches. These include pragmatism (e.g. Onwuegbuzie & Leech, 2005), bricolage (Denzin & Lincoln, 2000; Kincheloe, 2001; 2005) and multiperspectival analysis (Kellner, 1995). All seek to access as much meaning as possible from data but are applied in slightly different ways depending on the research questions and rationale for the research.

Pragmatism

Pragmatism is commonly regarded simply as a means with which research questions can be addressed and an approach that does not take too much account of the underlying epistemologies of the approaches used to do this. Pragmatic researchers may use science, art and social interaction in any combination in order to obtain a richer account of experience (Yardley & Bishop, 2008). They are less concerned with the epistemological debates underlying method, and instead set out to use whichever techniques will answer or address the research question. For example, they may use a mixed-method approach in the pursuit of practical outcomes, as seen in clinical practice, or for other pragmatic reasons such as to satisfy funders. The research question becomes central to the research process, and the issue of deciding which methods to use to answer it becomes more important than the philosophies or paradigms underlying the methods. The 'pragmatic' approach (Tashakkori & Teddlie, 1998; Onwuegbuzie & Leech, 2005), in common with the bricolage approach (Denzin & Lincoln, 2000; Kincheloe, 2001; 2005), advocates the combining of methodological ontologies in the pursuit of a more extensive understanding of the needs of human beings (Howard, 1983).

> ### *Problem-based question*
>
> You are a student researcher interested in pursuing a career in counselling psychology. While on placement you have been invited to join a research team made up of psychotherapists, psychiatrists and mental health service users. The aim of the research is to investigate the outcomes of six weeks of cognitive behavioural therapy sessions. It is decided to use both quantitative and qualitatively orientated approaches to investigate this. Why might you use each approach to research this topic?

Bricolage

Bricolage, first outlined by Denzin and Lincoln (2000), is a research approach that promotes interdisciplinarity as a way of drawing on many methods of inquiry. It regards the research process as consisting of many elements and is concerned with the theoretical and philosophical underpinnings of these as well as with the object, topic or phenomenon or other artefact under study. It is an approach that seeks to avoid the limitations imposed by employing a single method, such as limitations of its **epistemology**, and the 'traditional practices of' (Kincheloe, 2001: 681) or 'the historicity of certified modes of knowledge production' (Kincheloe, 2001: 681), by seeking out a **rigour** that leads to new ontological insights. This means that context is paramount in the bricolage approach, and objects of inquiry are regarded as firmly embedded within their social and cultural construction, historical situatedness and the language used to describe them. By examining the object within this context, using whatever methods necessary the bricoleur views the research from many perspectives in order to gain multiperspectival insight to its complexity.

Question

What do you think are the main differences between bricolage and pragmatism?

Multiperspectival analysis

The notion of multiperspectival analysis has been promoted by Kellner (1995). It too draws on multimethodological research strategies and does so to introduce a variety of ways of 'seeing and interpreting in the pursuit of knowledge' (Kincheloe, 2001: 682). This approach reduces the impact of assumptions and limitations brought to the research process by allowing the researcher to see the phenomenon in more dimensions than if they employed a single-method approach. The multiperspectival approach can be taken by employing flexible use of one particular method (see Mason, 2006) or by drawing on many methods or disciplines to enhance dimensional insight and illuminate the complexity of the phenomenon under study.

The three approaches highlighted above are described in order to enable some of the issues that may arise in considering a pluralistic qualitative approach to be illuminated. Issues of the role of epistemology, **ontology**, purpose and approach to the research are all of great importance when considering how you will find out more about your topic of inquiry.

Research Example

Employing a flexible narrative analysis approach (Frost, 2009b)

In a flexible use of narrative analysis I employed different models of narrative analysis to work with data gathered to explore the transition from first- to second-time motherhood among middle-class British white women (see Frost, 2006; 2009b). I sought to extract as much meaning as I could about each woman's hopes, fears, fantasies, expectations and realities during this time from the transcripts of semi-structured interviews I conducted with them. I used different approaches to analyse narratives I located within the data. These included systematically reducing the text using approaches such as Labov's structural model (1972), Gee's linguistic model (1993), Riesmann's performative model (1993), and Emerson and Frosh's critical model (2004). This allowed me to examine the meaning brought to the text by particular linguistic features, and to critically consider my role in the research process by investigating the stories and the way they were told in the interviews. The flexible narrative analysis approach draws on the strengths offered by each model it employs to privilege the narrator's words. It takes guidance from the interview text in each phase of analysis, and layers of understanding of the account are built up. The initial understanding of the story is gradually enriched by systematic exploration of the text until a new story emerges. Each finding contributes to the resultant multidimensional understanding of the meaning of the narrative. The approach resembles triangulation methods in its ambition to view data from different perspectives, seeking not to verify meanings but to add texture to the interpretation of them.

For full details of this study, see Frost, N. (2009b) 'Do you know what I mean?': the use of a pluralistic narrative analysis approach in the interpretation of an interview. *Qualitative Research*, 9(1), 9–29. It is also discussed further in Chapters 5 and 7.

Triangulation

The notion of using more than one method to 'find out more' about a phenomenon has traditionally been used to verify or support findings. Researchers use more than one method (often a qualitative one with a quantitative one) in order to 'triangulate' the outcomes of measurements and observations (Todd *et al.*, 2004). Qualitative researchers, however, are not seeking to validate any claim about the experiences or their possible meanings, but to explore how understanding of them can be enhanced. Qualitative researchers using phenomenological or constructivist paradigms are not in pursuit of a definitive truth about experience. They do not regard reality as fixed, but instead understand individuals to bring a unique perspective to the way they see and comprehend the world around them. The researcher into these experiences may use different methods to bring different ways of understanding the data, and to highlight complementary, contradictory or absent findings within it.

Recent work (Moran-Ellis et al., 2006) has identified different forms of triangulation that can be derived from the combining of methods in pursuit of 'knowing more' (Moran-Ellis et al., 2006: 45) about a phenomenon. These researchers distinguish between 'integration' of methods, which can be understood as 'a particular, practical relationship between methods, sets of data, analytic findings and perspectives' (Moran-Ellis et al., 2006: 46), and 'triangulation', which 'incorporates an epistemological claim about the research' (Moran-Ellis et al., 2006: 46). They emphasise that the meaning of triangulation has been extended beyond seeking increased confidence (or validity) in results, as might traditionally have been its reason for use in mixed qualitative-quantitative research. This is an evolution of the traditional approach to triangulation, which uses different methods in order to counter biases and assumptions brought by one method alone, and regards differences in findings as examples of flaws or biases in measurement. When using methods of different epistemologies (whether positivist and interpretivist, as may be found in some quantitative-qualitative combinations, or social constructionist and critical realist, as may be found in some qualitative-qualitative mixing) triangulation can offer a more in-depth, multidimensional insight to the complexity of the social world. It can generate 'complementarity' (Moran-Ellis et al., 2006: 48) instead of highlighting flaws in measurements. It can 'reflect different aspects of a phenomenon' (Moran-Ellis et al., 2006: 48), and inform researchers about both the phenomenon under study and the research process. This broadening of the meaning of triangulation within social science supports the pragmatic researchers who are more concerned with the technical framework of pluralistic research than the epistemological or theoretical one.

Research Example

In our pluralistic work with interviews elicited from women making the transition to second-time motherhood (Frost, 2006; Frost et al., 2010) none of our findings appeared to contradict each other and so we understood this approach to have provided us with a way of 'generating complementarity' (e.g. Greene, Caracelli & Graham, 1989). It provided us with different understandings of the phenomenon under study to be reflections of its different aspects (Moran-Ellis et al., 2006). Our approach was a pragmatic one that was interested in both the insight gained to the phenomenon of transitioning to second-time motherhood, and the process by which we came to derive our understanding of individual experience. In adopting this approach we focused on the role of the researchers as well as on the techniques of analysis that they employed. Epistemological claims were social constructionist so that we took the view that each researcher entered into their own relationship with the data, and that this played a unique role in transforming the data to a presentation of the findings (see Frost et al., 2011).

Paradigms in competition

While both qualitative and quantitatively orientated approaches to research serve valuable purposes in furthering research aims, mixed-method approaches have been criticised for combining qualitative and quantitative paradigms. It is argued by some that the differing philosophies underlying each of these designs mean that they cannot be combined. The results of such criticisms have been to see the paradigms placed in competition with each other. Many eminent researchers have taken issue with this. Ann Oakley labelled the criticisms 'a paradigm war' (Oakley, 1999); she argues against this, saying that there is a place for both approaches and that without both it is not easy to see whether, for example, personal experiences are individual or collective oppression (1999: 251). She highlights that she has perceived animosity directed at her work on the basis that it leans too much towards one paradigm or another. She expresses her 'puzzlement' (1999: 248) at having her work labelled as 'old Oakley' and 'new Oakley', based on the methodologies that she employed over the years, at being asked to account for the difference in her writing and at being accused of 'letting the qualitative and feminist sides down' (1999: 248). Importantly, Oakley emphasises that 'all methods must be open, consistently applied and replicable by others' (1999: 252). She stresses that, instead of undergoing some sort of conversion away from qualitative research, it is more important to ask why different research methods are seen as opposing in the first place.

This question, first asked in 1999, is now increasingly regarded as moot. Subsequent debates about mixing methods (e.g. Tashakkori & Teddlie, 1998; 2003) have led to a 'paradigm peace' (Bryman, 2006), and other questions, such as those about quality criteria and evaluation of mixed-method research, are being asked (Bryman, 2006). Researchers have taken positions in which they either choose to overlook or marginalise issues of coherence/incoherence in epistemology and ontology in favour of applying methods best suited to the research question. The research question is paramount and it is assumed that 'Mixed methods research can answer research questions that the other methodologies cannot.' (Teddlie and Tashakkori, 2003: 14, cited in Bryman, 2006: 118).

CASE STUDY

As a final-year undergraduate student you have the choice of choosing any topic you like to carry out research. You decide to focus on something of which you have personal experience: the death of a close family member. You decide to research how other students have experienced bereavement. To begin the study, you want to find out how many students in your cohort have had this experience. How will you do this, bearing in mind that this is a sensitive topic that may upset people?

▶

▶ Once you know who has been bereaved you want to explore what it was like for them. How would you gather such data?

Once this decision is made you start analysing the data you have collected. You have some numbers and some words. What might you do with them?

In doing the analysis you sometimes find yourself feeling upset and reliving your own experience of being bereaved. What will you do about this?

You may not be able to answer all these questions yet, particularly if you are new to research. They are designed to start you thinking about how much you already know about conducting research and what aspects you may want to focus on when using this book. For example, were you clear about which methods to choose? What about defining your research question? How were you going to address the ethical considerations of this study, and how were you going to bring reflexive practice into your research?

Pluralism in qualitative research

In our research we have adopted many of the same reasons for combining qualitative methods with each other as mixed-method researchers do: we take a largely pragmatic view that it is important to find the best methods to address the research question; we are concerned to conduct research that is useful and worthwhile. We concur fully with Oakley that the research methods must be open, and would also agree with Bryman and others that quality criteria that are applicable to one method are not always the best to be applied to another (e.g. Bryman, 2006; 2007). The pluralistic approach that we adopt may be seen to be more towards the agnostic end of a range that places methods as a means of profiling political and ethical issues at one end (e.g. Parker, 1992) and a focus on understanding how methods can illuminate specific phenomena or processes at the other (Willig & Stainton-Rogers, 2008). As Bryman says in relation to mixed-method research, we are concerned to 'access as much as possible within the data' (Bryman, 2006) in our adoption of a qualitative pluralistic approach.

Areas of research in which pluralism has been used include studies into anomalous experience (Coyle, 2010), the movement of youth identity through space and time (Katsiaficas *et al.*, 2011), and the management and repair of shame (Leeming & Boyle, 2004). It has been discussed in a Special Issue of *Qualitative Research* (2006) in relation to triangulation (Moran-Ellis *et al.*, 2006) and multi-modal **ethnography** (Dicks, Soyinka & Coffey, 2006). The PQR team have published papers on the impact of researchers on pluralistic work (Frost *et al.*, 2010), and on issues of interpretation in pluralistic work (Frost *et al.*, 2011). A forthcoming Special Issue of the *Qualitative Research in Psychology* journal will focus on a variety of questions raised by employment of a pluralistic qualitative approach through invited papers (Frost & Nolas, Eds 2011). Some research methods incorporate pluralistic working as an essential part of their approach. One example is memory work, in which researchers form a collective within which each member contributes a memory and the group analyses it (see Frost *et al.* (forthcoming) for more details of some of the issues that arose for one group in carrying out this approach). With the re- emergence of pluralism in psychological research (early calls were made in 1983 (Howard) and have surfaced periodically since then (e.g. Burck, 2005; Mason, 2006)) the arguments about whether, and how, methods with differing assumptions can be combined with each other considered what constitutes knowledge and reality.

We examine some of these arguments throughout this book by considering the perspectives and insight brought by each method. Perspectives may be informed by epistemological or ontological positions and also by the personal assumptions, cultural knowledge and other contextual information that each researcher brings to their employment of the chosen method(s). The chapters about the different ways in which each method might be employed (Chapters 2, 3, 4 and 5) consider in detail the epistemological and reflexive practice arguments and their influence on application. The remaining chapters (Chapters 6, 7 and 8) consider practical and theoretical concerns in carrying out research with a pluralistic approach.

Why might you want to carry out qualitative research pluralistically?

As we have seen, there can be many reasons for carrying out research pluralistically. It may be to achieve the richest experience possible, as in the pragmatic approach, to draw on the most appropriate tools to address the research question, as in the bricolage approach, or to gain different perspectives on a phenomenon, as in the multi-perspectival approach. Different methods may be employed in combination in order to achieve different forms of triangulation of the data. In this book we focus on using only qualitative methods in combination. We discuss how this may help in gaining greater insight to a number of research topics. As researchers you may want to gain as much insight as you can to individual experience, you may want to gain insight to previously under-researched areas, to include participants in the research process, to find news ways of looking at a previously researched phenomenon, to highlight lack of research in some areas of psychology or to use your own experiences to gain insight to others' experiences of culture or language difference. In all cases you will be considering, at the very least, the context in which the research is being conducted, the uniqueness of the participants' perspective in their recounting of their experiences, your role in the process and the methods you have brought to the transformation of the data. By bringing **reflexivity**, context and interpretation to the research process the qualitative approach is distinguished from the objective, positivistic assumptions brought to quantitatively orientated research. It allows researchers to access some insight to the meanings that individuals make of their experiences. Researchers can go further, using other methods to consider other aspects of the phenomenon. For example, using narrative analysis researchers can inquire into how this meaning-making informs individual sense of identity, or using discourse analysis to see the context within which individuals create meaning through language in their social interactions. Methods such as IPA seek out chains of understanding so that from the accounts provided by individuals the illumination of themes can lead the researcher through the linguistic, to the affective, physical and cognitive lived experience of the individual. Each chapter in this book focuses in detail on the way in which each method, used singly or in combination with another, can facilitate these insights.

The background to the book

In our own research the authors of this book came to develop their individual interest in pluralistic qualitative research in different ways. Much of our initial curiosity was piqued during our doctoral research, in which many of us were supported and educated in qualitative ways by knowledgeable and informed supervisors. We were enabled to think around our topic and its method of inquiry and, in taking ownership of our work, to start questioning some of the aspects of our approach. We asked questions that we considered essential to conducting high-quality research, such as:

- How do we know as lone researchers that other researchers using the same method would have found (or not found) similar meanings in the data we have?
- How do we know that the same data examined using different methods would not have illuminated different insights?
- Where is a space for contradiction or qualitative triangulation in single-method research? Is it needed?

Overall we were wondering if there was more meaning that could be accessed in our data, and how we could find out about this while retaining our desires to prioritise the participant and the recounting of their experiences. Pluralism seemed to offer a way to do this and in exploring this we came across a number of further questions: questions about epistemology, ontology, reflexivity, data transformation and research presentation, for example. Along the way we presented our work to many other researchers, academics and practitioners in several fields of psychology from across Europe. These researchers now form the Network for Pluralism in Qualitative Research (N-PQR; see www.npqr.wordpress.com) and a quick glance at its site shows the varied topics of research in which this approach is being applied.

The pluralistic approach can now be considered in detail, and this book aims to present the discussions and debates that have been held about this approach so far.

Book structure

This book is organised in two parts, but each chapter follows broadly the same structure. In Part 1, we take each method and discuss it in detail in a way that aims to show how and why you can employ it in your own research. We present some background to its development and use, and describe various ways in which it is applied. Typical research questions are described alongside several examples of its use. Challenges and particular considerations of each method, such as application, ethics, data elicitation and participant recruitment, are considered. Each chapter is liberally scattered with contemporary research examples as well as with some problem-based questions to get you thinking. Each method chapter is written by a researcher who has personally employed this method (Sevasti-Melissa Nolas – grounded theory, Pnina Shinebourne – IPA, Amanda Holt – discourse analysis, and Cigdem Esin – narrative analysis) and to illuminate their experience of it each chapter includes a 'Reflection on Practice'. We hope that in addition to providing you with a way to get closer to the experience of applying this method to some of the questions that arose for the individual researchers when they did that, this feature will enable you to reflect on your own use or contemplation of using this method.

In Part 2 we extend the discussion to consider how and why the methods might be used in combination. In this part of the book we focus on the particular issues, challenges and benefits of pragmatics in pluralistic research, interpreting data pluralistically and writing up pluralistic research. The concluding chapter looks at how this approach has been applied and considers the next steps in its use within psychology. The chapters in Part 2 follow a similar structure to those in Part 1 and include the same useful features of research examples drawn from around the world, problem-based questions and reflections on practice.

Whether you choose to use this book as a reference book to dip in and out of, as an essential textbook to support your qualitative research methods learning during your undergraduate or master's degree or as a supplement to your broader introduction to conducting research in psychology, it will provide you with a solid foundation for understanding and using qualitative methodology in your own work. We hope you enjoy it and are always pleased to hear about your work at our website: www.npqr.wordpress.com.

My early research work was very quantitatively orientated. As a science graduate first and then a psychology graduate, the focus of research had usually been on measuring, testing and verifying things. It was with my introduction to working with people in a hospital setting that I began to consider other ways of carrying out inquiry. As a student working alongside experienced medical and other researchers I became increasingly aware of how qualitatively orientated research could bring some understanding of what it might be like to be a patient in a hospital. With this foundation and subsequent psychodynamic counselling training, I became interested enough in pursuing this type of research to undertake a PhD in qualitative research. This was a narrative analysis study of the transition to second-time motherhood, in which I was surrounded, guided and supported by highly experienced and knowledgeable qualitative researchers. As I learned more and more about the narrative analysis approach my delight in it grew alongside an increasing concern that I was still at risk of imposing my story on the participants simply through the fact that I had been the one to select a method with which to analyse and interpret their stories. Out of these thoughts grew the seed of investigating a pluralistic use of qualitative methods.

With the help of funding from Birkbeck, University of London, I put together a small team of analysts so that we could together explore what else might have been found in the data that I had analysed for my PhD, using a flexible approach to narrative analysis. Some of our findings have been published in academic journals but, more than that, I have been immersed, engaged and excited by the questions we have asked, been asked and addressed along the way, as well as by the debates and arguments that have ensued. The PQR team organised two successful international symposia to present our work and to invite responses to and discussion of it. These led to a continuing engagement with researchers in academia, clinical practice, commercial psychology, NHS governance and medicine. I am often approached by PhD students wishing to employ a pluralistic approach in their study and several colleagues have discussed the strengths and limitations of it with me.

Now I almost cannot help but think of researching phenomena pluralistically. It seems to me that most questions about human experience, understanding and perception should be approached from as many viewpoints as possible. Only then can we seek to begin to understand the complexity within which we negotiate our everyday lives and sense of self. My research interests on mothers and identity, and experiences of mental illness would all seem to benefit from a pluralistic approach. As important as seeking to learn as much as we

Reflection on Practice

can from data, I think, is the notion that the adoption of a pluralistic approach reduces the likelihood of imposing my truths, realities and assumptions on to those that are donated to me by participants. Through careful reflexive practice the pluralistic approach allows for some blurring of the researcher/researched boundaries that have been prevalent in psychology up until relatively recently. Given the time and other resources that a pluralistic approach can command I would like to say that I do not always employ it in my research. However, this is not quite true as I find it is always going on in my head even if resources in the external world do not permit!

Further reading

Forrester, M.A. (Ed.) (2010) *Doing Qualitative Research in Psychology.* London: Sage Publications Ltd.
A detailed guide to conducting qualitative research with accompanying web resources.

Lyons, E. & Coyle, A. (Eds) (2007) *Analysing Qualitative Data in Psychology.* London: Sage Publications Ltd.
This book provides detailed consideration of single-method analysis of one piece of data, and a useful chapter (Chapter 11) that draws comparative reflections on the similarities and differences across the four methods.

Smith, J.A. (Ed.) (2009) *Qualitative Psychology: A Practical Guide to Research Methods* (2nd edn). London: Sage Publications Ltd.
In addition to chapters dedicated to different methods, this book includes a useful chapter on **phenomenology** (Chapter 3), and one on validity and qualitative research (Chapter 11).

Todd, Z., Nerlich, B., McKeown, S. & Clarke, D.D. (Eds) (2004) *Mixing Methods in Psychology: The Integration of Qualitative and Quantitative Methods in Theory and Practice.* Hove: Psychology Press.
This book provides informative discussion of the history, employment and applications of mixed-method research.

Willig, C. (2008) *Introducing Qualitative Research in Psychology: Adventures in Theory and Method.* Maidenhead: Open University Press.
This book includes chapters on less common methods such as memory work (Chapter 8) and the case study approach (Chapter 5).

CHAPTER 2

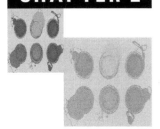

Grounded Theory Approaches

Sevasti-Melissa Nolas

Introduction

This chapter is about using grounded theory. It focuses on the development of grounded theory, the underlying assumptions of the approach and the ways it is used in research. The chapter will cover theoretical as well as practical issues relating to the use of grounded theory. The origins of grounded theory lie in the micro-sociological tradition of research and, as such, each section has been written with a view to relating that tradition to research topics in psychology. The chapter begins with a background and history of grounded theory. It continues with a discussion of the ontological and epistemological issues that underpin the grounded theory approach. The chapter provides a detailed description of what one needs to consider and do in carrying out a piece of grounded theory research. Examples and reflections on practice are given throughout, and ethics considerations are also discussed.

History

Grounded theory is an approach used to study action and interaction and their meaning. It was developed by Barney G. Glaser and Anselm L. Strauss, two American sociologists working at the University of California, San Francisco, in the 1960s. They developed the approach while studying the way in which health professionals cared for the ill in American hospitals, and especially how they managed the issues of death and dying. Their interest in the topic developed from the observation that discussions of death and dying were at the time absent from the American public sphere. They wanted to explore how that absence affected those contexts in which death and dying occur and so their study explored how a social issue (absence of public discussion on death) impacted on professional practice in a clinical setting. The social issue they identified was the lack of public discussion around death and the process of dying. *Awareness of Dying* (1965) is now a seminal text, as is *The Discovery of Grounded Theory* (1967), which Glaser and Strauss wrote to outline the research approach they were using.

Glaser and Strauss continued to work together for a number of years before developing separate intellectual trajectories. Glaser's approach emphasises the emergence of theory from the data without the imposition of the analyst's conceptual categories onto the data. Glaser's work emphasises the opportunity grounded theory offers for developing 'formal theory' (see, for example, Glaser, 2007). Strauss's take on grounded theory emphasised the symbolic interactionist roots of the approach, which concentrate on the construction of meaning through everyday interaction. Strauss, with Juliet Corbin (1990), wrote a detailed book on 'how to do' grounded theory, *Basics of Qualitative Research*, which is still widely used. Anselm L. Strauss passed away in 1996 (Bryant & Charmaz, 2007: 5). Barney G. Glaser is still writing and teaching on grounded theory, and runs workshops in a number of cities.

Since its early days, grounded theory has been developed by a number of Glaser and Strauss's students as well as others (Bryant & Charmaz, 2007). It is still a popular approach for studying action and interaction and, although Glaser has always maintained that it is or can be a mixed-method approach, it is frequently used for qualitative research in areas such as nursing, social work, clinical psychology and other helping professions.

Ontology

The ontological orientation of grounded theory has its roots in early sociological thought, pragmatism and **symbolic interactionism** (Star, 2007), which draw on European (French) and North American social science at the end of the nineteenth and turn of the twentieth centuries.

Grounded theory follows in the path opened by the founder of sociology, Emile Durkheim, in espousing the idea that social facts exist and that the empirical study of these facts constitutes a true scientific endeavour (Bryant & Charmaz, 2007: 22). From the pragmatist tradition, we find in grounded theory the idea that our understanding is built on consequences and not antecedents (Star, 2007: 86). This means that knowledge is created retrospectively. This is in contrast to other philosophical orientations that emphasise the prospective creation of models, which subsequently await verification. Like pragmatism, grounded theory also assumes the existence of an objective reality, but one that is complex and consists of a number of overlapping, complementary as well as contradictory perspectives (Star, 2007: 87); grounded theory also draws our attention to action and interaction as meaningful units of analysis in their own right. Action is created through the relationships between people; it is treated as an ongoing, continuously unfolding social fact (Star, 2007: 90).

The way in which grounded theory understands action and interaction has its roots in the symbolic interactionist tradition that emerged out of the Chicago School of micro-sociology. According to symbolic interactionism (Blumer, 1969; Stryker, 1981; Prus, 1996; Rock, 2001; Sandstrom, Martin & Fine, 2003), social reality is intersubjective, it consists of communal life with shared linguistic or symbolic dimensions that is also reflective of those shared meanings. Reflexivity means that people are able to attribute meaning to their being and in doing so develop lines of action. People are also able to take the perspective of the other (Mead, 1934).

Activities organise human group life. While we create meaning out of behaviour intersubjectively, it is activities that organise human life. In turn we tend to spend a good deal of time negotiating such activities and building relationships through these activities. We are able to both accept and resists others' influences and, as such, activities are multidimensional, implying cooperation, competition, conflict and compromise. At the same time, the relationships we form say something about the role and identities we create, as well as how our communities are organized. Symbolic interactionism deals with process by thinking about human lived experiences as 'emergent or ongoing social constructions or productions' (Prus, 1996: 17).

The emphasis in symbolic interactionism on action, interaction and activity has been inherited by grounded theory and has led to the approach being adopted as a preferred method for understanding practice in a number of disciplines and applied settings.

Epistemology

When thinking about the epistemology underlying grounded theory it is common to categorise the various historical periods of grounded theory as either positivist or constructivist. Certainly, as Bryant and Charmaz (2007: 50) point out, Glaser and Strauss's initial work (1967) espoused a number of positivist assumptions about the existence of an objective reality that is unmediated by the researcher's or others' interpretations of it. Later developments of grounded theory that have taken their inspiration from social constructionism are more amenable to a view of reality that is mediated through language and other forms of symbolic representation (Burr, 1995). However, categorising grounded theory approaches in this way, as either positivist or constructivist, is unhelpful because it risks missing what is most useful and enduring about these approaches (Clarke, 2005; Bryant & Charmaz, 2007). This section looks at key epistemological underpinnings of grounded theory to help to determine the usefulness of each for designing and carrying out grounded theory research.

The epistemology of grounded theory is essentially one of resistance to pre-existing knowledge, and of managing the tensions between the empirical phenomena and abstract concepts. Grounded theory's various legacies play a key role here. In symbolic interactionism, the distinction is made between knowing about a phenomenon and being acquainted with a phenomenon (Downes & Rock, 1982: 37, cited in Van Maanen, 1988: 18). The shift of emphasis from knowledge about something to acquaintance with a phenomenon has resulted in the creation of a small niche within the discipline of sociology, not so much concerned with building broad conceptual models but instead with creating understanding of 'the vigorous, dense, heterogeneous cultures located just beyond the university gates' (Van Maanen, 1988: 18–20). Grounded theory embodied this tradition when Glaser and Strauss encouraged their students to challenge the 'theoretical capitalism' involved in the fine-tuning of existing theories (Bryant & Charmaz, 2007: 17). The call to leave armchair theorising behind also has implications for how research is conducted, but we will return to this point in the next section, on method.

The tension between the empirical and the conceptual is managed through an iterative process of data collection and analysis. Knowledge in grounded theory is arrived at through this process. The approach relies on the analyst moving back and forth between their empirical data and their analysis of it (Bryant & Charmaz, 2007: 1). In this process there are three distinct analytical practices employed towards the creation of knowledge, as described below.

Constant comparison

Knowledge in grounded theory is derived through a process of constant comparison. Comparison in grounded theory is not used to verify existing theory (see above). Instead it is used to generate and discover new categories and theories by juxtaposing one instance from the data with another (Covan, 2007: 63). Comparing and contrasting instances in this way enables the analyst to look for similarities and differences across the data in order to elucidate the meanings and processes that shape the phenomenon being studied. Similarities can be grouped together into categories. Categories are more abstract than initial codes, and begin to group together codes with similar significance and meaning, as well as grouping common themes and patterns across codes into a single analytical concept (Charmaz, 2006: 186). Categories are then compared with each other to produce theory. Differences, on the other hand, far from presenting a problem to the analyst, are treated as opportunities to extend the analysis in order to account for the role that such differences play in the phenomena under investigation. In fact, Glaser and Strauss (1967) placed a good deal of emphasis on the value of analysing extreme cases that might challenge, and therefore enrich, an emerging theory (Covan, 2007: 63). The process of using extreme cases, or negative cases, to extend the analysis is called theoretical sampling (see page 28).

Abduction

Reichertz (2007) defines abduction as 'a cognitive logic of discovery'. It is a form of inference used especially for dealing with surprising findings in our data. It directs the analyst to make sense of their data and produce explanations that make surprising findings unsurprising (Reichertz, 2007: 222).

Abduction is different to deduction and induction. Deduction subordinates the single case into an already known rule or category, and induction generalises single cases into a rule or category by focusing either on quantitative or qualitative properties of a sample and extending them into a rule or category. Abduction, on the other hand, creates a new rule or category in order to account for a case present in the data that cannot be explained by existing rules or categories (Reichertz, 2007: 218–219).

There are two *strategies* involved in abduction, both of which require creating the conditions in order for abductive reasoning to take place (Reichertz, 2007: 221).

1 The first is a 'self-induced emergency situation' (Reichertz, 2007: 221). This means that in the face of not knowing what to make of a surprising finding, rather than dwelling on the infinite number of possibilities, the analyst puts pressure on themselves to act by committing to a single meaning.
2 The second strategy is completely antithetical to the first. It involves letting your mind wander without any specific goal in mind, or what Pierce (1931–1935), a key writer on abduction, called 'musement' (Reichertz, 2007: 221).

What these two quite antithetical strategies have in common is tricking the thinking patterns of the conscious mind in order to create 'an *attitude* of preparedness to abandon old convictions and to seek new ones' (Reichertz, 2007: 221).

Reflexivity

Reflexivity is not often associated with Glaser and Strauss's original formulation of grounded theory. Yet the impetus behind *Awareness of Dying* was deeply personal, both men having experienced bereavement in the period preceding the study (Bryant & Charmaz, 2007: 7; Star, 2007: 82). Lempert (2007: 247) notes that grounded theory in its original formulations presumed that the researcher as a research instrument was a 'neutral knower'. Mruck and Mey (2007: 518) suggest that Glaser's emphasis on allowing theory to emerge means that there is little room for reflexivity in Glaserean grounded theory, which would impose on that emergence. On the other hand, Strauss and Corbin's approach, rooted far more in symbolic interactionism, takes the view that the researcher's biography, and the sociocultural influences therein, influence the researcher's theories and interests (Mruck & Mey, 2007: 518).

Given developments in qualitative research methods in psychology and the central role that reflexivity has played in those (Willig, 2000) we would encourage a reflexive stance to grounded theory. The approach's emphasis on action, including that of the researcher(s), indicates that there is ample room for developing a reflexive stance in grounded theory. Indeed, like Mruck and Mey (2007), I have in my own teaching of research methods always put forward the view of research as a continuous process of decision making (Marshall & Rossman, 1989: 23). Accordingly, and at the very least, reflexivity is a way of making the research process less esoteric, and more transparent and accountable to one's colleagues and the public. It is also a way of developing theoretical sensitivity (another staple of grounded theory) of the context and processes one is researching. For instance, early experiences of action research and my reflection on the meaning and dynamics of those experiences led me to formulate my own research project that looked at the gaps between formal and informal **discourses** of action (Nolas, 2009; see Reflection on Practice on page 37 of this chapter). In this regard, reflexivity plays an epistemological role in opening a space for the creation of new knowledge.

Methods

Grounded theory's focus is on action and interaction, and it is suitable for answering event-orientated questions such as 'What is happening?' (Glaser, 1978, cited in Bryant & Charmaz, 2007: 21). The symbolic interactionist tradition lends itself to exploratory questions of *how*, while the emphasis on constant comparison provides the tools for the more explanatory questions of *why* to be answered.

In this process in grounded theory everything is considered to be data, though notably, and because of the emphasis on building theory, data is certainly not everything in a research project (Bryant & Charmaz, 2007: 14). This is because the parameters of research design are drawn up according to the action or activity that one is studying. Everything in relation to that action then becomes data. This is quite a different approach to what many psychologists might be used to. In psychology we tend to make strong demarcations between our theories, methods and data. These boundaries are much more blurred in grounded theory, which is often described as an iterative process of data collection, analysis and further data collection. We will deal with the practicalities of data collection and analysis in the next section. Here we will explore the methods themselves, starting with a discussion of theoretical sensitivity – a starting point, if there is such a thing, in grounded theory.

Theoretical sensitivity

Grounded theory begins with theoretical sensitivity, which is defined as 'the researcher's ability to understand subtleties and nuances in the data' (Singh, 2003: 310). For example, when Singh (2003; 2004) was researching attention deficit hyperactivity disorder (ADHD) her historical analysis of the ADHD literature and her own immersion in the field through participant observation in a clinical setting and teaching at a primary school had sensitised her to a number of issues relating to the study of ADHD. For instance, she observed that in the clinic setting fathers tended to be less involved in issues relating to their child's (mainly sons) diagnosis and management of ADHD. She also found that articles that referred to 'parents' and 'children' in relation to ADHD very often meant mothers and sons. As such, she decided to sample and interview both mothers and fathers about their experiences of being the parent of a child diagnosed with ADHD.

Ethnographic fieldwork

Like grounded theory, ethnography is also a boundary-spanning (Tedlock, 2003: 165) activity. It is an approach widely used in sociology and anthropology. With some notable exceptions in social psychology (Jahoda, Lazarsfeld & Zeisel, 1972;

Thomas & Znaniecki, 1996; Bradbury, 1999), cultural psychology (Cole, 1996) and clinical psychology (Bloor, McKeganey & Fokert, 1988; Gubrium, 1992, both cited in McLeod, 2001), for the most part the ethnographic approach is not widely used in psychological research. Similarly, and as Timmermans and Tavory (2007) point out, while grounded theory has its roots in ethnographic research, over time the link between grounded theory as an approach to both data collection as well as analysis has weakened considerably, making grounded theory 'first and foremost a systematic qualitative data analysis approach' (2007: 494).

There are two reasons to focus on ethnography when conducting grounded theory research. On the one hand, it is the bedrock of the symbolic interactionist tradition from which one form of grounded theory emerged. It broadens the scope for collecting types of data that are not readily amenable to more common qualitative research methods, such as cultural practices that we engage in with others that do not always form part of our conscious or codified knowledge – knowledge that is communicated through language. These might include such things as the systems of classification that shape our work and everyday lives (Bowker & Star, 1999), how village life is organised around an open psychiatric community keeping the sane and the mad apart (Jodelet, 1991), or the ritual processes in the discourses that surround death in contemporary Britain (Bradbury, 1999). It also provides us with a useful framework of 'fieldwork' for organising a range of data (such as documents, letters, internet postings, news articles) that crop up in the process of and are related to the activities being investigated. As such, there are a number of useful lessons that can be drawn from thinking about data collection methods ethnographically.

Participant observation

Ethnographic fieldwork relies on the researcher spending a considerable amount of time in the context in which their research interests reside. This could be an organisation or community, a network of people or any other relevant grouping. The aim of the approach is to achieve an 'intimate familiarity' (Prus, 1996) with the subject matter. Ethnographic studies are 'naturalistic' (Hammersley & Atkinson, 1995: 3) meaning that the researcher seeks to observe people and their interactions as they occur, in situ. Observation here is in stark contrast to the usual meaning found in psychology; its meaning lies much closer to the everyday activities of noticing, paying attention to and taking note of particular situations or interactions of interest in a purposeful manner. It frequently crosses over into participation of various degrees as researchers apprentice themselves to the routines of others' lives. Such an approach is in contrast to experimental approaches to psychological research where people are removed from their context and daily activities and their behaviour is manipulated through experimental design. It is also different to interviewing and focus groups, which while allowing participants to use their own language and give meaning to discussion topics still brackets these moments of recounting experience from the rest of daily life. It is also different to clinical uses of observation, such as one-way mirrors, because its aim is not to compare actions with, and the extent to which they deviate from, previously established norm. Instead, observation in ethnographic research is a way of collecting contextual information, inclusive of people's interactions. It is largely unstructured by the researcher and has to follow the rhythm of the situation or context. The researcher is, depending on their prior familiarity with the research context, largely unaware of the social norms but ends up learning about those by purposefully, but quite often inadvertently, disrupting them with their presence.

Informal interviews

In the ethnographic process, informal interviews abound. They are part and parcel of participant observation. The term 'informal interview' refers to unplanned research-relevant or related conversations that might take place and which the researcher records in their fieldnotes after the event. Such interviews are much closer to conversations and do not necessarily follow a structured or semi-structured format. The interviews are often prompted by the researchers' questions as they try to find out what is going on and why certain things are being carried out in the way they are. They might also be prompted by individuals in the field wanting to communicate information to the researcher that they think might be relevant to the study. Informal interviews can be individual interviews as well as group interviews.

Formal interviews and focus groups

Interviewing can be regarded as the formalised method of interpersonal communication used for research. It is 'essentially a technique or method for establishing or discovering that there are perspectives or viewpoints on events other than those of the person initiating the interview' (Farr, 1982, in Gaskell, 2000: 38). There are a number of excellent publications on the topic of interviewing (e.g. Kvale, 1996) and, for this reason, I will not go into it in a huge amount of detail here. In outline, interviews have been described as a 'purposive conversation' (Kvale, 1996). The structure and formality of interviews ranges from fully structured with standardised questions, to semi-structured that include a few guide questions but are generally informed by the interviewee, and completely unstructured in which the participant directs the interview in its entirety. Similarly, focus group discussions are often organised around topics but can equally involve structured activities, such as viewing videos or pictures, or sorting through issues relevant to the research, as a way of engaging participants, developing conversation and accessing views on and experiences of the topic under investigation (see Gaskell, 2000).

Documents, archives

In psychological research we tend not to include documents in our data other than perhaps as protocols for guiding our own action (e.g. research proposals, interview topic guides). Yet if you think about psychology and its practices (experiments, surveys, interviews, clinical interventions) as a socio-cultural activity you will find that documents play a central role in that practice. In clinical psychology, for instance, manuals are a very important aspect of practice, especially if one is interested in empirically testing the efficacy of the therapeutic approach with which one practises. Consider change practices in different types of organisations. These are often launched with the production of a strategic document or a policy change, which spells out new expectations and behaviours (Prior, 2003). As such, documents often form an important part of more formalised activities. In my own research on evaluating a youth inclusion programme it was possible to trace the development of the programme and policy thinking by analysing the language used to talk about the programme in official documents and on government websites. As the monitoring and evaluation strategy got under way and its findings were fed back into programme development, the programme itself began to change – for instance, by becoming more inclusive of young women's interests and needs.

Other methods

There is a range of other methods that might be included in a grounded theory project. For instance, Dilks, Tasker and Wren (2010), in researching the links between therapy and recovery in psychosis, used audio recordings of therapy sessions. In my own research using participatory video (Nolas, 2009), the videos produced by our young participants were similarly included as part of the material to be analysed to extend understanding of what happens when we say that we are working in a participatory way. For further information on other methods see Denzin and Lincoln (2000), and Banks (2007).

Ethics

Research in the grounded theory tradition adheres to the same ethical guidelines as any other piece of qualitative research. Data are collected anonymously, including in instances of participant observation where the identity of those being observed is concealed in the subsequent analysis and writing-up of the study. What participants tell the researcher is kept confidential and the identity of participants is protected. Different ethical considerations do, however, come into play when thinking about the participant observation and informal interviewing aspects of a grounded theory project. Here access to the field is usually negotiated through a 'gatekeeper'. A gatekeeper is a key member of a group, community or organisation who becomes known to the researcher (either through the researcher's network or through a formal introduction and sometimes even a chance encounter) and through whom access to the rest of the group, community or organisation is discussed (Hammersley & Atkinson, 1995: 63–67). At this point researchers should be clear about the methods they are using (e.g. formal and informal interviews) and how the data will be used. However, researchers should not rely on gatekeepers communicating the details of the research and the role of the researcher to other members of the gatekeeper's community. Researchers should always identify themselves as such, explain their research to other community members and ask permission from those they talk to for using the information provided in their research (e.g. in the context of informal interviews).

Ilana Singh's work (2002a; 2002b; 2003; 2004; 2005) on mothers' and fathers' experiences of parenting a child with ADHD is an example of a robust use of grounded theory analysis. In her approach she practised a number of the grounded theory principles. Her study began with a historical analysis of ADHD. Debates around ADHD have come to be dominated by biological and pharmacological discourses of the diagnosis. Singh's work sought to explore the relationship between the historical context that gave rise to ADHD and Ritalin, and mothers' acceptance of medical intervention for their sons with ADHD. Her historical analysis of the ADHD literature and her own immersion in the field through participant observation in a clinical setting and teaching at a primary school, sensitised her (theoretical sensitivity) to a number of issues relating to the study of ADHD (Singh, 2003). For instance, she observed that in the clinic setting fathers tended to be less involved in issues relating to their child's (mainly sons') diagnosis and management of ADHD. She also found that articles that referred to 'parents' and 'children' in relation to ADHD very often meant mothers and sons. As such, she decided to sample and interview both mothers and fathers about their experiences of being the parent of a child diagnosed with ADHD, and compared their experiences throughout her analysis (Singh, 2003; 2004). She sampled one group of parents from a clinical setting and another set of parents outside the clinic from relevant support networks, mailing lists and educational conferences. In initial interviews, Singh asked mothers and fathers to respond to an open-ended question: 'How do you think and feel about Ritalin (or other psychostimulant) treatment?' (2004: 1195). She used a 'picture-oriented interviewing' method where parents were asked to spend up to 30 minutes leafing through a series of magazines before the interview, selecting up to ten pictures they felt captured or could help them express how they thought and felt about psychostimulant treatment for ADHD. Parent interviews were then organised around the pictures, with parents leading the discussion and illustrating their views and experiences through the pictures. As Singh (2003) continued her interviewing and the simultaneous analysis of her interviews, she started to concentrate 'on exploring representative concepts and emerging hypotheses' (2003: 311). Her initial 'open coding' was conducted as a group activity with 'a small community of coders work[ing] together to explore key themes and categories in the data' (2003: 310). Early interviews with mothers suggested that they spoke about their experiences of parenting a child with ADHD through

Research Example

Research Example

what Singh (2003: 311) calls a 'transformation narrative' in three acts: before diagnosis, diagnosis and post-diagnosis. Singh began to use the three phases of the narrative as a way of exploring parents' experiences. In comparing mothers' and fathers' responses to the three phases it emerged that fathers' experiences of their sons' behaviour and diagnosis did not conform to the same narrative. This is an important, if preliminary, finding because fathers bring a different perspective to the construction and lived experience of ADHD, which has, by and large, been missing from our understanding of ADHD. Her analysis (Singh, 2004) also explored the meaning and function of mothers' narrative of transformation from the mothers' perspective. Singh argues that biological discourses of ADHD appear on the surface to offer mothers the opportunity to replace 'mother-blame' with 'brain-blame' for ADHD, and thus enable mothers to reposition themselves as 'good mothers'. At the same time, however, Singh shows that the consequences of this transformation narrative are far from simple or as liberating as they appear at first sight. This is especially the case when the medication associated with 'brain-blame' is taken into the picture and mothers can be blamed afresh for 'irresponsible uses of Ritalin' (Singh, 2004: 1203).

Practice

In this section we look at the analytical tools that grounded theory employs and we discuss how to use them.

Pragmatics

Recruitment and sampling

Recruitment in grounded theory is determined by the action or activity that is being researched. In this sense the sample is *purposive*. When sampling purposively, you seek to recruit people to the study who are relevant and involved in the phenomenon being investigated. Samples of *convenience* might also be common (Morse, 2007). When sampling in this way you seek to recruit participants or informants who are more accessible to you than others, or more available to do interviews. It provides a way in which at the beginning of a project, such as in a pilot, you might identify some of the characteristics and scope of the activity you want to research (Morse, 2007: 235). From here you may use a *snowball* sampling method where subsequent, relevant participants are identified for you by initial interviewees.

In grounded theory the sampling process is not demographically representative as it might be in a quantitative study or in some qualitative approaches that require working with homogeneous samples. Representation in grounded theory works in a different way along the lines of relevance and involvement in or knowledge of a particular activity. This means that when you are recruiting participants to your study they have to have some relationship to the activity you are studying. For instance, if you were interested in researching the ways in which 'giving birth' takes place in contemporary society you might begin by sampling a group of mothers in the first instance as well as a group of relevant professionals (e.g. midwives). Both groups are directly involved with the birthing process. As your research developed it might become relevant to include other groups in the sample (e.g. fathers, or other professionals) in order to test your emerging theories about giving birth in a contemporary western society. Morse (2007: 231) goes further by saying that researchers need to seek out 'excellent' informants who have been through, or observed, the activity under investigation, and who are reflective and articulate enough to be able to recount that experience to you in detailed and nuanced terms. For instance, in the previous example this might involve talking to midwives with a number of years of experience and mothers who have had more than one baby. While this is sound advice that will save you considerable time in terms of creating a detailed and in-depth picture of the context and the actions you are studying, it is also an exclusionary sampling strategy that marginalises less articulate experiences and less expert experiences that nonetheless form part of the fabric of the field of action (e.g. first-time mothers or less experienced midwives). You might want to think about talking to more experienced informants as part of the pilot stages of your research, who have been through various permutations of the activity you are studying, before expanding your sample to include a broader range of relevant informants.

Example from using grounded theory to study psychotherapy and the experiences of being in therapy

Dilks, Tasker and Wren (2010) studied individuals' subjective experiences of psychosis and the role of therapy in that experience. They began their study using tape-recorded therapy sessions and interviews with clinical psychologists and their clients. Their analysis of this material suggested that the client's ability to 'function in the social world' was an important aspect of clinician–client encounters and constituted therapy goals for both clinicians and clients. The authors wanted to test this emerging theory and, as such, went on to collect published personal accounts of the experience of psychosis. The analysis of these accounts helped them to refine their initial theory. The published version of their theory suggests that functioning in the social world was achieved by clients through a range of strategies ('doing recovery', 'negotiating selfhood', 'making sense' and 'balancing act'), which in turn helped them to manage the impact of psychosis so that they could function in the social world.

Example

The sampling approach that is most associated with grounded theory is that of *theoretical sampling*. This means that sampling strategies are developed as analysis takes place. As categories emerge or are constructed through the analysis of your material and you begin to develop a grounded theory of the activity you are studying, you may find gaps or anomalies in the story emerging from your analysis. Theoretical sampling refers to further sampling of participants or events based on the categories that you are working with. It also refers to testing your theory with negative cases. Negative cases are participants or situations that present a challenge to the theory that you are developing. They are the cases that do not fit the theory. Such cases should be engaged with in terms of what they teach you about the theory that you are putting forward.

Eliciting and gathering data

Participant observation and fieldnotes

In the previous section, ethnography was presented as an approach to data collection derived from the symbolic interactionist legacy of grounded theory. Participant observation was discussed as the particular research strategy to be used. In this section we look at some of the practicalities of doing participant observation and practical advice about how participant observation can be documented by the researcher.

As noted previously, participant observation is the time the researcher spends in the field living alongside the people they are doing research with. It can take a number of forms, ranging from the more detached and observational to the more involved and participatory. The degree of your involvement in the field might depend on what you are interested in. For instance if you wanted to observe children's interactions during breaks at school you might decide that the best way to do this would be to sit at the edge of the playground and observe the children from a distance. You could, however, imagine a situation where, as part of your research, you work in a school as a teaching assistant for two days a week. In that case you might decide to organise games for the children and reflect on how they engage with the game and each other. In any piece of fieldwork, levels of participation and observation will often vary depending on what is happening in the context. Sometimes it is helpful and possible to acquire or create a role in the context of study (e.g. by becoming a volunteer teaching assistant). Performing some aspect of the activities that others do, or closely shadowing their activities, gives the researcher some first-hand experience (albeit perhaps superficial, depending on duration of involvement) of the processes they are studying. Sometimes, however, such a strategy is neither feasible nor desirable, especially if it places an undue burden on those in that context (by imposing additional training or supervision needs).

The written record of time spent in the field is compiled into a set of what are called fieldnotes. These are 'accounts describing experiences and observations the researcher has made while participating in an intense and involved manner' (*Emerson, Fretz & Shaw, 1995: 5*). There is no prescribed way of taking fieldnotes;

both formal and anecdotal advice varies. I have found Emerson, Fretz and Shaw's (1995) *Writing Ethnographic Fieldnotes* a very useful and accessible guide. These authors write about fieldwork from a symbolic interactionist perspective and their analytical strategies draw on grounded theory. In their book they outline two main strategies for taking fieldnotes. The first strategy 'values relating naturally to those encountered in the field' (Emerson *et al.*, 1995: 17) and advises the researcher to immerse themselves fully in the experience of local activity and worry about writing down fieldnotes later. The second strategy requires the field worker to prioritise the writing activity by selecting events that they think should be recorded, and to simultaneously witness and record these events. It is often the case that field workers use a bit of each strategy (Emerson *et al.*, 1995: 18), with some written notes being taken in the field alongside a number of 'mental notes' (Emerson *et al.*, 1995: 19) – mental bullet points intended to help the researcher remember important conversations or sequences of events. In my own experience I have often made notes or bullet points about my day in the field (about people, conversations, events and activities) on trains and buses while returning home or to the office. My more extensive, and more narrative descriptions and reflections, based on these notes, are written and typed up the following day.

Formal and informal interviewing

Grounded theory uses open-ended questions that will allow someone to describe an experience, an action or a process. Formal interviewing tends to follow some process or degree of structuring. Semi-structured interviews will have a range of questions and prompts that you as the interviewer prepare before the interview. In formal interviewing a lot of the work takes place beforehand in terms of thinking exactly what you want to ask people and preparing your topic guide. During this time you might find it useful to test questions out on friends and colleagues to make sure that the questions you are considering asking are as unambiguous as possible and that they elicit the type of response you are looking for. For instance, this might be about making sure that questions are written in such a way as to enable your interviewee to talk about an action or a process instead of merely giving an opinion about it. I tend to think in terms of 'how' or 'what happens' to help me formulate appropriate questions. I also try to make my questions initially quite broad so as to allow my interviewee to respond to them in ways that are meaningful to them. For instance, if I am doing research on people's experiences of a particular public service I would not ask them what they thought about the service ('Can you tell me what you think about Service X?') but instead I might begin by asking what brought them to the service in the first place ('Can you tell me what were the circumstances that led you to make contact with Service X?' or 'Can you tell me a bit about your involvement with Service X?'). These are quite broad opening questions that are asking for a story or experience in response ('I first heard about Service X when …').

During the interview you need to concentrate on what people are telling you and especially how what they are telling you relates to (inter)actions, activities, events or processes. Interviewees will often repeatedly return to the main ideas of what they want to convey to you. It is important to pick up on these ideas and explore them with the interviewee, and not just dismiss them as being 'off topic' because they are not covered in your initial topic guide. Remember, in this style of interviewing everything that the interviewee says (and sometimes what they choose not to say) is potentially relevant and important to informing your study. Charmaz (2001) also advises that researchers pay attention to pauses, 'ums' and 'you knows', as the struggle to find the words to express something can indicate a taken-for-granted meaning (Charmaz, 2001) or shared knowledge assumption. You also need to pay attention to the absence of talk about (inter)actions, activities, events or processes, and try to elicit such talk or at least find out why no reference is being made to such areas. Formal interviews are usually audio recorded with the consent of the interviewee. Sometimes interviewees are not happy to be recorded and the researcher might have to rely on their notes and/or memory with regard to key issues and themes from the interview.

Informal interviews can often occur spontaneously. For instance, while conducting participant observation, someone from the community or organisation might speak to you about your research and the exchange turns into an informal interview; it might be an exchange that starts off as more of a conversation but turns into an interview. These moments give you the opportunity to ask questions relating to your research and to find out more about people's experiences and the actions and interactions involved in a more natural way. A word of caution though: it also means that you may sometimes be caught off guard without the necessary preparation that you might have done. Or you will need to rely on your memory much more in terms of the sorts of questions that you want to ask. You should know your research topic well in terms of the research focus and what it is that that interests you. This interest should guide your questions. Once again your questions here should be invitations to explain, expand and above all recount actions, as opposed to opinions about actions.

Useful phrases for asking people to expand on meaning, and focus on actions and activities

'Tell me about ...'
'How ...'
'What happened ...'
'Can you give me an example ...'
'Could you describe that further ...'
'What exactly do you mean when you say ...'
'What does that look like in practice ...'
'What would I need to know and do to participate ...'
'How is that different to previous times ...'
'How does that compare with ...'

Useful Phrases

It is possible to record or take notes in informal interviews if you carry a recording device or notepad with you all the time during the research, and providing the person you are talking to gives their permission. However, you would need to consider what it might do to the quality of the interaction if you take out a notebook or recorder. Instead, and where for whatever reason recording devices are not available, you will need to follow the same advice given above for recording ethnographic fieldnotes.

Documents, archives

Document research covers a range of areas including archives and historical documents, government documents, internal documents in a service or organisation, and letters. One of the founding studies of attitude research (Thomas & Znaniecki, 1927; 1996) was based on people's personal letters. More contemporary equivalents could include email correspondence and blogs as well as online documents. Relevant documents will need to be located. Many archival and historical documents require the researcher to physically visit an institution where the document is stored. If you are using such material as part of your grounded theory study then you will need to factor in the time that you will need in order to visit the institution, access and study the document, especially when copying is not permitted.

Analysis and interpretation

Constant comparison, abduction and reflexivity

As noted in the section on epistemology, the processes of constant comparison, abduction and reflexivity are the main ways in which knowledge is created in grounded theory. It is expected that while coding and categorising, as well as in the later stages of theoretical coding and sorting, you will be continuously comparing your codes, categories and memos in order to refine your selections and interpretations. Comparison involves looking at the similarities and differences in selection in order to make sure that the data instances coded and the codes categorised merit the labels that they are given, and that codes and categories are distinct enough from one another. It is also expected that you will be practising your abductive reasoning skills by cultivating 'an *attitude* of preparedness to abandon old convictions and to seek new ones' (Reichertz, 2007: 221). Finally, think about the role of reflexivity, a questioning stance to your own assumptions as well as openness to using the experiences of practice to shape your research, in guiding your analysis.

Coding and categorising

Coding is the first step of the analytic process in grounded theory. It involves labelling your research materials with smaller, meaningful units of text (a word, a phrase). The resulting labels are often referred to as codes. There are two types of coding in grounded theory: substantive coding and theoretical coding (Holton, 2007). We will return to theoretical coding after we discuss substantive coding in this section and memo writing in the next.

Substantive coding is bottom-up coding that follows the logic of the text and takes its labelling cues from the text. It is referred to as 'open coding', which can either be a line-by-line examination of the text or a distillation of key ideas that emerge through the text (Stern, 2007: 118). In substantive coding it is helpful to keep codes in the language or meaning of the person speaking or the context being researched.

Example of coded text

The following extract has been taken from the evaluation of a youth inclusion programme (Humphreys, Nolas & Olmos, 2006). This was a participatory evaluation where young people created audiovisual stories about their views and experiences of their areas and of the youth inclusion programme they were participating in. Young people were asked about their areas, positive and negative aspects of their areas, what they would change and what their hopes were for the future, and how they had found the youth inclusion programme.

Transcript	Codes
Young person: … the positive things about my area is that when you know lot of people that you can get on with everyone, a lot of people know … this is small area where every one knows every one, so it's a friendly place.	Knowing a lot of people Getting on with everyone Small area, everyone knows everyone 'A friendly place'
The negative things about my area is that there is different groups so say that someone new who was actually moving to the area they might find it hard to like fit in because they might not know a lot of people …	Different group, would be hard to fit in as a newcomer
One benefit of, about my area is the gym because gym is the place you can come, like young people will come on Saturdays and it's for cheap, it's not expensive so a lot of people can come and like just work out and get fit, like in a fun way because all your friends will come and join here, you just work out together.	Gym is a good thing You can be calm there Its cheap Everyone goes there Do things together
If I had power to change certain things about my area the things I would change would probably be like, like some centre, youth centre, like where every one knows about it, its not just certain people, where like it is well known where young people can come like at different times, and do different activities so that everyone feel welcome, like you would come and do different activities. Like it would bring people off the street like young people off the street so that they don't feel like they have to go and do crime so that you know, they can feel better about themselves …	A youth centre that everyone knows Where everyone feels welcome Bring young people off the streets Getting involved in crime to feel good about oneself

Example

For instance, imagine you were evaluating a youth inclusion programme and the young people taking part on the programme spoke about having 'nothing to do' and 'nowhere to go'.[1] In initial coding of their transcripts you might use both these phrases as codes to indicate each instance when those words are mentioned. Not all your young people will talk about those experiences in the same way, however. Imagining that they talk about 'the youth centre closing down' or 'we are not allowed to hang out in that park' you might create the following codes, respectively: 'youth centre closed down' and 'hanging out in park not allowed'. You have now coded all your transcripts and you realise that a number of these codes are very similar in expressing a similar experience. Borrowing the label from your code you might decide to create the category 'nothing to do' as a key category in the analysis. All your codes then begin to represent instances or examples of 'nothing to do'. By examining all your codes under the category of 'nothing to do' you can begin to explore the particular circumstances in which young people have nothing to do (e.g. after school, in public spaces). This is the first phase of your analysis. It is a process of creating initial codes and then moving from codes to categories. The latter part of this process is one of abstraction, going from more detailed, local and descriptive information, to more abstract, theoretical categorisation. What you will find is that while you are coding and then categorising, a number of ideas or theoretical concepts will come to mind. It is important that you do two things at this stage. First, do not impose these concepts on the data at this stage. Instead, and this is the second thing to do, write them down on a separate piece of paper, remembering to link the code to the note (so you can cross-reference later). This latter process is very important and is called memo writing. We turn to it next.

Memo writing

Writing memos is the fundamental process in which the researcher engages analytically with their data (or artefacts) (Lempert, 2007). Memo writing takes place throughout the research process. It is a way of capturing ideas, interpretations, hunches or analytical responses that you as a researcher have to your data. Memos are fragments of nascent theory, a bridge and footpath between the detail of the data and the abstractions of theory. Lempert (2007: 246) defines the research practice of 'memoing' as 'the dynamic, intellectually energizing process that captures ideas in synergistic engagement with one another and, through naming, explicating, and synthesizing them, ultimately renders them accessible to wider audiences'. Initial memoing might be quite tentative and uncertain without much coherence or connection between memos (Lempert, 2007: 247). Lempert suggests that memos can take many forms including jotted notes, diagrams, drawings or whatever form of expression the researcher has used in order to engage with their data.

An example of this from my own analysis was when I was analysing 'What happens when we say that we are doing participation?' My analysis was based on the next phase of evaluating the youth inclusion programme mentioned in the previous section. Young people in the programme I was involved in evaluating were predominantly boys, and the staff I was meeting appeared to have much expertise

1 The example used throughout this section is based on the work of Humphreys, Nolas and Olmos (2006).

of working with boys. Their comments about girls' activities suggested that they were more comfortable working with boys because they knew how to engage the boys. I also experienced project workers in one project being much more judgemental and critical of the views and experiences expressed by the few young women participating in our evaluation activities, than the views and experiences of the young men in the group. I began to think about what this meant for a programme for *youth* that aimed to be *inclusive*. Who were the 'young people' the programme referred to? Who was being included? My memoing process involved jotting notes (single words and phrases) on to a piece of A4 paper, trying to literary draw the problem. I then started to think about, and created a new memo about, the relationship between girls and boys, inclusion and exclusion. The memoing process helped me to begin to think about these categories dialectically and I began to develop the theory that the 'youth' in youth inclusion tended to signify boys and that inclusion was then related to engaging boys. In mixed groups the inclusion of one group (boys) had, as I had experienced and the programme early monitoring figures suggested, the unintended consequence of sometimes excluding girls from the programme.

Example of memo writing

The following memos were generated while analysing the fieldnotes from a visit to a local youth inclusion project. The fieldnotes documented the discussion with those involved in managing and delivering the youth inclusion programme locally.

1. The 'problems' here are discussed from the perspective of the managers/youth workers – 'bouts of antisocial behaviour' and 'criminal families', ex-traveller families living there and the need to break cultural stereotypes around traveller families.

2. Within the discussion and discourse around the problems of the area, 'solutions' are weaved in – so, the discussion might start by saying what the issues are and then it will follow by saying what actions have been taken locally in order to deal with the problems. So, for example, the young mothers on the estate initiated a public meeting that generated some hostility and in particular anger towards the police because of lack of response on the police's side to neighbours' complaints of nuisance behaviour on the estate [this is interesting, I know from my own experience of noisy and disruptive neighbours that the police cannot really intervene and that it's the council that deals with this, e.g. a phone number that can be called for noise at antisocial hours, a diary that needs to be kept before action can be taken – collecting an evidence base that will justify action]; since the meeting, some of the 'notorious

Example

families' have moved away and so the problem seems to have subsided ...

3. I need to think about what it means that the discourses of problem and solutions are intertwined – is this done to demonstrate to us outsiders that things are being dealt with locally? That we want to preserve our identity for outsiders? For example, one of the managers uses the metaphor of things bubbling under the surface [of the calm sea], he tells us that on the outside the area looks 'quaint' but that there is an undercurrent of problems (such as older people feeling vulnerable in their homes). Or, for example, when I was talking to Mary (pseudonym) and asked her about the demographics of the area she avoided answering my question both in terms of age and race. From the conversations of the day it seems like a family area; we were told that there is a large cohort of young people; family and young people seem to be categories that neutralise any potential racial tension that could be said to exist in the area given the fascist graffiti on the vandalised house.

Theoretical coding and sorting

You now have your codes, categories and memos. In the next phase of the analysis you are performing three overlapping analytical tasks. The first task is theoretical coding: 'theoretical codes conceptualize how the substantive codes may relate to each other as hypotheses to be integrated into the theory' (Holton, 2007: 283). The aim here is to look for latent integrative patterns in your research material and analysis that can in turn be used to propose theories of social behaviour (Glaser, 2005, cited in Holton, 2007: 283). In other words the relationships and associations in your research material will not be initially obvious but implied in the action and interactions being researched and your role, through the analysis, will be to make the tacit pattern explicit. Holton (2007: 283) suggests that reading widely can help to recognise patterns and make the researcher more open to 'serendipitous discovery of new theoretical codes' as you take inspiration from theoretical languages in other disciplines. The second task is sorting. Sorting is the 'physical display of [the analyst's] thought processes' (Stern, 2007: 120). It involves writing out all of your memos and displaying them on a large surface (a table or the floor) and sorting through them, grouping them, categorising them, telling a story with the memos, until 'the appearance of theory begins to take shape' (Stern, 2007: 120). It is a key process in developing your theory by helping to develop the initial scaffolding of that theory (Holton, 2007: 283).

In my own research (Nolas, 2007) I found that project workers told a number of different stories about the young people they worked with. In my substantive coding I analysed these stories for their content, what the stories were about. My theoretical coding of the stories concentrated on the intended purpose of telling these stories. The theoretical coding suggested that the stories served a communicative function in which stories were used to open new spaces and preserve old spaces for youth inclusion to take place.

Using the literature

The role of existing literature in grounded theory is much contested (Bryant & Charmaz, 2007: 19). Strictly speaking, grounded theory calls for the researcher to enter the field without any preconceived ideas and allow theory to emerge. However, it has been argued (Emerson, Fretz & Shaw, 1995) that this suggests a decontextualised view of research, almost as if the researcher emerges from a vacuum to collect their data and then returns to that vacuum in order to analyse it. Furthermore, and especially where it is necessary to write proposals, you will need to review some literature to situate your research topic. As Stern (2007: 123) says, 'in order to participate in the current theoretical conversation, I need to understand it'. Being familiar with the literature is also useful in order to avoid situations in which what you think is a finding turns out to be known already in the field. As such, an initial review of the literature on the topic that you are researching can usefully orientate your research strategy by indicating what is already known and has been extensively researched, versus areas where gaps exist.

In my project (Nolas, 2007), in the initial stages of the research I carried out an extensive review of social psychological approaches to participation and working with communities. A lot of the literature in this area involves working with adults in the context of health. At the time, and within social psychology, there was comparatively much less written on the social psychology of participation with children and young people, and working with young people in community contexts, and especially in the more nebulous area of 'social exclusion' (for an exception see Bostock & Freeman, 2003). Having conducted my analysis I found that a key characteristic of the youth inclusion programme was its relationship to older notions within youth work. At that point I returned to the literature and began to look for research on youth work, social exclusion and youth inclusion, in order to compare my analysis to existing knowledge and refine my emergent theory.

Presenting the research

In a very early, and often forgotten, social psychological study of community resilience in which combined social action with the ethnographic (or 'sociographic' as the authors referred to it) study of that action, Marie Jahoda (Jahoda *et al.*, 1972: 98) wrote about the need to put 'before the reader a living picture of some of these people with whom we have had such close contact for a few months'. I have always found this metaphor very compelling. It also indicates that writing is an important part of the research and, in fact, analysis continues to take place through writing (Wuest, 2006, cited in Stern, 2007: 121). This also means that the researcher needs to be *something of a storyteller* (Stern, 2007: 122) in conveying the research journey and its outcomes to a reader. But grounded theory is not about storytelling, it is about theory development. In this respect you might find Wuest's (2006, cited in Stern, 2007: 122) interpretation of Glaser (1978) helpful. Glaser (1978) argues that grounded theorists should write about theory and not people. Wuest (2006) achieves this by first writing about her concepts, then providing the supporting data and, finally, drawing on relevant literature (Stern, 2007: 122).

Susan Leigh Star (2007: 76) has argued that grounded theory provides a way of looking at the world that simultaneously incorporates formal and informal understandings of it. While not aware of Star's work at the time, my motivation for adopting a grounded theory approach to looking at change work was similar (Nolas, 2009). The specific change strategy that I was looking at was participation. Participation refers to a way of working that strives to include people in the decision-making processes that are relevant to them and to empower people to take decisions on issues that affect them. I wanted to explore the gap between formal and informal ways of talking about participation – in other words, the differences between professional/scientific ways of understanding participation and the everyday experience of participation. My own experience pointed me towards a gap between the formal and the informal, and the increased publication of reflective pieces that contemplated the messiness of participation suggested that others had had similar experiences. Participation looked at as a way of working with people, a strategy for change, presents us with a field of action and interaction. As such, I began to look for appropriate social psychological theories for studying action and interaction. This led me to the literature on symbolic interactionism and to a version of the ethnographic tradition heavily inspired by grounded theory (Emerson, Fretz & Shaw, 1995). Symbolic interactionism, ethnography and grounded theory were especially useful for studying 'what happens when we say we are working in a participatory way'. I was attracted to symbolic interactionism's 'theoretical self-silencing' (Rock, 2001: 27), which is also a prominent feature of grounded theory. The study of participation is theoretically laden and ideologically loaded (in many cases for very good reasons – see Freire, 1970; 1994) making it sometimes difficult to disentangle the possibilities and limitations, and to produce theoretically nuanced and practically sensitive conceptual articulations about the process itself. The grounded theory approach provided an opportunity to conduct a study that focused on action and interaction in the field, and on emergent categories, as opposed to imposing theoretical frameworks of participation onto the field. My case study of a youth inclusion programme presented me with two fields of action in

Reflection on Practice

which to explore these ideas. The first was that of the programme of youth inclusion, which drew on ideas of participation such as empowerment and the need to build relationships with young people in order to bring about change. The second field was that of programme evaluation, especially the evaluation of young people's views, which was explicitly designed using ideas of participatory action research and critical pedagogy (Freire, 1970). My theoretical sensitivity on the topic was developed through previous experience of action research and prior training in social psychological approaches to public health and community development. During the fieldwork I persistently looked for negative cases to challenge the dominant understanding of participation as necessarily empowering for targeted groups. It was through working with negative cases that I discovered the gendered dimensions of participation in this particular programme (see page 34 and the text on memoing). Looking for negative cases also meant that when young people spoke about and demonstrated change, or new awareness, these instances presented themselves as genuine moments of surprise as opposed to being expected. I also used comparisons in my interviewing, asking youth workers and other project workers how current experiences of working with young people compared to past experiences or other contexts they had worked in. I also compared the experiences of the different local youth inclusion groups, and compared their experiences with policy and media discussions of young people, in order to understand the meaning and practice of what was being called 'youth inclusion'.

Common uses and applications

Grounded theory, as a research design and analytical tool, has been used in a range of psychological research as well as in related disciplines. It is has proved particularly useful in applied settings such as nursing, social work, counselling and psychotherapy. Because the study of action and interaction is at its core, when grounded theory is used as an 'entire package', it is most often used as a way of understanding practice. Susan Leigh Star (2007: 76), for instance, whose work looked at classification systems and how they impact on professional and daily life, adopted a grounded theory approach to her work because she was 'looking for a way simultaneously to incorporate formal and informal understandings of the world'. In my own work the approach lent itself well to exploring the gap between formal and informal ways of talking about one particular change strategy used in community work, namely participation. The grounded theory approach allowed me to answer the question: 'What happens when we say we are working in a participatory way?'

Glaser and Strauss's (1965) work has become the inspiration behind the widespread adoption of grounded theory in clinical settings. Their study explored how a social issue impacted on professional practice in a clinical setting. The social issue they identified was the lack of public discussion around death and the process of dying. They also observed that this lack of public discussion was present in the very context it was most relevant to: the medical context of palliative care. Professionals' behaviour in that context also exhibited the same moral attitude implied by the lack of public discourse on dying (that it is better to live than to die, unless someone is in extreme pain). Glaser and Strauss (1965: 7) reasoned that, as more and more Americans were beginning to die in hospital as opposed to dying at home, the problem of 'awareness of dying' would become increasingly salient for all those involved. As such, they set out to explore what happened around terminally ill patients in American hospitals. In looking at the kinds of interactions between dying patients and hospital staff, the sorts of tactics used by staff to engage with patients and the different conditions under which interaction took place, Glaser and Strauss found that 'awareness' was a pivotal explanatory concept that explained interactions and tactics under different conditions.

Grounded theory becomes useful for studying practice because, as Star (2007: 79) puts it, it makes invisible work visible. It helps to surface the tacit and taken-for-granted aspects of practical work by asking questions about what people are doing and trying to accomplish, how exactly they are going about the 'doing', and how

---

An example of using the grounded theory to study chronic illness

Cathy Charmaz's seminal work looks at ways in which people with chronic illness manage their illness and construct their sense of self. In her own words, her study consists of studying 'the private face of a public problem – what illness and disability mean to people who have them' (Charmaz, 1991: 4). The study is based on 170 interviews with 90 participants over a period of 11 years. Charmaz's doctoral work developed from the experience of working as an occupational therapist. During this time she found that much of her work, rather than delivering on the rhetoric of rehabilitation about maximising human potential, focused instead on supporting patients to manage their disabilities on an everyday basis in a way that would enable them to stay at home and avoid being institutionalised (1991: vii). She became fascinated by the way in which people with a chronic illness managed their identity and time in light of their illness. Her study shows that people experience chronic illness in three different ways: as an interruption, an intrusion and/or an immersion. Each of these experiences has consequences for how people define themselves and manage living with their illness. Chronic illness also affects people's experience of time, as their illness often determines how they go about their daily activities.

Example

people understand what is going on (Emerson, Fretz & Shaw, 1995). In this respect, grounded theory is also commonly used with action research approaches, a common participatory change practice with roots in the work of social psychologist Kurt Lewin. It has been argued that theory *building* is one of the biggest challenges for action research (Huxman, 2003: 243, cited in Dick, 2007: 402). At the same time, both action research and grounded theory concentrate on the 'emergence' of theory from the bottom up. In this respect Dick suggests that action research can strengthen its theory-building potential by borrowing the language and analytical practices of grounded theory. This is an example of using grounded theory as an analytical tool that brings rigour to and systematises analysis. Similar uses of grounded theory can be found in qualitative research (see Dilks *et al.*, 2010) also for the purpose of organising the research.

An example of combining grounded theory and participatory action research to inform professional practice

Eli Teram and colleagues (Teram, Schachter & Stalker, 2005) used grounded theory and participatory action research to explore the experiences of female survivors of childhood sexual abuse and to create a handbook for physical therapists that would enable them to develop sensitive practice for working with this population. Their study developed in response to evidence about the health problems experienced by survivors of childhood sexual abuse, and their own experiences of working with survivors as physiotherapists and social workers. They faced the challenge of producing usable knowledge in an unexplored area. Grounded theory, as we have seen in this chapter, is an appropriate methodology for developing a conceptual under-standing of a phenomenon where little prior knowledge exists. The primary aim of action research, on the other hand, is to put such knowledge to use (Reason & Riley, 2008). The study involved inter-viewing 27 Canadian women survivors of childhood sexual abuse who had either received physiotherapy or were considering physiotherapy. The three authors analysed the data independently and then shared their analysis with the participants. The authors and the women then met on a monthly basis for a period of six months in order to turn their analysis into practical suggestions and guidelines for sensitive practice (Teram *et al.*, 2005: 1133–1134). The final output of the project was a handbook on sensitive practice for health professionals.

Example

Another use of grounded theory is in research on lived experience in domains that have come to be dominated by 'expert knowledge', such as science and technology, engineering, and medical and other clinical sciences. The orientation of grounded theory in privileging emergent theory, as opposed to existing theory, as well as its symbolic interactionist roots, makes the approach suitable for exploring the everyday lived experience and capturing both the construction of expert views as well as how expertise is experienced and the impact it has on ordinary people's everyday life. For example, Ilana Singh's work (2002a; 2002b; 2003; 2004; 2005) on mothers' and fathers' experiences of parenting a child with ADHD, and now also including children's experiences of ADHD (http://www.adhdvoices.com/), took a grounded theory approach (see the Research Example box on page 25 for more details). Similarly, Dilks *et al.*'s (2010) work looks at how individuals with psychosis and therapists co-construct the role and purpose of therapy. They use grounded theory as a way of bringing rigour to their analysis as well as a way of capturing experiences of therapy from different perspectives.

CASE STUDY

The press in your country does not often carry very positive stories about young people. Most of the stories that appear in the press are about young people getting into trouble with the law, disrupting town centres on a Saturday night, and generalised 'bad' behaviour. You would like to find out how widespread this negative view of young people is. You decide to interview members of your local church congregation. You also interview your friends and fellow students from university. Finally, you also decide to interview Saturday shoppers, who you recruit at the local shopping centre. You recruit ten people from each group and conduct 60–90-minute interviews with each person, which you later transcribe. You analyse the material using the grounded theory method. You find that each group holds the following views of young people. Those in the church congregation speak well of young relatives but have an ambivalent view towards young people to whom they are not related. The student and peer group have favourable views of those in their networks, but suggest that not all young people are like them. Your Saturday shoppers have a broad range of views about young people and talk a lot about public spaces for young people.

1. How is grounded theory being used here?
2. Given the emerging findings from the church congregation group and the student peer group, what seems to be presenting itself as a key category and potential nascent theory?
3. What do you make of the findings from the Saturday shoppers group? How do they relate to the other two groups?

4. Given these initial findings, and following grounded theory principles of theoretical sampling, what would you do next?
5. What are the similarities between the case study (in terms of impetus for the study/initial observations) and Glaser and Strauss's (1967) study (described on page 39)?
6. Glaser and Strauss (1967) started with the observation of a social issue (absence of a public discussion about death and dying), and went on to understand how this social issue affected professional and patient interactions in a context where one might expect discussions of death and dying to be the norm. Taking the initial starting point of the above case study (negative stories of young people in the media) how might you design a grounded theory study that engages with the symbolic interactionist roots of grounded theory?
7. Leaving the above case study as it is, what other methodological approaches might it be appropriate to use? (See other chapters in this book for ideas.)

Chapter summary

In this chapter we have focused on the grounded theory approach to qualitative research in psychology.

- The ontological and epistemological underpinnings of the approach were discussed. These were traced to early sociological thinking, the pragmatist and the symbolic interactionist tradition. The epistemology of grounded theory was described as being composed of three main practices: constant comparison, abduction and reflexivity. We saw that grounded theory poses a number of ontological and epistemological challenges to conventional psychological thinking, especially to those approaches that focus exclusively on individuals and ignore group life. Grounded theory's focus is not on individuals or psychological states or experiences. Its main unit of analysis is action and interaction, especially as that continuously unfolds in and is shaped by different social settings. It presents us with a deeply social psychological view of the world, and especially one informed by theories of society and culture.
- The chapter then focused on the methodological tools used in a grounded theory approach. We saw that grounded theory relies on a number of research methods, such as fieldwork and participant observation, and their recording, as well as interviews, focus groups and archival documentation. It was noted that such approaches have much more in common with sociological and anthropological approaches to research that will perhaps be familiar to the psychological researcher (with the exception of those

researchers working in critical traditions). As such, doing grounded theory requires a fundamental shift in perspective from focusing on entities to looking at processes, and from what people say to what people do together. It also reintroduces context into psychological analysis, both in its ontological as well as epistemological orientation.

- The chapter looked at a number of practical examples where grounded theory has been applied. It was noted that the approach has been used in a number of applied research settings. It offers a system for studying the formal and informal dimensions of an activity and so is often used in the study of professional practices. The tendency of the approach to privilege emergent theory has also led to its use in the domains where lived experience has come to be dominated by 'expert knowledge'. In these contexts grounded theory creates space for engaging with non-expert views and experiences.

Problem-based questions

1. Everything is data but data isn't everything. What does that mean exactly, with reference to the grounded theory approach?
2. Grounded theory emphasises the study of action and interaction. How might this be relevant to psychology?
3. What would you say is the difference between grounded theory and *a* grounded theory?
4. If one's research does not subscribe to all the historical legacy of the grounded theory approach, can one still be said to be doing grounded theory?

Further reading

Bowkers, G. & Star, S.L. (1999) *Sorting Things Out: Classification and its Consequences.* Cambridge, MA: The MIT Press.

Bryant, A. & Charmaz, K. (2007) *The Sage Handbook of Grounded Theory.* London: Sage.

Charmaz, K. (2006) *Constructing Grounded Theory: A Practical Guide through Qualitative Analysis.* London: Sage.

Glaser, B.G. (1978) *Theoretical Sensitivity.* Mill Valley, CA: Sociology Press

Glaser, B.G. & Strauss, A.L. (1965). *Awareness of Dying.* Chicago, IL: Aldine.

Glaser, B.G. & Strauss, A.L. (1967) *The Discovery of Grounded Theory: Strategies for Qualitative Research.* Chicago, IL: Aldine.

Strauss, A.L. & Corbin, J. (1998) *Basics of Qualitative Research* (2nd edn). London: Sage.

CHAPTER 3

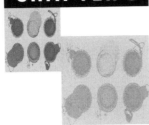

Interpretative Phenomenological Analysis

Pnina Shinebourne

Introduction

This chapter is about interpretative phenomenological analysis (IPA). IPA is an approach to qualitative research that explores in detail personal lived experience to examine how people are making sense of their personal and social world. It tries to understand what the world is like from the point of view of the participants. At the same time, IPA acknowledges that this understanding is always mediated by the context of cultural and socio-historical meanings. Therefore, the process of making sense of experience is inevitably interpretative and the role of the researcher in trying to make sense of the participant's account is complicated by the researcher's own conceptions.

The first part of this chapter presents the history of IPA, and shows how it has evolved to take its place in psychological research. The theoretical underpinnings of the approach are discussed, and this is followed by a consideration of the epistemological and ontological frameworks IPA employs. A detailed presentation of the stages involved in doing IPA follows, with illustrations taken from a study exploring the experience of women in rehabilitation for their problems of addiction. The chapter concludes with reflections on using IPA.

History of IPA

IPA was first used as a distinctive research method in psychology in the mid-1990s. Smith (1996) drew on theoretical ideas from phenomenology (Giorgi, 1995), **hermeneutics** (Palmer, 1969), and on an engagement with subjective experience and personal accounts (Smith, Harré & Van Langenhove, 1995). IPA is also influenced by symbolic interactionism (Eatough & Smith, 2008). Symbolic interactionism provides a theoretical perspective with basic assumptions that people act on the basis of the meanings that things have for them and that meanings emerge in the processes of social interaction between people (Blumer, 1969). Thus, meanings are constructed and modified through an interpretative process that is subject to change and redefinition (Blumer, 1969). In this way 'people form new meanings and new ways to respond and thus are active in shaping their own future through the process of interpreting meaning' (Benzies & Allen, 2001: 544).

By combining insights from phenomenology, hermeneutic philosophy and engagement with subjective experience, IPA proposes a middle way between different qualitative methods. In common with phenomenological psychology it offers researchers an avenue to study subjective experiences and the meanings that people attribute to their experience. In common with discursive psychology, IPA accepts that the research process is fundamentally hermeneutic, with both researcher and participants engaging in interpretative activities that are constrained by shared social and cultural discourses.

This synthesis of ideas from different perspectives has led to the development of a distinctive qualitative psychological methodology. As Willig (2008) contends, the introduction of IPA into psychology has made phenomenological methodology accessible to those who do not have a philosophical background. In addition, by developing detailed descriptions of the analytic process, those new to IPA are encouraged to use it in their own research (Willig, 2008).

Much of the early use of IPA was concerned with health and illness (for a recent review of IPA's use in health psychology see Brocki & Wearden, 2006). Other key areas for IPA research are sex and sexuality, psychological distress, and issues of life transitions and identity (for overviews of research in these areas see Smith, Flowers & Larkin, 2009). As Smith *et al.* (2009) point out, issues of identity are intertwined with most of the research in health and illness, sexuality and psychological distress. They contend that, as IPA research often concerns topics of considerable existential significance, it is likely that the participants will link the specific topic to their sense of self/identity.

Ontology of IPA

Although IPA is grounded in the experiential dimension in its concern with a detailed examination of individual lived experience and how people are making sense of that experience, it 'endorses social constructionism's claim that sociocultural and historical processes are central to how we experience and understand our lives, including the stories we tell about these lives' (Eatough & Smith, 2008: 184). In this respect it can be located at a centre-ground position between experiential approaches such as descriptive phenomenology and discursive approaches such as discourse analysis. In the experiential approaches the focus is on participants' experiences and how they make sense of their experiences. The discursive approaches are focused on language as a social action that is used to construct and create the social world (Reicher, 2000).

The different qualitative methods are grounded in different epistemological stances (Henwood, 1996; Willig, 2008). These vary significantly, as 'they have different philosophical roots, they have different theoretical assumptions and they ask different types of questions' (Reicher, 2000: 4). However, there is considerable overlap between qualitative methods (Lyons, 2007; Charmaz & Henwood, 2008;

Smith *et al.*, 2009) and the distinction between the different approaches can be conceived in terms of a continuum from the experiential to the discursive, and from the empiricist to the constructionist (Lyons, 2007; Willig, 2008). With its focus on content and systematic analysis of a text to identify themes and categories, IPA shares some similarities with grounded theory (Willig, 2008). Through its concern with meaning-making IPA also shares strong intellectual links with narrative analysis (Crossley, 2007; Smith *et al.*, 2009). Eatough and Smith (2006) maintain that 'IPA shares some common ground with **Foucauldian discourse** analysis [FDA], which examines how people's worlds are discursively constructed and how these are implicated in the experiences of the individual' (2006: 118–119).

In this respect IPA can be described as located at the 'light end of the social constructionist continuum' (Eatough & Smith, 2006) in relation to discourse analysis. Smith *et al.* (2009) suggest that 'while IPA studies provide a detailed experiential account of the person's *involvement* in the context, FDA offers a critical analysis of the structure of the context itself and thus touches on the resources available to the individual in making sense of their experience' (2009: 196).

Why do IPA?

IPA has been described as 'an approach to qualitative, experiential and psychological research which has been informed by concepts and debates from three key areas of philosophy of knowledge: phenomenology, hermeneutics and **idiography**' (Smith *et al.*, 2009: 11). IPA draws on each of these theoretical approaches to inform its distinctive epistemological framework and research methodology.

Phenomenology is both a philosophical approach and a range of research methods concerned with how things appear to us in our experience. Edmund Husserl (1859–1938) initiated modern phenomenology at the beginning of the twentieth century and since then it has become a major philosophical movement that has impacted on many strands of contemporary philosophy (Zahavi, 2008). Other phenomenological philosophers – namely, Heidegger, Sartre and Merleau-Ponty – contributed to the philosophical perspective of a person as embodied, embedded and immersed in the world in a particular historical, social and cultural context (for a comprehensive overview of phenomenology see Moran, 2000). Phenomenology as a research method draws on the phenomenological philosophy initiated by Husserl. Although a number of diverse approaches have been developed, the focus on subjective experience has remained a fundamental principle of all phenomenologically informed research methods, including IPA (for a discussion of various phenomenological approaches in psychology, see Langdridge, 2007).

Hermeneutics, the theory of interpretation, constitutes another major theoretical underpinning of IPA. Historically, hermeneutics developed from interpretations of biblical texts but was subsequently established as a philosophical foundation for a more general theory of interpretation. Although phenomenology and herme-neutics were developed as two separate philosophical movements, Heidegger

(1962) presented hermeneutics as a prerequisite to phenomenology. According to Heidegger, the meaning of hermeneutic resides in 'the whole manner in which human existence is interpretative' (Moran, 2000: 235). Thus, Moran contends that:

> Phenomenology is seeking after a meaning which is perhaps hidden by the entity's mode of appearing. In that case the proper model for seeking meaning is the interpretation of a text and for this reason Heidegger links phenomenology with hermeneutics. How things appear or are covered up must be explicitly studied. The things themselves always present themselves in a manner which is at the same time self-concealing. (Moran, 2000: 229)

In this view, interpretation is a necessary part of phenomenology because the entity's mode of appearing may conceal something that is hidden. The task of interpreting is therefore to engage in the dynamic of conceal/reveal, making manifest what may lie hidden. In Heidegger's conception, every interpretation is already contextualised in previous experience in a particular context, as according to Heidegger, human existence is fundamentally related to the world: human beings are thrown into a world in a particular historical, social and cultural context (Heidegger, 1962). From this perspective, understanding of events or objects in the world is always mediated and constrained by already existing knowledge: 'Interpretation is grounded in something we have in advance' (Heidegger, 1962: 191). Heidegger recognises the danger that such preconceptions may present an obstacle to interpretation (Smith *et al.*, 2009) and, therefore, in interpretation priority should be given to the new object rather than to one's preconceptions. Interpretation is thus envisaged as a dynamic process, an interplay between the interpreter and the object of interpretation.

Idiography constitutes the third theoretical underpinning of IPA. An idiographic approach aims for an in-depth focus on the particular and a commitment to detailed finely textured analysis of actual life and lived experience (Smith *et al.*, 2009). A commitment to idiography is linked to a rationale for single case studies. Smith (2004) suggests that a detailed analysis of a single case would be justified when one has a particularly rich or compelling case. A detailed single case study offers opportunities to learn a great deal about the particular person and their response to a specific situation, as well as to consider connections between different aspects of the person's account. It is also possible to consider a case study as a part of a larger study involving a number of participants. The individual case can be used as a starting point in the process of analytic induction, affording an opportunity for working from the ground up by drawing together additional cases to move towards more general claims. Perhaps the important point to consider is that the details of a single case also illuminate a dimension of a shared commonality, as 'the very detail of the individual also brings us closer to significant aspects of a shared humanity' (Smith, 2004: 43).

IPA draws on each of these theoretical approaches to inform its distinctive epistemological framework and research methodology, as described below.

- IPA is phenomenological in its detailed examination of the personal lived experience of practical engagement with the world and in exploring how participants make sense of their experience. IPA acknowledges that the understanding of an event or an object is always mediated by the context of cultural and socio-historical meanings. The term *lived experience* is often used 'to encompass the embodied, socio-culturally and historically situated person who inhabits an intentionally interpreted and meaningfully lived world' (Eatough & Smith, 2008: 181). In agreement with Heidegger's views, IPA considers phenomenological inquiry as an interpretative process. In this view, interpretation is necessary because the entity's mode of appearing may conceal something that is hidden. Consistent with its phenomenological underpinning, IPA is concerned with trying to understand what it is like from the point of view of the participants. At the same time, a detailed IPA analysis can also involve asking critical questions of participants' accounts. Thus, interpretation can be descriptive and empathic, aiming to produce 'rich experiential descriptions', and also critical and questioning 'in ways which participants might be unwilling or unable to do themselves' (Eatough & Smith, 2008: 189).

- IPA is interpretative in recognising the role of the researcher in making sense of the experience of participants. Smith (2004) refers to 'double hermeneutics: The participant is trying to make sense of their personal and social world; the researcher is trying to make sense of the participant trying to make sense of their personal and social world' (2004: 40). The researcher's point of access to participants' experience is through their accounts, usually obtained through direct contact with participants. The concept of 'double hermeneutics' refers also to the researcher's own involvement through their own preconceptions and 'prejudices', which may constitute an obstacle to interpretation (Smith, 2007) unless priority is given to the phenomenon under investigation. Drawing on Ricoeur's (1970) distinction between two strategies for understanding meaning – namely, a hermeneutics of meaning recollection, of empathic engagement, and a hermeneutics of suspicion, of critical engagement – Smith (2004) has argued that both modes of hermeneutic engagement can contribute to a more complete understanding of the participant's lived experience. However, 'within such an analysis the empathic reading is likely to come first and may then be qualified by a more critical and speculative reflection' (Smith, 2004: 46). Smith *et al.* (2009) maintain that IPA occupies a 'centre-ground position' whereby it is possible to combine a hermeneutic of empathy with a hermeneutic of questioning 'so long as it serves to "draw out" or "disclose" the meaning of the experience' (2009: 36), in contrast to employing a theoretical perspective imported from outside the text. Larkin, Watts and Clifton (2006) contend that the strategies chosen by the analyst 'may be informed by prior experience and knowledge, psychological theory, or previous research – provided that they can be related back to a phenomenological account' (2006: 116).

- IPA is idiographic in its focus on detailed examination of particular instances, either in a single case study or in studies of a small group of cases. In such studies the analytic process begins with the detailed analysis of each case, moving to careful examination of similarities and differences across cases to produce detailed accounts of patterns of meaning and reflections on shared experience. A single case study offers an opportunity to learn a great deal about a particular person in a specific context, as well as focusing on different aspects of a particular account. In addition, through connecting the findings to existing psychological literature, the IPA writer can help the reader to see how the case relates to other relevant research. IPA is particularly suitable for research where the 'focus is on the uniqueness of a person's experiences, how experiences are made meaningful and how these meanings manifest themselves within the context of the person both as an individual and in their many cultural roles, for example as an MS or epilepsy sufferer, as a parent, sibling, employee, student, friend, spouse' (Shaw, 2001: 48). For example, in health psychology, in order to understand the meanings and the significance of a particular condition for a person's everyday life, the researcher may need to gain access to in-depth accounts of individuals' experiences. At the same time, studies of several participants also highlight the shared themes and concerns. In addition, the individual case can be used as a starting point in the process of analytic induction, affording an opportunity for theory development from the ground up by drawing together additional cases to move towards more general claims.

Examples of suitable research include explorations of questions like:

- How do people make decisions about taking a genetic test?
- What is it like to experience anger?
- What is it like to donate a kidney?
- What is it like to be the carer for a person with Alzheimer's?
- How do couples make the decision to have children?

The approach to recruiting participants for an IPA study follows from the theoretical account of the epistemology of IPA. This means that participants are selected purposively. **Purposive sampling** refers to a method of selecting participants because they have particular features or characteristics that will enable detailed exploration of the phenomena being studied. Because the primary concern of IPA is with a detailed account of individual experience, IPA studies usually benefit from an intensive focus on a small number of participants. Sample size can vary according to the research question and the quality of the data obtained. In the studies reviewed by Brocki and Wearden (2006) participant numbers vary from one to thirty, although they point out that a consensus towards the use of smaller sample sizes seems to be emerging. As discussed above, IPA also makes a strong case for a single case study, which could be justified when one has a particularly rich or compelling case. Smith *et al.* (2009) suggest a sample size between three and six for undergraduate or master's-level IPA projects.

IPA researchers usually try to identify a homogeneous sample. With a small number of participants it seems helpful to think in terms of a defined group of participants for whom the research questions will be meaningful. Making a decision on the extent of 'homogeneity' is guided by the focus of the study. An investigation of a phenomenon that is rare (for example, living with a rare genetic disorder) may in itself define the boundaries of the relevant sample. Alternatively, with less specific issues the sample may be drawn from a population with similar demographic or socio-economic status.

IPA requires a data collection method that will invite participants to offer rich, detailed, first-person accounts of experiences. Semi-structured, one-to-one interviews have been used most often, as they are particularly useful for in-depth idiographic studies exploring how participants are making sense of experiences. Such interviews enable the researcher and participant to engage in a dialogue, modify questions and follow interesting aspects that come up during the interview (for overviews of quality and concerns over the status and use of interview data see, for example, Atkinson, Coffey & Delamont, 2003; Roulston, 2010). However, other methods suitable for colleting rich verbal accounts have been used – for example, diaries (e.g. Smith, 1999), focus groups (e.g. Flowers, Knussen & Duncan, 2001) and email dialogues (Turner, Barlow & Ilbery, 2002).

It is helpful to envisage the interaction during interviews as a conversation, which although guided by the researcher's pre-prepared questions, opens up a space for participants to provide detailed accounts of experiences guided by their own concerns. During the interview, it may be more fruitful to follow unexpected turns initiated by the participant's accounts, rather than adhering to the specific questions in the original sequence. As Smith *et al.* (2009) contend, 'unexpected turns are often the most valuable aspects of interviewing: on the one hand, they tell us something we did not even anticipate needing to know; on the other, because they arise unprompted, they may well be of particular importance to the participant' (Smith *et al.*, 2009: 58).

Arroll, M. & Senior, V. (2008) Individuals' experience of chronic fatigue syndrome/ myalgic encephalomyelitis: an interpretative phenomenological analysis. *Psychology & Health*, 23(4), 443–458.

Background

Chronic fatigue syndrome/myalgic encephalomyelitis (CFS/ME) is a condition of unknown aetiology that consists of symptoms such as fatigue, muscle and joint pain, gastric problems and a range of neurological disturbances. Previous qualitative research in the area of CFS/ME has focused on participants' beliefs about the cause of their illness and symptomatology, but the factors that influence how individuals with CFS/ME perceive their symptoms have not been investigated from a phenomenological epistemology. The authors contend that as CFS/ME has a wide-ranging influence on individuals' lives, investigating this condition within the patients' phenomenological experience will provide depth and detail to our present understanding of CFS/ME.

Method

Participants

The sample consisted of two male and six female participants with ages ranging from 35 to 67. The average length of time the participants had been living with CFS/ME was 21.4 years, although this varied widely from 6 to 53 years.

Data collection

Semi-structured, one-to-one interviews consisted of a range of open-ended questions, including prompts that allowed further elaboration of the topic under discussion. The interview started with a broad question – 'Can you please describe to me how you became ill with CFS/ME?' – and was followed by more specific topics: the cause of CFS/ME, the effect on one's life, the process of diagnosis, and advice that one would give another individual who believed that he/she might be suffering from CFS/ME. The duration of the interviews was between 26 and 90 minutes, with an average interview lasting 40.8 minutes. The interviews were recorded and transcribed verbatim.

Analysis

The transcripts were analysed using IPA. The analysis followed the staged process described in Smith and Osborn (2003), first for one transcript and then repeating the procedures for each transcript. In the final stage the superordinate themes and sub-themes for the study as a whole were established. Six distinct themes that illustrated the participants' experience and perception of their symptoms were identified.

Research Example

Research Example

Findings

The paper illustrates the shared themes but also the particular details of individual participants' experiences. In the present study, symptomatology and illness course, interference with daily and working life, frequency of symptoms, external information, diagnosis and treatment each played a part in the recognition of individuals' symptoms as CFS/ME. Although the interviewees stated that fatigue was the predominant symptom of their illness, they listed a range of other symptoms including pain, gastrointestinal problems, cognitive difficulties and sleep impairments. The narrative is constructed as a journey from the initial experience of bodily sensations, through the disruption these symptoms imposed on individuals' lives. Trying to make sense of their experiences, participants initially evaluated their symptoms in terms of known diseases. When the known disease provided inadequate explanations of their symptoms, participants sought external information and a diagnosis to shed new light on their personal experience. However, a diagnosis of CFS/ME was not the end of the journey and, in fact, may have only been the beginning in the search for treatment.

Discussion

The symptomatological findings in this study were in accordance with previous studies … As in the Cohn (1999) study, the participants described their predominant symptom in terms of energy levels, where an individual is allocated a set amount of energy and any expenditure that exceeds this amount will result in ill health. Equally, the description of CFS/ME symptomatology as fluctuating in nature (Ware, 1999) was also apparent in the present study. However … it was not the symptoms themselves that concerned the interviewees, but rather the frequency of bodily disturbance (Radley, 1994). This incidence of symptoms prompted the interviewees to question whether their complaints were 'everyday' occurrences or a sign of a more serious underlying disorder. However, even with an increased understanding participants still had a struggle for recognition of their condition. Furthermore, even with a positive clinical diagnosis of CFS/ME the journey continued with a search for treatment.

The authors suggest that as the participants in the study had CFS/ME for many years, in future research it may be useful to look at individuals at different points in their condition. The authors conclude that by using a method of investigation that does not constrain the findings to be interpreted in terms of pre-set hypotheses, their study has highlighted the lived experience and meaning-making of those with CFS/ME. The findings should be useful for researchers and/or practitioners to increase their understanding of the process by which individuals recognise their symptomatology as being consistent with CFS/ME.

Methods: how to do IPA

This section outlines step-by-step guidelines for conducting an IPA study, illustrated with an extended example from a study exploring the experience of women in rehabilitation for addiction problems. However, the stages described below should not be treated as the 'correct' method for doing IPA as IPA provides a flexible framework that can be adapted by researchers in accordance with their research aims.

The research question

The main reason for choosing a research methodology is that it is consistent with the epistemological position of the research question. As IPA is concerned with the in-depth exploration of personal lived experience and with how people make sense of their experience, the type of research question suitable for an IPA study is likely to involve issues and experiences of considerable significance to the participant. Often these are transformative issues concerned with personal and social identity. These could be current, emotive, dilemmatic issues or issues involving longer-term reflection across the life course. The example box below lists the type of research question suitable for IPA studies.

Examples of research questions suitable for IPA studies

- How do people with chronic back pain describe the impact on their sense of self? (Smith & Osborn, 2007)
- How do people experience chronic fatigue syndrome? (Arroll & Senior, 2008)
- What does it mean to be a donor offspring? (Turner & Coyle, 2000)
- How do HIV-positive women experience partner relationships? (Jarman, Walsh & DeLacey, 2005).

Example

An IPA study starts with formulating suitable research questions. The questions are open and exploratory, designed to focus on exploring participants' accounts of lived experience, understandings and sense-making within the particular context of their lives. The example box below illustrates the research questions that guided my project exploring the experience of women in rehabilitation for addiction problems (Shinebourne & Smith, 2009).

> Example
>
> ***Research questions from project exploring the experience of women in rehabilitation for addiction problems***
> - How do the participants describe their experiences of addiction and recovery?
> - In what contexts do their experiences occur?
> - How do the participants understand and make sense of their experiences of addiction and recovery?
> - How are individual differences reflected in the participants' accounts of their experiences with alcohol/drug addiction and recovery?

The first two questions are descriptive, in line with a phenomenological approach, and they frame the accounts in the context of the participants' world. The third question opens up an interpretative avenue for participants to reflect on their own accounts in their attempts to make sense of their experiences. The fourth question provides a prompt to remain focused on the particular, the detail, texture and nuance of the participants' lived experience.

Sample and recruitment of participants

Potential participants can be reached by approaching relevant groups, agencies or gatekeepers, through personal contacts, or through '**snowballing**'. Snowballing refers to a method of selecting a sample in which potential participants are asked whether they know of other people with relevant characteristics and experiences who might be approached. Snowball sampling is often used to find and recruit 'hidden populations', groups not easily accessible to researchers through other sampling strategies. Participants in the rehabilitation study were recruited through agencies offering treatment and recovery programmes for people with problems of addiction. Considering that some participants in rehabilitation may be vulnerable, it seemed sensible to secure agencies' support, not only in suggesting suitable possible participants, but also in providing follow-up support for participants. However, using agencies required obtaining consent both from the agency and the participant. The sample for the rehabilitation study consisted of six female participants who had been involved in their programmes for between one and two years. The age range was between 31 and 52 years.

Data collection

As noted above, IPA requires a data collection method that will invite participants to offer a rich, detailed, first-person account of their experiences and phenomena. Semi-structured, one-to-one interviews have been used most often, and this method is used in the following example. An interview schedule should be prepared in advance to help the researcher to anticipate and prepare for possible difficulties – for example, in addressing sensitive issues and in question wording. Interview questions should be open and expansive, to encourage participants to talk at length. Questions should not make too many assumptions about participants' experiences and should not lead towards particular answers. As some questions may be too abstract for some participants, it is helpful to prepare more specific prompts to be used if required. It is usually helpful to start the interview with a descriptive question about the present, as in the example box below, which illustrates the interview schedule for the rehabilitation study.

Interview schedule from project exploring the experience of women in rehabilitation for addiction problems (extract)

1. Can you tell me what place alcohol/drug has in your life at the moment?
   Possible prompts: What happens? How do you feel? How do you cope?
2. Can you tell me about a recent time when you used alcohol/drugs?
   Possible prompts: What happened? How did you feel? How did you cope?
3. Can you describe how alcohol/drinking/using drugs affects your relationships with other people?
   Possible prompts: Partner, family, friends, work colleagues?
4. Can you tell me how you started drinking/using drugs?
   Possible prompts: How long ago? What do you think brought this about? Can you describe how you felt about alcohol/drugs at that time?
5. Have you changed the ways you used alcohol/drugs over time?
   Possible prompts: In what ways? Does anything make it better? Does anything make it worse? How do you feel about these changes?
6. What would be for you a positive development?
   Possible prompts: How can your situation improve? Can you imagine what it would feel like?

Example

The schedule starts with a question about the present, which provides a focus for participants to describe current issues in their life at some length. Questions about potentially sensitive issues and questions inviting reflection appear later in the schedule. This allows time for participant and researcher to become more comfortable with each other and with the interview situation, and to feel their way into the dynamics and rhythm of the interview. Prompts are prepared in case participants find it difficult to respond, and to offer them a range of possible routes. The schedule includes ten questions that tend to occupy between 45 and 60 minutes of conversation, depending on the topic.

CASE STUDY

Constructing an interview schedule for an IPA study

The study explores the psychological impact of chronic back pain through in-depth personal accounts of sufferers and the manner in which their sense of self unfolded and developed as their pain progressed.

Imagine a novice IPA researcher constructing an interview schedule for the first time asking for your help in redrafting and refining the interview questions.

A. Write down what you think is wrong with each of the questions in the schedule below.
  1. Was it a shock when the pain started?
  2. So you have been having this pain for five years then. Do you think it is going to get better or not? What do you hope will make it better?
  3. What is the most frightening thing about being in pain?
  4. Do you get angry when you are in pain?
  5. Living with chronic pain must be very tough. Do you describe yourself as a tough person?
  6. I can imagine the pain is demoralising – is that right?
B. How would you improve these questions? Draft alternative questions and add additional questions suitable for the study.
C. What would be a suitable sample to interview (characteristics, how many participants)?

To compare your answers with the interview schedule and the sample actually used in the study, see Smith, J. & Osborn, M. (2007) Pain as an assault on the self: an interpretative phenomenological analysis of the psychological impact of chronic benign low back pain. *Psychology & Health*, 22(5), 517–534.

Analysis

IPA provides a flexible framework of processes and strategies for analysis. Analysis in IPA is an iterative, complex and creative process that requires the researcher's reflective engagement in a dialogue with a participant's narrative and meanings. Although in practice the analysis is fluid, iterative and multi-directional, for the purpose of illustrating the process here it is useful to describe distinct stages.

Initial stage

The initial stage consists of reading the whole transcript a number of times to become thoroughly familiar with the data. It is useful to record some observations and reflections about the interview experience, as well as any other thoughts and comments of potential significance, in a separate reflexive notebook. This is accompanied by a detailed textual analysis that starts with writing notes and comments on the transcript. The process of engaging with the transcript in close analysis involves focusing on content, use of language, context and interpretative

Interview: initial comments (extract)

Exploratory comments	Original transcript
Issues from the past – upheaval of life as lived at present	Not being able to work and going into rehab which was very difficult and having to go back into my past so it's been a huge upheaval of everything you know, you know like the hornet's nest
Using metaphor – indirectly pointing to problematic experience underneath image of conventional ordinary life	[ ] P: What was in your hornet's nest? C: Erm, what was in there quite a lot really I mean, as I said nothing major, nothing major has ever happened to me in the sense of the conventional kind of stuff, you think it was because I was abused, it was because, that didn't happen, but you know my
Dysfunctional childhood family – father alcoholic	childhood wasn't as functional as I thought you know I had a very, yeah my dad was an alcoholic but I
Intense relations with mother and sister, female bond, no male	didn't really see him as one because he was a functional and sociable one you know, good job it was all of that kind of thing he wasn't there a lot so my home life was kind of like that and then he left erm so it was just me and my mum and my sister so it's been very much like that ever since it's always
'Penetrate' – man as hostile, aggressive sexual image, yet feeling of loss	been the three of us so it's always been this very intense thing that no men can never penetrate us three do you know what I mean, we've always been very close like that and I suppose I find it quite hard to trust people you know, a sense of loss I suppose
Repeated pattern of dysfunctional relationship with men – attributes to childhood experience of father	as well and the way I got over that was to have a drink it made me more confident well I thought I did it made me ease in erm, you know disastrous relationship with men all my life you know there's always been like my father
Drinking as means of dealing with painful feelings	
Initial positive experience of drinking (more confident)	

Example

comments arising from the engagement with the material. Other notes include initial interpretative comments and reflections. This process is illustrated in the example box above, which contains a short extract from an interview with Claire (name changed).

Second stage

The next stage involves returning to the transcript to transform the initial notes into emerging themes. The main task involves an attempt to formulate concise phrases that contain enough particularity to remain grounded in the text and enough abstraction to offer a conceptual understanding. Although still focusing on the immediate text, at this stage the scope broadens as the researcher will also be influenced by having already analysed the transcript as a whole. The example box below represents the emergent themes for the extract from the interview.

Developing emergent themes (extract)

Original transcript	Emerging themes
Not being able to work and going into rehab which was very difficult and having to go back into my past so it's been a huge upheaval of everything you know, you know like the hornet's nest	*Facing the past – upheaval*
[]	*Dealing with painful emotions*
P: What was in your hornet's nest? C: Erm, what was in there quite a lot really I mean, as I said nothing major, nothing major has ever happened to me in the sense of the conventional	*Dysfunctional childhood family*
kind of stuff, you think it was because I was abused, it was because, that didn't happen, but you know my	*Alcohol in childhood family*
childhood wasn't as functional as I thought you know I had a very, yeah my dad was an alcoholic but I didn't really see him as one because he was a functional and sociable one you know, good job it	*Intense bond with mother and sister*
was all of that kind of thing he wasn't there a lot so my home life was kind of like that and then he left	*Loss*
erm so it was just me and my mum and my sister so it's been very much like that ever since it's always been the three of us so it's always been this very intense thing that no men can never penetrate us	*Drinking as means of dealing with painful feelings*
three do you know what I mean, we've always been very close like that and I suppose I find it quite hard	*Drinking as support*
to trust people you know, a sense of loss I suppose as well and the way I got over that was to have a	*Dysfunctional adult relations with men*
drink it made me more confident well I thought I did it made me ease in erm, you know disastrous relationship with men all my life you know there's always been like my father	

Example

Third stage

The next stage consists of examining the emerging themes and clustering them together according to conceptual similarities. The task at this stage is to look for patterns in the emerging themes and produce a structure that will be helpful in highlighting converging ideas. The clusters are given a descriptive label that conveys the conceptual nature of the themes in each cluster (see the example box below).

Initial clustering of themes (extract)

Focus on addiction	Relationships with others	Focus on recovery
Intensity of engagement in addictive behaviours	Dysfunctional family dynamics	Recovery as arduous experience
Harmful experience of being drunk	Dysfunctional adult relationships	Feeling safe
Drinking as means of dealing with painful feelings	Obsessive patterns of relationships	Self-awareness
Drinking as support	Social isolation	Support from others

Example

Final stage

In the final stage a table of themes is produced. The table shows the structure of major themes and sub-themes. An illustrative data extract or quote is presented alongside each theme, followed by the line number, so that it is possible to check the context of the extract in the transcript. As Eatough and Smith (2006) write:

> for the researcher, this table is the outcome of an iterative process in which she/ he has moved back and forth between the various analytic stages ensuring that the integrity of what the participant said has been preserved as far as possible. If the researcher has been successful, then it should be possible for someone else to track the analytic journey from the raw data through to the end table. (2006: 120)

Moving on

The next step in projects involving more than one participant consists of moving to the next case and repeating the process for each participant. Inevitably the analysis of the first case will influence further analysis. However, in keeping with IPA's idiographic commitment, it is important to consider each case on its own terms, trying to 'bracket' the ideas and concepts that emerged from the first case. In following the steps rigorously for each case separately, it is important to keep an open mind to allow new themes to emerge from each case. As the analysis of subsequent transcripts continues, earlier transcripts are reviewed, and instances from earlier transcripts added and included in the ongoing analysis.

Once all transcripts have been analysed and a table of themes has been constructed for each, a final table of themes is constructed for the study as a whole (see the example box below). In the process of constructing the final table, the tables of themes for each participant are reviewed and, if necessary, amended and checked again with the transcript. The process is iterative and requires repeated returns to the data to check meanings. In constructing the final table of themes it may be possible to amalgamate some themes or to prioritise and reduce the data included in the individual tables. In selecting themes it is important to take into account prevalence of data but also the richness of the extracts and their capacity to highlight the themes and enrich the account as a whole.

Example

Table of themes (part)

Superordinate theme 1 – focus on addiction

Addiction as an affliction

Katherine: Addiction is like you have this big boil here and it's like full of poison	682
Tracey: I am on the floor, pissed and throwing up and crying	178–9
Susie: the paranoia and the fear every time I woke up without knowing where I've been	284–5
Meera: Just normal everyday things like bathing, like cooking, didn't bother to eat properly	218–19
Claire: This feeling of complete despair [ ] if I could kill myself	291–2

Intensity of engagement in addictive behaviours

Claire: I can't stop until there's nothing left or until I pass out [ ] continue, continue, continue	131–2
Meera: Was all all consuming as well, the alcohol consume me	44
Susie: I walked around with a bottle of vodka everywhere I went, I couldn't survive	259
Tracey: All I wanted was cocaine, I didn't give a shit about friends or anything	263
Katherine: I still force it into my body, my body tried to tell me no but I still do it	33–4

Addiction as support

Susie: My first, my only love which was drugs and alcohol	241
Meera: I drink alcohol sometimes to enhance whatever I am feeling	568–9
Julia: I didn't feel safe to face it sober, I mean it is also crutches	199

* The number in the right column indicate line number in the transcript

Claire: The way I got over that was to have a drink, it made me more confident	70–1

Superordinate theme 2 – focus on self

Perception of self

Claire: I'd always kind of hit myself down for it like this isn't good enough	590–1
Susie: Felt I'm not good enough 'cause I always compared myself to other people	304
Katherine: I never really liked myself in my life I was never good enough	495
Tracey: Thoughts like oh I'm worthless or no one cares about me	537
Katherine: I value myself I didn't before but now [in recovery] I do	758
Susie: I've discovered [in recovery] there are good things about me which I never saw	127–8

The table of themes provides the basis for writing up a narrative account of the project. The narrative account consists of the interplay between the participants' account and the interpretative activity of the researcher. It is sensible to take the superordinate themes one by one and write them up in that order. The writing style reflects the IPA approach to analysis, beginning with a close reading grounded in participants' accounts before moving towards a more interpretative level. The narrative account should aim to be persuasive and to mix extracts from participants' own words with interpretative comments (see the example box below). In this way it is possible to retain some of the 'voice' of the participant and at the same time to enable the reader to assess the pertinence of the interpretations.

Narrative account (extract)

The engagement with addiction was portrayed metaphorically as the deep attachment evoked by love and friendship: 'My first, my only love which was drugs and alcohol' (Susie), 'you've got a bottle of wine and that's your best friend' (Tracey). Embracing the love object, all other attachments are abandoned, as described by Claire ('my relationship ended, my friends disappeared') and Tracey:

> All I wanted was cocaine, I didn't give a shit about friends or or anything like that if you do, if you weren't a cocaine user than you're no use to me, d'you know what I mean, so I have lost a lot of friends because ahm of the cocaine and stuff like that.

Example

All participants described an all-consuming intense and obsessive experience, overshadowing all else in life. Yet the insatiable hankering turns out to devour the self and presents a being reduced to its one desire:

> Meera: I couldn't answer the front door without having a drink, answer the telephone without having a drink, ahm I I didn't want to see anybody so it was very much ahm it was just me and ah whatever I was drinking was all was all important, was all all consuming as well, the alcohol consumes me.

> Claire: I can't stop until there's nothing left or until I pass out [ ] continue, continue, continue and just mentally obsessed that I need more when am I gonna get more.

> Katherine: All my life it's either been slimming pills, uppers, downers, I was very hooked on pain killers, codeine erm, for many years, in fact anything I touch I become addicted to actually.

Katherine's account highlights the transferable pattern of addictive behaviour. Like Katherine, other participants described a range of addictive behaviours. Julia, Claire and Katherine described problems of addictive behaviour with food. Susie, Julia and Claire were engaged with obsessive exercising, swimming and running. Susie, Julia and Claire also described themselves as perfectionists, having to do everything to the best. Engaging in addictive behaviours seems to offer participants a strategy to escape from facing negative feelings towards themselves:

> Susie: I didn't realise that the level of self-loathing, I don't allow myself um to look at that self-loathing because I drank alcohol or picked drugs to fix that [ ] that's part of why I drank because I didn't like who I was.

> Katherine: Everything in my life is to do with escape you know the drinking the drugs whatever I mean the sleeping around it's you know, all being because I couldn't be with who I am just everything is a bad escape.

Presenting the research

The final report starts with an introduction that describes what the project is about and outlines the rationale for the project. The introduction also explains the rationale for using IPA and describes the stages in the process. Following the introduction, in IPA studies the 'literature review' is quite short as the primary research questions are phenomenological and the process is inductive rather than theory-driven. The literature is used concisely to develop some picture of the current state of research in the specific area. The literature review is useful to identify gaps in the field that the study aims to address, outline some existing key contributions and offer an argument why the study makes a contribution to the field. It is recognised that during the analysis issues may arise that were not anticipated at the outset. These will be picked up at a later stage by engaging with literature in the 'Discussion' section.

In a typical IPA study the next section provides a step-by-step guide to the actual method used in the research, including details of participants, data collection method and the process of analysis. This is followed by presentation of the analysis in narrative form which includes detailed extracts from participants' accounts (see the example box on pages 61–62). In the final section, the discussion shifts the focus towards a wider context of a dialogue with existing literature, complementing, illuminating or problematising other perspectives in the literature. The reader is then able to engage in the process of considering the study in relation to their professional and personal experience as well as the relevant literature. The discussion and conclusion may point towards applications in practice and provide suggestions for further research.

I was attracted to IPA through the commonality with my background in existential psychotherapy, which is grounded in a phenomenological approach and encourages clients to explore their own experiences, interpretations and meanings in the context of their life. In my research work I have always enjoyed the process of thematic analysis and clustering concepts and ideas according to conceptual similarities. For me the added excitement in working with IPA was twofold. First, retaining the idiographic perspective, giving voice to the experiential accounts of the participants and at the same time exploring commonalities across cases. The possibilities for developing multiple levels of interpretation offered another attraction. Using IPA enabled me to develop a more holistic concept of the research process from a perspective congruent with my worldview. It enables me to combine ideas of phenomenological and existential philosophy with a flexible analytic approach that is focused on both subjective experience and interpretative possibilities.

Reflection on Practice

Chapter summary

- Interpretative phenomenological analysis (IPA) is an approach to qualitative research concerned with exploring in detail personal lived experience, and examining how people are making sense of their personal and social world.
- IPA considers that understanding is always mediated by the context of cultural and socio-historical meanings, and therefore the process of making sense of experience is inevitably interpretative.
- IPA considers that the role of the researcher in trying to make sense of the participant's account is complicated by the researcher's own conceptions.
- IPA shares some common ground with other qualitative approaches. It can be located at a centre-ground position between experiential and discursive approaches.
- IPA draws on concepts and debates from three key areas of philosophy of knowledge – phenomenology, hermeneutics and idiography – to inform its distinctive epistemological framework and research methodology.
- Research questions in an IPA study are likely to involve experiences and issues of considerable significance to the participant.
- In line with its idiographic focus, IPA encourages the study of small, relatively homogenous samples.
- IPA makes a strong case for a single case study, justified when one has a particularly rich or compelling case.
- IPA requires a data collection method that will invite participants to offer detailed, first-person accounts of experiences. Semi-structured, one-to-one interviews have been used most often.
- IPA provides step-by-step guidelines for conducting a study. The guidelines constitute a flexible framework of processes and strategies that can be adapted in accordance with the aims of the research.
- Analysis in IPA is an iterative, complex and creative process that requires the researcher's reflective engagement in a dialogue with a participant's narrative and meanings.
- The final narrative reflects the IPA approach to analysis, beginning with a close reading grounded in participants' accounts before moving towards a more interpretative level.

Further reading

Eatough, V. & Smith, J.A. (2008) Interpretative phenomenological analysis. In Willig, C. & Stainton-Rogers, W. (eds) *The Sage Handbook of Qualitative Research in Psychology* (pp. 179–194). London: Sage.
This chapter discusses the theoretical foundations of IPA and considers a range of current issues.

Smith, J.A. (1996) Beyond the divide between cognition and discourse: using interpretative phenomenological analysis in health psychology. *Psychology and Health*, 11, 261–71.
This paper provides a summary of the theoretical basis for IPA.

Smith, J.A., Flowers, P. & Larkin, M. (2009) *Interpretive Phenomenological Analysis: Theory, Method, and Research*. London: Sage.
This book is the most comprehensive and up-to-date guide to IPA. The book covers the theoretical foundations for IPA, detailed step-by-step guidelines to conducting IPA research and extended work examples from several areas.

Smith, J.A., Flowers, P. & Osborn, M. (1997) Interpretative phenomenological analysis and health psychology. In Yardley, L. (ed.) *Material Discourses and Health* (pp. 68–91). London: Routledge.
This chapter illustrates IPA applied to three different areas in the psychology of health.

CHAPTER 4

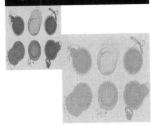

Discourse Analysis Approaches

Amanda Holt

Introduction

This chapter is about approaches to discourse analysis. Discourse analysis is a methodological approach that aims to highlight the ways in which 'knowledge' is *socially constructed*. It aims to expose the implicit values and hidden assumptions that underpin taken-for-granted knowledge – knowledge that legitimises existing institutional practices that may be considered unjust. This chapter begins by briefly describing the historical and intellectual context of this methodology, and outlines the assumptions *about the world* and the assumptions *about psychological knowledge* upon which it is based.

The chapter then discusses two distinct theoretical approaches to discourse analysis that are used in psychology: 'Foucauldian discourse analysis' and 'discursive psychology'. The chapter explores the commonalities between these two approaches and considers the ways in which they might be combined. The latter part of this chapter includes detailed descriptions of how to use discourse analysis. Examples throughout the chapter illustrate the differences in the findings reached by each approach. Practical issues such as recruitment and sampling, data production, analytical coding and presenting research are discussed. The chapter concludes with a summary of some common research uses and applications.

History (or histories?)

It has been suggested that there are at least 57 varieties of discourse analysis (Burman & Parker, 1993). These are encompassed within a number of broad theoretical traditions that foreground language, such as *social semiotics*, *ethnomethodology* and *conversation analysis* (Gill, 2000). The method itself transcends subject disciplines: you will find it being frequently used in film, media and cultural studies, languages and literature, politics and law, the visual arts, as well as more traditional social sciences such as sociology and criminology. Therefore, it is impossible to provide a coherent narrative that can outline '*the* history of *the* method'.

However, within psychology, the 1970s is often pinpointed as the time when many psychological researchers were drawn to the discourse analytic methods that were already established within other subject disciplines. Furthermore, many historical overviews of social psychology (e.g. Burr, 2003; Richards, 2009) suggest this 'turn to language' was the outcome of an epistemological 'crisis', which resulted in disillusioned social psychologists actively searching for alternative methodologies. This disillusion was mainly fuelled by a dominance of experimental methods within social psychology – methods that, in the endless quest to isolate 'variables', tended to 'bracket off' the very social processes that social psychologists were interested in. However, in the spirit of this chapter, which is attempting to encourage students to *question* taken-for-granted assumptions, it is important to remember that this version of history is *one of many possible versions*. Over time, it has managed to achieve legitimacy as *the* history of discourse analysis in psychology. But this is not The Truth. It is one truth of many 'truths'. This is an important point, to which this chapter will return.

Ontology of the approach

Discourse analysis is underpinned by a *constructionist* ontology. As such, it is at odds with, and attempts to challenge, the *realism* that underpins more mainstream research methods (such as quantitative experimental methods). Such mainstream realist methods tend to be based on the assumption that pre-existing 'structures' determine social life. Such structures might be assumed to exist 'inside our heads' as more psychological paradigms, such as *cognitivism*, might suggest. Or they might be assumed to exist 'out there' in the world, as more sociological paradigms, such as *Marxism*, might suggest. In contrast, constructionist methodologies (such as discourse analysis) make no assumptions about the social world, and instead aim to expose and highlight the *constructedness* of these assumptions. They also aim to question the implications of taking for granted such assumptions. (Hence the term 'post-structuralism', a term that is often associated with an intellectual approach that rejects, or challenges, the assumption of 'pre-existing structures'!)

As well as making assumptions about the social world, mainstream realist methods also make assumptions about *being a person*. That is, they take as their (unquestioned) starting point an *essential, rational and boundaried subject* (or person). While in our everyday interactions it is perfectly reasonable to draw on common-sense assumptions about the world and the people in it, this does become problematic if we do the same thing in our research and fail to ever question the nature of what it is we are researching. One of the good things about constructionist methodologies is that they won't let us take for granted alleged 'truths' about the world. And, once we start questioning these 'truths', and start seeing them as only one of many possible 'truths', then we are liberated to consider alternative ways of thinking about (or constructing) the world and the people in it. Constructionists would argue that it is here where research can produce *real change* – rather than the *superficial change* that more realist research might produce (which, in the process, leaves underlying fundamental 'truths' unquestioned and, therefore, still in place).

All of this means that one of the defining features of discourse analysis is the way in which the questioning of taken-for-granted 'truths' is intrinsic to the research question itself. That is, the research question should always aim to be looking to uncover particular assumptions that we make about the world and to consider what the effects of it might be (see the research example box).

Research Example

Developing a research question that is underpinned by a constructionist ontology

Jane Ussher's (2003) research focused on women's experiences of pre-menstrual dysphoric disorder (PMDD), which was classified as a psychiatric disorder in the DSM-IV in 1994. However, her research question did not aim to explore whether menstruation *causes* PMDD, as *realist* ontological paradigms (using *experimental* methods) might dictate. Instead, Ussher aimed to expose this notion as one particular and dominant 'truth'. Therefore, she developed a research question that asked: 'What are the effects of this particular hegemonic truth for the women who are the subjects of it?' (i.e. for women whose experiences are medicalised and consequently constructed as pathological). Ussher also aimed to explore what possibilities for change may be enabled or disenabled by this particular 'truth' for the women in question. What this example shows is the way in which Ussher's decision of whether to investigate this issue through a *constructionist* lens or through a *realist* lens is a political one, since each will have 'effects' by either maintaining or disrupting the current 'truth'.

Given the centrality of constructionism to discourse analysis, the potential for its combination with other analytic methods will inevitably be shaped by the extent to which those methods are also underpinned by constructionist ontologies. For example, traditional grounded theory, such as that developed by Glaser and Strauss (see Chapter 2), assumes a *realist ontology* in that the knowledge produced is assumed to be grounded in the data that *pre-exists the researcher looking at it*. However, Charmaz (2006) has developed a grounded theory more in keeping with constructionist principles, with which discourse analysis methods would certainly be compatible. Similarly, the more constructionist approaches to psychoanalysis are also compatible with discourse analysis (for an overview, see Branney, 2007). Nevertheless, in some cases it may be very useful to combine discourse analysis with quantitative methods, if done appropriately. For example, a brief quantitative survey that looks at 'stop and search' patterns among different ethnic groups may be a useful precursor to interviewing police officers and using discourse analysis to examine the ways in which they account for their seemingly discriminatory practices.

However, within the field of discourse analysis itself, there have been a number of discussions regarding the extent to which different approaches (e.g. Foucauldian discourse analysis and discursive psychology) can be combined. This is something to which this chapter now turns.

Epistemology: why do discourse analysis?

While realist approaches to social research view language as a means to access 'The Truth', constructionist approaches view language as *constitutive of truth*. This means that it is through language that meanings are negotiated and 'realities' are produced. In effect, *nothing pre-exists language*. Thus, our knowledge about the world is produced through the organisation of language and particular behaviours (or 'practices') into particular *discursive formations* that comprise 'discourses'. Discourses serve to seemingly provide a coherent and credible 'truth'. To take an example, 'cognition' – and the internal structures on which it is assumed to be based – does not pre-exist language: it is *talked into being* by the use of words such as 'operation', 'perception' and 'higher/lower order processing'. It is also *practised into being* through the performance of controlled laboratory experiments, through a lecturer's PowerPoint slide, which shows a flow chart with 'memory' at the top and the categories of 'episodic' and 'procedural' underneath, through the writing and publication of journal articles, and so on. That is, the way it is *talked about* and the way *things are done* are organised into a specific formation which constitutes a 'cognitive discourse'. Similarly, 'social class' – and the external structures on which it is presumed to be based – does not pre-exist language.

Question

In what ways is a 'discourse of social class' talked into being and practised into being?

It might help to think about the different 'agents' (e.g. social scientists – including university students! – doctors, politicians) and 'institutions' – (e.g. research institutes, social services, the police, mass media) that produce and reproduce particular discourses of social class.

You might take this exercise a step further and think about which groups are privileged by these discourses and which are disadvantaged (and in what ways).

In relation to Ussher's (2003) work, then, she wants to look at the 'effects of' a 'medical discourse' that is dominant enough to shape the way that women understand their experiences. One could also speculate on the assumptions upon which this discourse is founded: the *idea* of Cartesian dualism (i.e. the mind/body split) and, within this, the *idea* that there is a causal relationship between *biological* changes and *psychological* effects. These are only ideas, yet they have been *talked into being* to such an extent that they are taken for granted. They are also *practised into being* by a woman visiting her doctor, or through the institutional practice of classifying PMDD within the DSM-IV. The seemingly coherent and credible 'truth' that emerges from this medical discourse is that *menstruation causes psychiatric disorders*. Such a 'truth' will have all sorts of implications for the women who are subject to them, and the medical institutions that gain or lose from them. And the fact that different groups of people gain or lose from the dominance of different discourses means that when we are thinking about discourses, we also have to think about *power*.

So, given the centrality of language to power relations in constructionist approaches, we need a research methodology that similarly foregrounds language and power in social analysis. Discourse analysis does this, and two distinct approaches have emerged within psychology – one that arguably foregrounds power, known as Foucauldian discourse analysis, and one that arguably foregrounds language, known as discursive psychology. It is to these two approaches that we now turn.

Foucauldian discourse analysis

Foucauldian discourse analysis (FDA) is an approach associated with the work of Ian Parker (1992) and Burman and Parker (1993). It is derived from post-structuralism and, in particular, from the work of Michel Foucault and his conceptions of power (see Foucault, 1975/91; 1976/90; 1991). FDA aims to examine how 'objects' (things) and 'subjects' (people) are constructed in discourse and to explore what the effects of this might be for people who are *subjected to* them (hence the term 'subjects'). One of the key ideas in FDA is the notion of **subject positions**. This term refers to the possible social locations that either afford or delimit particular ways of being a subject. For example, if you recently experienced a burglary, a particular *subject position* will have been made available to you: that of 'victim'. Once this subject position is taken up, a number of ways of being will be opened up to you (such as access to victim support resources or eliciting sympathy from friends), but other ways of being will be closed down (such as sleeping soundly for a few nights!). This is one reason why there has been a movement to rename women who experience sexual violence as 'survivors', rather than 'victims' – because the 'discourse of victimhood' upon which the subject position of 'victim' is based enables some very limiting and disempowering ways of being.

A further example of this can be found in Ussher's (2003) work, discussed above: the dominant medical discourse that 'menstruation causes psychiatric disorders' offers up very few subject positions to the women who experience bodily changes beyond that of 'ill, unstable or mad' (2003: 142). Such a subject position may be reinforced by (and may, in turn, reinforce) particular institutional practices, such as doctors prescribing medication or psychological treatment to such women. Thus, this subject position offers both rights (such as access to particular forms of 'treatment') and duties (such as permitting the medical regulation of one's body). As this example illustrates, the subject positions offered may afford multiple and contradictory experiences and practices, and these may need to be negotiated carefully by the subject in question.

In order to enable analysis of this process, an FDA approach to data analysis asks the data a number of questions:

- How do subjects utilise particular *discourses* that are available to them to construct their experiences?
- What 'subject positions' are made available to subjects *within the discourses* that are drawn upon?
- How do subjects *negotiate* these subject positions?
- What *ways of being* do these subject positions enable or delimit? The role of power is particularly explored in this final question: who wins from this discursive process … and who loses?

Discursive psychology

A second approach within discourse analysis in psychology is commonly referred to as discursive psychology (DP), and is associated with the work of Jonathan Potter and Margaret Wetherell (1987; Wetherell & Potter, 1992). While FDA enables a more macro-level analysis, DP takes analysis to a more micro-level by focusing almost entirely on the immediate interactional setting that produces the data. In this sense, DP is particularly concerned with the 'action orientation' of discourse in its recognition that language is a social practice that has a performative function. In many ways, it focuses in on the third of the four questions asked by FDA outlined above (i.e. how do subjects *negotiate* subject positions, albeit specifically in the context of the communicative setting?).

Potter and Wetherell's influential *Discourse and Social Psychology* (1987) takes particular interest in the role of accounts, which they identify as explanations of behaviours that might be 'unusual, bizarre or in some way reprehensible' (1987: 74).[2] Researchers working in this area (not all would necessarily identify as being 'discursive psychologists') have suggested a number of verbal and non-verbal **rhetorical devices** that may enable excuses and justifications in a speaker's explanation of their actions. These devices are fashioned from the speaker's culturally available linguistic resources. A summary of some of these devices can be found in Table 4.1.

DP also identifies wider cultural explanatory frameworks that are taken for granted as 'truths'. These are known as 'interpretive repertoires' and are similar in

---

[2] That is not to suggest, of course, that accounts cannot be rather more ordinary than this, but the point is that accounts nevertheless involve the negotiation of a subject position that is *morally justifiable*. The manoeuvres that are made to get to such positions are of particular analytical interest to discursive psychologists (they also tell us much about the moral context of the interaction).

Table 4.1 Rhetorical devices suggested by researchers interested in discursive analysis

Rhetorical device	Example and function	Reference
Active voicing	He said 'don't do that ...' Increases facticity of account, establishes objectivity and rhetorical distance from account	Hutchby & Wooffitt (1998)
Contrasting discourse	I was like this ... now I'm like this ... Emphasises transition by listing competing descriptions	Smith (1978)
Disclaimers	I'm not being sexist but ... Disclaimers anticipate (and reject) potential negative claims	Hewitt & Stokes (1975)
Extreme case formulation	It was 'phenomenal' Strengthens claims by taking claims/evaluations to their extremes	Pomerantz (1986)
Use of passive language	I found myself ... Precludes possibilities of agency and choice	Abell et al. (2000)
Use of 'realise'	An interactional resource that suggests authenticity	Edwards (1997)
Temporal markers	Then I ... when you ... first I ... Marks temporal relationships between events (often to signal developmental progression)	Shiffrin (1987)
Vague descriptions	Vivid details can easily be undermined: vague descriptions produce just enough material to sustain action without opening to attack	Potter (1996)

flavour to the notion of 'discourses' used in FDA. However, Gill (2009) argues that 'interpretive repertoires' are perhaps more fluid concepts in that they tend to be more specific to the context of their use and are in a continual state of flux (in contrast, the FDA concepts of a 'medical discourse' or a 'consumer discourse' are more singularly encompassing and, as such, suggest greater rigidity).

The strength of a DP approach is its recognition that accounts will vary according to their situational context. Therefore a focus on the immediate data-producing setting is an important aspect of DP discourse analysis to illustrate how subject positions are not only grounded in wider material and institutional power relations (as an FDA approach would suggest) but are also 'local, highly situated and occasioned' (Wetherell, 1998: 401). For example, in an interview setting where a researcher asks a participant about her/his experiences, the participant will draw on a specific set of linguistic resources that are tailored to the researcher, the environment, the dialogue, the purpose of the interview, and so on.

Research Example

Identifying 'interpretive repertoires' in the sex and relationships articles in a UK women's magazine

In her DP analysis of *Glamour* magazine sex and relationship advice articles, Gill (2009) identifies three *interpretive repertoires* that she claims serve to privilege men and heterosexuality. These are the 'intimate entrepreneurship' repertoire, which draws on the idea that a successful relationship (constructed as a 'goal') is founded on *strategy, planning* and *tactics* (similar emotion-less 'skills' to those deemed necessary in the western workplace). The 'men-ology' repertoire draws on the importance of studying and learning about 'what men want' – in effect, making relationship-building an educational project that requires expertise. The third repertoire is 'transforming the self', which draws on notions of self-change, particularly in the field of sexual and bodily 'confidence' and 'attitudes'.

Gill argues that these three interpretive repertoires 'intermingle and co-exist' (2009: 361) in the same text and work together to perpetuate not only unequal gender relations (in their promoting the servicing of men) and hetero-normativity (it is always men who are the relationship goal) but also a neoliberal ideology in the way that they impel women to survey and regulate their *selves*. However, as Gill points out, by each drawing on notions of women's agency, choice and empowerment, the three interpretive repertoires work together to effectively disguise the rather questionable overall message of *Glamour* magazine.

In order to enable analysis of this process, a DP approach examines how discursive resources (including the use of rhetorical devices and interpretive repertoires) are used to 'do things' in a particular context and to examine their particular effects. In particular, the analytical process involves *identifying* such discursive resources in a text and looking at how they vary, and how they are consistent across different texts and within the same text (Potter & Wetherell, 1987).

Commonalities between Foucauldian discourse analysis and discursive psychology

There are clearly commonalities between these two approaches to discourse analysis. Both FDA and DP foreground the role of language in the construction of social reality by 'de-centring the subject'. They also both emphasise the importance of *reflexivity* in the research process – that is, as a researcher you need to be reflexively aware of how your own cultural, social, political, linguistic and epistemological location shapes your production of research knowledge. Reflexivity is consistent with an epistemology which recognises that knowledge claims are 'ideological, political and permeated with values' (Schwandt, 2000: 198) and the

Using discursive psychology (DP) to examine transcripts of children's calls to a telephone helpline

Hepburn (2005) analysed two transcripts from calls to the NSPCC helpline; the first concerned a 12-year-old girl who reported concerns over the possible sexual abuse of her best friend. In this transcript, Hepburn identified the use of 'active voicing' and the provision of vivid details as particular *rhetorical devices* used by the girl to persuade the counsellor of the facticity of her account:

```
 7 She said 'oh: I dunno what you're
 8 ta:lking about. (.).hh my little
 9 [sist]er must 'ave wrote that' an
10 Coun: [°Mm°]
11 I says .hh (0.3) 'like your- but I know
12 your handwritin:. what-who is the devil.' (2005: 259)
```

Hepburn then identified the way in which the caller *justifies* why she has not told her friend's mother about her concerns (because 'he'll hit 'er' (2005: 260)) – an option that Hepburn suggests would be the 'normal' course of action for somebody located in this particular subject position (as a 12-year-old girl). Hepburn argued that the discursive analysis highlights how children are compelled to *convince* they are telling the truth and to *justify* why they are taking up valuable time and resources. In turn, this tells us much about the problematic institutional requirements of calling such helplines, which appear to demand more of children and young people, in terms of their credibility and motives, than they do of adult callers.

reflexive process involves continual re-examination of initial analyses and an exploration of alternative interpretations (Alvesson, 2002). It also means acknowledging that the researcher's interpretation is a privileged one that silences possible others, and a consideration of the implications of this. However, while many researchers (e.g. Finlay, 2003) suggest that the use of reflexivity in social research turns a potential 'problem' (of subjectivity) into an 'opportunity', the use of reflexivity is not unproblematic. Its use has often been suggested as a way of hiding the lack of democracy that characterises most kinds of social research – after all, it is the researcher's reading that is ultimately privileged (Burr, 2003). It is also important to recognise that reflexive insights are also subject to the same discursive processes as participants' insights, and so any reflexive analysis must be recognised for the range of 'functions' that it may perform (Gough, 2003a). That is, it may tell us less about the ways a researcher's professional and personal identity shapes research and more about the discursive moves made by a researcher to claim a moral subject position for themselves (for example, they could do this by 'reflecting on' their interest in social justice or their concern for the well-being of the participants).

FDA and DP also share a similar stance towards issues of **reliability** and **validity**. Clearly, the positivist meaning of these terms is not appropriate for research methods that are underpinned by a constructionist methodology, but there does need to be some way of evaluating discourse analytic work. Useful conceptual suggestions include 'quality' (Willig, 2008), 'transparency' (Coyle, 2007) and 'coherence' (Harper, 2006), concepts that have been suggested in more general debates about evaluation in qualitative research (see Elliott *et al.*, 1999; Elliott, Fischer & Rennie, 2000; Madill, Jordan & Shirley, 2000; Reicher, 2000). Stenner (1993) suggests that discourse analysis produces a *reading*, rather than an *interpretation*, as there is no supposition of an 'outside truth' against which the analysis can be assessed. Thus, judgement of its quality must be in terms of its usefulness, rather than any kind of accuracy. This brings attention to the fact that the aim of discourse analysis is not to produce generalisable findings that can establish universal laws of behaviour (as more mainstream psychological scientific methods do). Instead, it aims to highlight particular processes that are anchored to their context – and perhaps to provide a guide for political practice in the light of such findings.

Differences between Foucauldian discourse analysis and discursive psychology

In terms of distinctions between FDA and DP, perhaps most apparent is their differing emphases: while DP focuses on the immediate situational interaction and how subjects adapt their talk according to its needs, FDA is more focused on the relationship between discursive formations and wider social and institutional practices. Thus, it has been argued that their differences mainly concern the different kinds of research question that they each address, rather than any profound differences in the practice of data analysis (Burr, 2003). As you may already have noticed, in practice there is little difference between 'discourses' in FDA and 'interpretive repertoires' in DP. Similarly, both concern themselves with subject positions and the ways in which moral contexts shape these. However, while some theorists (e.g. Parker, 1992) have suggested that these two techniques should not be

---

Question

You want to investigate the reasons why Members of Parliament have chosen their particular line of work, and have used 'life story interviews' to produce rich qualitative data that, among other things, taps into their account of their occupational history. This data could be analysed in a number of ways, but you have decided that discourse analysis is most appropriate. Would you choose Foucauldian discourse analysis, discursive psychology or a combination of the two? What factors drive your reasoning?

CASE STUDY

Combining Foucauldian discourse analysis and discursive psychology

Depending on the topics of a particular research study, it can be useful to integrate both approaches. For example, my research aimed to explore parents' experiences of their child's involvement in offending (see Holt, 2009), their receipt of a Parenting Order through the courts as a result of this (see Holt, 2010a), and their subsequent attendance of 'parenting classes', which was a condition of the order (see Holt, 2010b).

A DP approach was essential to enable an understanding of how the specific research interview setting (which includes the questions that are asked, the mode of interaction and the researcher–narrator relationship) shaped the data produced. Consequently, each participant's account needed to be understood within each situated and local (or 'micro') interview context, which necessitated the need for a DP analysis at this immediate level.

However, the institutional context of this research project made an analysis of wider power relations essential: Parenting Orders are disproportionately issued to mothers, lone parents and those with fewest economic resources. Furthermore, receiving a Parenting Order has real material affects: the parent is compelled to attend court, pay court costs and engage in parenting support sessions.

However, and perhaps most importantly, it is only through acknowledgement of this wider 'macro' context that the assumptions inherent within the DP approach become comprehensible. For example, Riley, Sims-Schouten and Willig argue that the DP approach assumes that 'people want to appear in a good light, want to blame others, or that they want to disclaim responsibility' (2007: 142). But it is only when the subject's position is *contextualised* by reference to wider relations of power (i.e. having been *made responsible* through the courts and *experienced blame* through being labelled a 'bad parent') that such discursive actions within the immediate interview context become meaningful.

Questions for reflection

1. What might be the problems with combining the FDA approach with the DP approach? How important are concerns over theoretical consistency when undertaking social research?
2. How might the usefulness of this particular research study be evaluated? How can this study facilitate social, political or personal change? Is it ethically acceptable for the researcher to decide whether and what kind of change is necessary?
3. What kind of topics/research questions might be inappropriate for combining FDA and DP? When might using an FDA or a DP approach singly work better?

integrated, given their distinct theoretical foundations, others (e.g. Wetherell, 1998) suggest a more pragmatic approach that integrates both the need to attend to the discursive practices employed in the immediate setting and the wider social and institutional practices being drawn upon.

Methods: how to do discourse analysis

Now that we have outlined the theoretical context of discourse analysis, this section outlines the more practical aspects of employing discourse analysis. In particular, it discusses pragmatic issues including recruitment, sampling and data collection, interpretation and analysis, and the presentation of discourse analytic work. As the practice elements of FDA and DP are similar, they will be discussed together. Where there are differences, these will be highlighted.

Pragmatics

Recruitment and sampling

One of the strengths of discourse analysis is its applicability to a wide range of texts. Newspaper articles, policy documents, online texts (e.g. blogs, message boards, emails) and visual data (e.g. photographs, videos) can all be analysed using discourse analysis. However, given that discourse analytic approaches do not attempt to generalise from a sample to a wider population, it is not considered important to obtain data from a large sample. Indeed, given the level of detail that is required in the analysis, it is prudent (and perhaps more ethical) to avoid collecting data from a very large number of participants that is unlikely to be used. A rough guideline might be something like 20 interview transcripts or 'cases' elicited for analysis.

One issue that can arise when using discourse analysis is the ethical question of obtaining informed consent from participants. As Elliot (2005) acknowledges, outlining the nature of the research to participants becomes problematic once the research epistemology shifts from the 'common sense discourse' of *naturalism* to a more marginalised and complex *constructionism*. This raises a number of dilemmas: for example, should the researcher go into detail about the kind of analysis their data will be subject to? Given its shift away from the more 'mainstream approaches' that the participant is likely to expect, does the researcher have a duty to explain – at the risk of sounding opaque – that they are less interested in the *participant's experiences* in any realist sense, than in their *constructions of*

Question

What might be the ethical implications of Hepburn's published work (see the research example box on page 74), in which children's and young people's calls to a helpline were 'translated' into an exercise in identifying discursive resources in the context of conversational demands?

experiences, which will not be assumed to possess any real existence of their own? Does the research topic affect the importance of a researcher's duty to 'epistemologically explain themselves'?

Eliciting and gathering data

If interviews are going to be used, they do not necessarily need to be produced through face-to-face encounters; indeed, as I have argued elsewhere (see Holt, 2010c), in many ways discourse analysis lends itself very well to data produced from telephone interviews. This is because telephone interviews require the participant to fully articulate their responses since alternative means of communication (e.g. body language) are not available (and, in any case, cannot easily be produced within a typed transcript).

Regardless of mode, it is generally recommended that interview data is produced through unstructured interviews, since more structured interviews are likely to curtail both the detail that is required for a sophisticated analysis, and the inconsistencies and contradictions that occur in talk that discourse analysis aims to highlight. Thus, an interview guide or topic list, which provides a few open-ended questions and/or discussion themes, is most appropriate. An open approach during interviewing is also necessary to enable participants to conceptualise and construct experiences in ways *most meaningful to the participant* (rather than to the researcher). Harper *et al.* (2008) also suggest that adopting a 'devil's advocate' position in a research interview might facilitate the use of counter (and counter-counter) claims. That is, a more adversarial framework in interviews is likely to enable the *excuses* and *justifications* that are central to discourse analysis. However, such an approach could be problematic and should perhaps be considered in the light of the competing need to facilitate a positive social experience for the participant!

It is also useful to make notes immediately following the interview, using a research diary. This might include impressions of the interview, points of anxiety and any atypical incidents that occurred. This practice provides you with the opportunity to document any immediate analytical ideas that occur, as well as enabling you to reflect on your own role in the interview process. You might also take this process a step further and ask participants for their responses to their experiences of the research process. Such a request might constitute one way in which reflexivity *can* be made a more democratic process by enabling the participants as well as the researcher to take part in reflexive processes (Gough, 2003a).

Texts such as policy documents, political speeches or extracts from e-media are arguably easier and less time-consuming to obtain than interview data. However, as with any secondary data, queries concerning its quality and credibility need to be addressed. Furthermore, it is obviously more difficult to perform a DP analysis on such texts when the interactional context of their production is more ambiguous; indeed, Potter and Wetherell (1995) stress that DP should not be used on any texts that do not constitute 'naturally occurring talk', and this includes 'research interviews' (since the researcher is setting the interactional agenda). However, many researchers have usefully applied DP to analyse data from research interviews, and I would add that a very blurry line distinguishes 'naturally occurring' and 'unnaturally occurring' talk, and that the discursive moves that people make in a research interview are as worthy of exploration as in any other interactional setting.

Applying discourse analysis to online data: the production of 'pro-ana' identities

Giles' work illustrates how online communities are an increasingly important site for the negotiation and management of identities, and thus provide fertile ground for discourse analysts. In his research, Giles (2006) aimed to explore the ways in which young people who identify as 'pro-ana' (as in 'pro-anorexic') construct their identities in online 'pro-ana' communities. Such communities promote and attempt to normalise young people's engagement in anorexic practices (such as self-starvation and self-induced vomiting), and could therefore be seen as a 'resistance' to the dominance of medical discourses in 'offline' settings that serve to pathologise anorexic behaviours. Thus, data from such communities provided Giles with a rich and unique text to enable the analysis of particular identity-making practices that are silenced in more everyday mainstream settings.

Giles examined 20 'pro-ana' websites, and accessed archives from their discussion forums and message boards. He exported a sample of threads that involved conflicts/debates on to a Word document, which in total produced a data set of over 150,000 words. Analysis focused on the ways in which 'ana identities' were constructed, particularly in relation to other 'outsider' identity categories such as 'mia' (bulimia) and 'dieter'. Analysis also centred on the ways in which such 'outsiders' were managed within these communities. In conclusion, Giles reflected on the ways in which such websites provided individuals with a unique way of collectively (re)producing *counter-discourses* that served to undermine mainstream healthcare practices that construct anorexia within a dominant medical discourse.

Research Example

Analysis and interpretation

Many researchers have suggested a series of 'steps' (e.g. Parker, 1992; Willig, 2008) and 'worked examples' (e.g. Gill, 2000; Wood & Kroger, 2000) to aid the practice of discourse analysis. However, the notion of a *procedural prescription* is both theoretically problematic and difficult to articulate, as it is a rather intangible and idiosyncratic process. Perhaps what is more useful is Walton's (2007) observation that discourse analysis is less to do with following prescribed steps and more about conducting analysis in the spirit of post-structuralist inquiry – that is, to avoid making 'truth-claims', to utilise appropriate analytic concepts and to report findings in a way that is consistent with its theoretical and epistemological underpinning. Nevertheless, what follows is an outline of some of the 'stages' (as much as they can be considered as such) and some of the key decisions that are involved when *I* have conducted discourse analysis. While clearly influenced by the academics' guidelines suggested above, what follows perhaps illustrates the intangibility of doing discourse analysis, in the sense that mere words may not be enough to convey an analytic process that, I would argue, mostly takes place in one's own head.

Transcription

If interviews are being used, they must be audibly recorded and a very lengthy stage of transcription is likely to follow. While often left unremarked on by social researchers, transcription is an important stage of the analytic process since the intensity of engagement with the text means that many analytical insights are produced at this stage (which should be noted, perhaps continuing the research diary started during the interview phase). Thus, while laborious, it is important for the researcher to perform the transcription themselves. Furthermore, transcription is also the first stage where data starts being shaped by the researcher's own theoretical decisions about what is important and what can be omitted (Dunne, Pryer & Yates, 2005). A further 'shape-shifting' decision concerns how 'fine-grained' the analysis should be and, consequently, how fine-grained the transcription should be to enable this. For example, many discourse analysts adopt Jefferson's (2004) notation technique, but decisions need to be made on what aspects of the talk should be included: you may decide to include pauses, laughter and the emphasis of words, but decide to omit intakes of breath and the timed length of pauses. This, then, is the first phase where participants' words slowly become yours.

Developing themes

After transcription, it helps to read each transcript/document a number of times to develop a sense of its context and the story 'as a whole' while continuing to make notes on emerging themes. It might also be useful to compare these notes with your earlier notes in your research diary to see whether they still make sense, or whether their importance has changed over time (one key distinction between constructionist methodologies and positivist methodologies is that, with the former, the analytic focus will frequently shift until the end of the analytical process). This stage is possibly the most difficult of the entire research process, as the lack of clarity and certainty can produce much anxiety in the researcher. (The best advice I ever received concerning this aspect is simply to 'keep your nerve'!)

If approaching the data using an FDA approach, the process involves identifying words and phrases that, together, constitute wider 'discourses'. These can then be highlighted and coded together under an appropriate name (e.g. 'medical discourse', 'parent-blame discourse', 'lifestyle choice discourse'). A qualitative data software package (e.g. *NVivo*) might be useful to help manage this process by saving each highlighted and coded phrase into its own file and storing these files in an organisationally coherent way (e.g. by using hierarchical 'trees' to differentiate 'higher-level' *discourses* and 'lower-level' *ideas*, which individually constitute parts of a discourse). However, such software is not essential and it does not perform the analysis for you. Indeed, many researchers find doing discourse analysis using software a rather alienating experience and prefer using a series of Word documents using the copy + paste function. Other researchers have told me that they 'go old skool' with paper and highlighter pens.

As the analysis progresses, codes may change in conception (which may involve a continual and tiresome renaming of them!). Codes may also become more or less encompassing, resulting in their deletion or blending into other codes. It is also important to identify patterns based on wider *structuring axes* such as gender, age and ethnicity. For example, you might want to explore whether particular groups of participants (e.g. older men) are using particular discourses, while others (e.g. younger women) are not (and question if there are any exceptions to such patterns). You might also identify and code the *materialities* that are being drawn on (e.g. community, work and employment, family), and consider how these might be constraining and/or enabling the participant. It is also important to be alert to silences: what is *not* being drawn on or spoken of? It is also important to be aware of your own reactions during this process: what are you expecting that has not been spoken of or drawn on? Why should this be? Thus, it is important for researchers to interrogate themselves as much as the data. At this stage, it is useful to consider the codes as performing a temporary role in helping to organise the data, rather than as demarcating any kind of permanent conceptual division between categories. They are likely to continually shift and regroup as analysis continues and as you develop a deeper understanding of similarities and differences, and continuities and discontinuities – both within and between individual participants/cases.

Using a DP approach, the analysis is likely to be at an even more detailed level, as you identify specific discursive resources (such as rhetorical devices and interpretive repertoires) and consider their function within the interview setting. What was said immediately prior to it and what was the response 'doing'? As with FDA, you will need to consider the implications of the speaker's use of particular discursive resources, for both the speaker themselves and their audience. Based on your preparatory reading of discourse analysis, which is essential to this process, it might also be useful to make a list of some of the established rhetorical devices that you might want to identify (see my own attempt to do this in Table 4.1). An important point to remember is that analysis should always 'stay at the level of the text' and avoid making assumptions about what the speaker is 'trying' to achieve at a psychological level. This is because, in keeping with the ontological assumptions of the methodology, intentions and motivations should be considered as 'constructions' (rather than as 'pre-existing entities') and therefore truth claims should not be made about them.

Throughout the analysis, you need to ask the data many questions. Such questions might include:

■ How does the interview setting, and the researcher's and the participant's responses to each other, produce that particular account?

- What *discursive resources* are used to enable the participants to move forward (or not) in their account?
- How do the accounts of people of different genders, or ages, or cultures, differ from each other?
- How are earlier episodes that are talked about made sense of in relation to later episodes?
- How do the *discourses* (or *interpretive repertoires*) drawn on when explaining one experience relate to those drawn on to explain other experiences?
- What *subject positions* are available within these particular discourses, and what does that mean for practice (ways of doing) and subjectivity (ways of being)?
- How does a participant's orientation to particular contextual factors circumscribe their specific experiences, particularly in terms of the extent to which *agency* can be exercised?

Possible responses to these questions should be explored for some considerable time, and may be generated not only through the researcher but also through lengthy discussions with colleagues, supervisors and other academic audiences in presentations – all of which should enable the researcher to reflect on the quality of their work and its potential usefulness.

Analysis of experiences of second-time motherhood

First reading

I read through the paper transcript and began to scribble notes (in black ink, in the margins) on thematic ideas. I focused on questioning what kind of relations of power and effects of power seemed to be underpinning the narrative. Key themes identified at this stage concerned the gendered binary between *self* (as mother) and *husband* (as father); tensions between the subject positions of '*mother*' and '*employee*'; and relationships between *gender*, *work*, **subjectivity** and *social class*.

Second and subsequent readings

Next day, I reread the transcript and (in green ink) made further notes – looking for new themes that I had not 'read off' on first reading. Second reading enabled a richer understanding of the narrator's experiences, and ideas seemed to link together more effectively. I consciously ensured that a more theoretical framework informed my thinking this time, and I started making links between *freedom, choice* and *responsibility*: 'freedoms' seemed very limited and very gendered, and I started questioning the narrative in Foucauldian terms – how was the narrator *regulated* through motherhood, and how did *resistance* play out in the text?

Reflection on Practice

While predominantly using FDA by analysing how power was played out in the narrator's life (as depicted in her account), I also attended to a micro-level analysis using DP by also thinking about how power was played out in the immediate interactional setting of the interview. For example, I noticed tensions where the narrator made claims about the world and then immediately negated them using statements such as 'well, that's my perception' and I wondered what the implications of this rhetorical device might be?

Noticing that my ideas ran thinner as a reading through the transcript progressed, third and fourth readings started at different points in the transcript, yielding a little more, albeit diminishing, analytical insight.

NVivo analysis

My readings produced a number of different kinds of categories: some could be conceptualised as structuring axes (e.g. 'gender'), others as effects of power (e.g. 'regulation'), and others as agents (e.g. constructions of 'self', 'husband'). I imported the transcript into *NVivo* and, reading through the transcript, I highlighted and coded (and continually recoded) these categories, creating (and re-creating!) 'tree hierarchies' in the process. At this stage, I wanted to create a convincing story that operated around core conceptual ideas (e.g. regulation, resistance) and that would be consistent with a constructionist ontology and that centralises (a Foucauldian conception of) power.

Write-up

Analysis continued 'on the page': themes were weaved together to produce an analytic narrative, which was punctuated by transcript extracts to provide supporting 'evidence' (perhaps a throwback from positivist research practices?). Often, it is only during write-up that one can test whether the analytic narrative is intelligible, and a key element of this stage was the continual monitoring of this from an 'objective' perspective (while simultaneously accepting that there is no such thing!).

A final anxiety concerned the writing of the 'Introduction' and 'Conclusion'. This 'top and tailing' seemed a further throwback from scientific methodology, which performs the role of maintaining the notion of linearity in the research process: I wondered if my analysis might have more integrity if I left it a little rough around the edges? For me, doing discourse analysis is 'top and tailed' with an intense anxiety – both when beginning the process and 'committing' to slicing up the text in a particular way, and then again on ending the process, which for me was characterised by an anxious re-rereading of the work and a reluctance to hit the 'send' button.

Presenting the research

 As with all stages of the research process, the presentation of discourse analytic research needs to be consistent with the theoretical and epistemological **positioning** of the approach. It is no good conducting discourse analytic research in a constructionist spirit if, at the final 'presentation stage', an awareness of and attention to language eludes the researcher (resulting in a research presentation that merely reinforces – rather than challenges – the status quo). Given that a key underlying assumption of discourse analytic research is that research does not merely provide an objective mirror on the social world, but that it actively constructs the social world, then every word needs to be scrutinised. Researchers have an authority and credibility that works to legitimise their construction of the social world, and with such power comes responsibility.

While by no means exhaustive, the following guidance suggests some of the things that researchers should be aware of when presenting their research.

Be continually aware of and alert to your use of a 'realist' language

Clearly, if the analysis is performed in the spirit of constructionism, then this needs to be reflected in the write-up. Truth-claims must be avoided – thus, participants do not 'think', but 'construct the world as …'. However, writing in this way is actually quite difficult to achieve for two reasons. First, because realism shapes everyday communication, it is difficult to avoid making slips in the write-up (for example, my own entrenchment in a 'positivist research discourse' often makes itself known by my frequent unchecked use of terms such as 'causes' and 'significant numbers of …' whenever I discuss research). This may be even more of an issue when presenting research orally at conferences when you are not able to scrutinise your every word quite as carefully as you might at a keyboard. Second, it is difficult because, to communicate to a wide audience (particularly those with the power to make changes, such as policymakers and practitioners) you cannot avoid drawing on language, terms and concepts that are compatible with mainstream psychological discourses. If you didn't, your research would quickly become incomprehensible (remember that discourse analysis – and therefore the language it is steeped in – is a very marginal methodology). This poses a dilemma, for if one wishes their research to enable social change, one must also implicate themselves in the maintenance of dominant ways of thinking and doing. At least for a while.

Make yourself visible

Kitzinger (1987) writes powerfully about the rhetorical devices that are used in the writing up of realist social science research. She describes how the 'discourse of scientific progress' pervades the text, enabling past research to be dismissed through phrases that describe its 'antiquated viewpoints', 'outdated references' and 'archaic practice'. She also describes how the scientific method is conceptualised in a way that makes it appear a neutral, objective and apolitical domain of technical expertise. Part of this discourse involves removing the researcher from the research process, which is most obviously achieved by using passive sentence constructions and writing up research in the third person. Any reference to the researcher, or to the ways in which the researcher's own identity might have shaped the research process, is avoided. While this is clearly in keeping with the spirit of realism, such practices are inappropriate when writing up discourse analytic research. Instead you should clearly document the role of the researcher (through the use of 'I') and enable a reflexivity that clearly positions aspects of the researcher's identity that she/he considers salient to the research process. For example, in their research into rape survivors' accounts of their experiences, Wood and Rennie (1994) positioned themselves by writing about their own experience (or not) of forced sex and how sharing this with the participants may have shaped participant responses. Similarly, in their study of 'gay men/heterosexual women' friendship dyads, the authors identified 'as three gay men' (Shepperd, Coyle & Hegarty, 2010: 210) to bring attention to the way their own personal sexual politics shaped their analytical emphasis (i.e. by attending more to *heteronormativity* than to *sexism*).

Be open to challenge

As discussed earlier, discourse analysis produces a reading rather than an interpretation, and so your analysis should not be presented as *the* definitive interpretation. Furthermore, openness to alternative readings should not only be welcomed, but encouraged by providing the original data in the appendix (or at least making large amounts accessible). If possible, provide a transparent account of the analytic process to enable the audience to evaluate the persuasiveness of the analytic account proffered (Langdridge, 2004), particularly in the light of your own acknowledgement of the personal and political values that informed the research (see above).

Provide data extracts in context

Following on from the previous point, unlike more mainstream realist research, which often provides brief sentences as 'supporting evidence' of a particular truth-claim, discourse analytic work often presents much larger chunks of data to provide a context for what is said (or written, or indeed placed if using visual data). When using DP in particular, often a participant's response can be made meaningful only when it is looked at in terms of what was said previously. Similarly, the interviewer's questions should be included within the extracts, as an *analysis* of the researcher's talk will enable a contextualised analysis of the data as a whole.

As this chapter has made clear, there are a number of ways in which discourse analysis can be used. First, as the research examples discussed in this chapter demonstrate, it can be used to address many different research questions, spanning topics as diverse as clinical psychology (e.g. Ussher), feminist psychology (e.g. Gill), communication psychology (e.g. Hepburn), criminological psychology (e.g. Holt) and health psychology (e.g. Giles). Furthermore, it can be applied to a range of primary and secondary textual data, which need not necessarily meet the criteria of

Research Example

The Social Construction of a Serial Killer

Bartels, R. & Parsons, C. (2009) The social construction of a serial killer. *Feminism and Psychology*, 19(2), 267–280.

Brief context and research aim

While there has been much psychological theory and research examining serial killing, this has tended to adopt a realist ontology by locating the 'causes' of serial killing within the agent himself (it is nearly always a 'he'). The most dominant explanations are those that mobilise the notion of sexual fantasy: a pathological category of person is constructed who is unable to control his instinctual urges, and who instead continually 'acts out' his fantasies. Such 'acting out' results in serial homicide.

However, rather than merely perpetuate this individualising discourse by investigating it within a realist paradigm, Bartels and Parsons adopted a discourse analytic approach. By analysing the courtroom testimony of Dennis Rader,[3] the research aimed to identify the ways in which Rader constructed himself and his crimes *within the courtroom setting*.

Method

Data were collected from a publicly available 78-page transcript of a court hearing that took place on 27 June 2005. The content of the transcript concerned Rader's confessions to and accounts of ten murders. Although Bartels and Parsons claim to have adopted a DP approach, and refer to Potter and Wetherell's (1987) germinal work as their touchstone, their identification of 'discourses' certainly draws on ideas consistent with FDA.

In outlining their method, Bartels and Parsons describe their rereading of transcripts before focusing their attention on 'the ways in which events, categories and emotions were discursively constructed and what functions they appeared to serve' (2009: 270). Their work was presented under three headings, labelled as 'discourses', and included extracts from the transcripts to support their analysis. Reference was also made to particular rhetorical devices and their functions within the courtroom setting. The analysis is followed by a discussion that summarises their findings, and suggests possible implications of the research and possible areas for further research.

---

[3]Dennis Rader was a notorious US serial killer who went by the name of BTK (Blind, Torture, Kill) and who was indicted for ten counts of murder in 2005.

Findings

Bartels and Parsons identified three discourses in Rader's talk. These all worked together to uphold the construction of serial killer as a sympathetic character who is taken over by sexual urges that he cannot control.

The first discourse identified is *'perpetrator as sympathetic'*; this discourse was constituted by a number of specific rhetorical devices. For example, in describing his crimes, Rader refers to how he tried to make Mr Otero [one of his victims] comfortable by placing '... "I think a parka or a coat underneath him"...' (2009: 270). Bartels and Parsons suggest that not only does this discursive move enable Rader to construct himself as sensitive to another's discomfort, the use of the term 'I think' functions 'to reflexively display him as an honest person [that] serves to validate his account' (2009: 271).

The second discourse identified is *'perpetrator as a serial killer'* and the authors identify Rader's references to expert literature (e.g. '... "I don't know if...[...]... you read much about serial killers, they go through what they call the different phases"...' (2009: 273), to enable him to position himself in the category of 'serial killer'. While by no means a flattering subject position, Bartels and Parsons suggest that it nevertheless affords Rader the possibility of mitigating responsibility for his crimes, by '[drawing on] the inference that he can't help doing what he did because it's what serial killers do' (2009: 274).

The final discourse identified is *'perpetrator as driven by sexual fantasy'*, which Rader draws on to construct his actions as sexual, thus obscuring the violence of them. For example, Rader talks about when '... "I was in the sexual fantasy"...' (2009: 275) and the use of the term 'in' suggests a different state of consciousness over which he had no control.

Discussion

Bartels and Parsons reflect on other research findings such as those in Coates and Wade's (2004) work, which identified similar discourses within judges' talk in sexual offences cases. These similarly served to minimise the perpetrators' responsibility by constructing them as 'overwhelmed by psychological forces' (Bartels & Parsons, 2009: 277).

They also refer to past research that identified such discourses within the talk of sex offenders, and they reflect on the implications of this for practice. In particular,

Research Example

Research Example

they question how professionals from the legal and psychological fields 'may attend to Rader and other serial killers in ways that are in accordance with this construction, for example, in terms of how they are treated, sentenced and researched' (2009: 277).

However, although Bartels and Parsons do not mention this, there are also wider political implications for their findings: serial killing is unequivocally a gendered crime, with the majority of perpetrators being male and the majority of victims being female (Wilson, 2009). However, the perpetuation of a psychologising and individualising discourse – perpetuated by judges, practitioners and the perpetrators themselves – obscures this structural context. Applying an FDA approach to the Rader data may have highlighted this issue. However, this may well have come at the cost of a clear and focused DP analysis, which highlights the ways in which talk is situationally contingent and performs functions beyond reflecting back 'reality'.

representativeness that one finds in scientific methodologies. One might take discourse analysis to a macro-level or a micro-level, and increasingly research is becoming more pluralistic as FDA and DP are integrated – perhaps with one or other approach having greater analytical emphasis. In terms of outcomes, there are a number of ways in which doing discourse analysis can produce a change for good – perhaps by exposing the implicit values and hidden assumptions that underpin particular kinds of knowledge that legitimise existing unjust institutional practices. Alternatively, it may have something to say more directly about the way communication is 'done' by particular professionals, and how it needs to be altered to work better for service users. Table 4.2 summarises and clarifies this diversity of application with reference to the five short research examples that were referred to in this chapter.

Table 4.2 Summary table: how discourse analysis can be used across a range of applications

	Ussher (2003)	Gill (2009)	Hepburn (2005)	Holt (2009; 2010a; 2010b)	Giles (2006)
Research question	How are scientific constructions of PMDD played out in women's narratives?	How are sexual relationships constructed in a women's magazine?	How do children manage institutional demands when making calls to a helpline?	How do parents construct experiences of parenting a child involved in offending?	How are 'pro-ana' websites used to enable identity work by its users?
Type of data	Face-to-face interviews with 108 women being treated for PMDD	20 magazine articles from 5 randomly selected issues of Glamour (UK) magazine	Transcripts from two telephone calls to an NSPCC helpline	Telephone interviews with 17 parents using narrative interviews	Archived threads from message boards and discussion boards from 20 websites
Analytic approach	FDA – with a focus on the role of scientific discourse	DP – with particular emphasis on interpretive repertoires	DP – also using elements from 'conversation analysis' such as script formulations	FDA – but also uses DP to attend to rhetorical devices	DP – using 'membership category analysis' technique – but also draws on FDA concept of discourse
Key findings	Five hegemonic 'truths' identified in women's talk that work to regulate femininity	While drawing on discourses of female empowerment, articles work in Glamour magazine to privilege men	Children struggle to make themselves credible in helpline interactions	The positioning of parents as 'bad parents' produces parental resistance to their social and legal regulation	Online communities are fiercely policed by those who identify as 'pro-ana'
Possibilities for personal, social and/ or political change?	Indirect change through highlighting current dominant discourses and possible alternative discourses that frame mental health practices	Indirect change through exposing the ways in which language works to promote gender injustice in the popular media	Although an exploratory study, it has future utility in offering practice guidance for helpline professionals when responding to interactional difficulties with children	Enforcing parents to 'take responsibility' through the criminal justice system will not work in engaging parents of 'young offenders' – more supportive policies are needed	While Giles claims no particular 'social goal' (2006: 475), there are clearly implications for the role of 'pro-ana' websites in undermining health professionals and in understanding the effects of such sites on their users

Chapter summary

- Discourse analysis is a methodology that incorporates a number of approaches and techniques. Two specific approaches commonly used in psychology are Foucauldian discourse analysis and discursive psychology.
- Discourse analysis is underpinned by a constructionist ontology that questions taken-for-granted assumptions about the world and the people in it. It emphasises the role of language in constructing the world, and the role of power in recognising that these constructions have different political effects for different groups of people.
- Foucauldian discourse analysis enables analysis of these constructive processes at a macro-level; a key aspect of analysis is the identification of wider social and institutional discourses and practices that shape people's experiences of the world.
- Discursive psychology enables analysis of constructive processes at a micro-level; a key aspect of analysis is the identification of the function of discursive resources used by speakers in interaction.
- Discourse analysis practice needs to remain faithful to its constructionist approach to knowledge. This means attending to issues such as reflexivity, researcher positioning and accountability, and scrutiny of the language used to present the research.
- Discourse analysis can be used to analyse a diverse range of texts. It can be used to achieve theoretical goals as well as more pragmatic goals in terms of making recommendations for policy and practice. It can also be used to highlight injustices and to offer alternative ways of thinking (that is, *counter-discourses*) about the world and the people in it.

Further reading

Burman, E. & Parker, I. (eds) (1993) *Discourse Analytic Research: Repertoires and Readings of Texts in Action.* London: Routledge.
A classic text for those interested in Foucauldian discourse analysis within psychology.

Burr, V. (2003) *Social Constructionism* (2nd edn). London: Routledge.
This is a very accessible text (which has quickly become a 'classic') for those new to this area, and who wish to gain a clear overview of social constructionist theory and its application to discourse analysis practice.

Lock, A. & Strong, T. (2010) *Social Constructionism: Sources and Stirrings in Theory and Practice.* Cambridge: Cambridge University Press.
A more advanced text that provides a thorough and thought-provoking discussion of the epistemological and ontological underpinnings of social constructionism in all its guises. Chapter 13 focuses specifically on its relationship to discourse analysis.

Potter, J. & Wetherell, M. (1987) *Discourse and Social Psychology: Beyond Attitudes and Behaviour*. London: Sage.
A classic text for those interested in discursive psychology within psychology.

Willig, C. (2008) *Introducing Qualitative Research in Psychology: Adventures in Theory and Method* (2nd edn). Buckingham: Open University Press.
This book has two excellent chapters on discourse analysis – one on discursive psychology (Chapter 6) and one on Foucauldian discourse analysis (Chapter 7).

Wood, L.A. & Kroger, R.O. (2000) *Doing Discourse Analysis: Methods for Studying Action in Talk and Text*. London: Sage.
This is a very accessible book that, while emphasising more 'discursive psychology' techniques, has a very practical focus and features a comprehensive glossary of terms.

CHAPTER 5

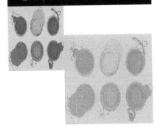

Narrative Analysis Approaches

Cigdem Esin

Introduction

This chapter is about using narrative analysis. Like the other approaches described in this book, narrative analysis is an umbrella term that covers a plurality of methods. The narrative analysis approach takes stories as the unit of analysis. The stories are usually gathered from the accounts of participants and each approach focuses on a different feature of the story. Features may be the structure (e.g. Labov, 1972), the content (e.g. Riessman, 1993; Lieblich, Tuval-Mashiach & Zilber, 1998) or the performative function (e.g. Riessman, 1993; Mishler, 1995; Denzin, 2001), for example. The chapter begins by describing the history of narrative analysis. It illustrates its migration from other social science disciplines to psychology. It then describes ontological and epistemological frameworks in which the different methods of narrative analysis can be located. The chapter provides detailed descriptions of analytical models used in narrative research and discusses the applications of each approach. It provides guidelines for their use and highlights the relevance of the research interview to this approach. Several research examples illustrating use of the different models are included.

History of narrative research

There are two parallel academic moves in the history of social sciences in which narrative research can be located (Andrews *et al.*, 2004). The first is the humanist tradition within western sociology and psychology. This tradition is person-centred; it treats storytellers and listeners as unified and singular. Researchers with humanist approaches paid attention to individual case studies, biographies and life stories. The second move emerged in connection with the postmodern ontology that emphasises the role of multiple subjectivities in the construction of narratives. Researchers in the second tradition are concerned with meanings produced in narratives, including unconscious ones. They pay attention to social conditions and power relations that shape the narratives (Squire, Andrews & Tamboukou, 2008: 3).

Different approaches to narratives and narrative analysis have developed within these two traditions. The focus of narrative analysis was the linguistic structure and content of narratives in the models located in the humanist tradition (e.g. Labov, 1972; Gee, 1991). The focus of analysis has shifted to the act of storytelling and construction of narratives through interaction in the models situated in the postmodern tradition (e.g. Riessman, 1993).

The use of narratives and narrative method in research positioned in both first and second moves has spread through a wide a range of social science disciplines over the past three decades. A burgeoning literature on narrative and narrative research practice has been published in various disciplines including sociology, history, anthropology and folklore, and sociology of education. Psychology is one of the disciplines in which the use of narrative methodological tools has gained momentum since the early 1980s. However, the interest in the history of narrative tradition in psychology can be traced back to the developments in studies of personality and life-span development using biography and case studies at the beginning of the twentieth century (Hiles & Cermák, 2008). The foundations for the new field of psychology were established by Theodore Sarbin's *Narrative Psychology: The Storied Nature of Human Conduct*, which was published in 1986. In the introduction to this book, Sarbin argued that narrative analysis as a model of contextualism could be used as a method in psychology in understanding human action because narrative analysis considers the meaning of stories as created within specific historical contexts. This approach also integrates the effect of time, place of telling and audience into analysis. The field of narrative psychology has been developed with the contribution of multiple theoretical and methodological perspectives on narrative and narrative methods (for examples see Emerson & Frosh, 2004; Hiles & Cermák, 2008).

Ontology

The assumptions that narrative analysis makes about the nature of social reality lie in the understanding and use of 'narrative' within this approach. The definition of 'narrative' varies depending on the discipline and approach to narratives.

What is narrative?

Narratives are stories with a clear sequential order, that connect events in a meaningful way for a definite audience. Story and narrative are often used interchangeably. Sequence is necessary for narrative. A narrative always responds to the question 'And then what happened?'

Narratives are powerful forms of giving meaning to experience. Mattingly and Garro argue that 'narrative mediates between an inner world of thought-feeling and an outer world of observable actions and states of affairs' (2000: 1). Events do not present themselves as narratives. It is through the experience of an event that it becomes a story. This means that the retelling of an event is always retrospective – the narrator already knows the ending.

Narratives are seen as the vehicle through which we talk about our world, lives and selves. Narratives do not simply express some independent, individual reality. Rather they help to construct the reality within relationships between the narrator and their external world. Narratives are produced in social interactions between individuals; they are not privately created (Smith & Sparkes, 2008).

Atkinson, Coffrey and Delamont (2003: 117) argue that, although people construct their own lives and those of others through biographical accounts, these accounts do not tell us unmediated personal experience. While personalised over time, stories are drawn from a limited repertoire of available narrative resources. Somers (1994) calls them public narratives. These are 'narratives attached to cultural and institutional formations larger than the single individual' (1994: 619). According to Somers (1994), narratives should not be considered 'natural' or as springing from the minds of individuals. People likewise are not free to fabricate narratives at will. While producing narratives of their lives, individuals use public narratives available in their culture. These public narratives are also used by people who listen to individual stories. They function as common sources that facilitate the communication between the storytellers and listeners.

Narrative analysis, therefore, perceives narratives as creative means of exploring and describing realities, which are arranged and bound in time. While interpreting the individual narratives, analysts take into account the individual and cultural resources people use to construct their narratives, as well as the interpersonal or organisational functions of narratives (Atkinson *et al.*, 2003: 117). Narrative analysis is not applicable to all research topics. If you intend to use narrative analysis in your research, you need to remember that the focus of your analysis will be narratives/ stories. Topics suited to narrative analysis include various aspects of identity, individual experiences of psychological processes, interpersonal and intimate relationships, experiences of body, beauty and health.

Example research questions

What are generational differences in the experiences of teenage pregnancy?
How does masculinity influence the success of boys in education?
Does gender have a role in the transformation of ethnic identities?
How do former drug users construct the self in their narratives of rehabilitation?

Source: *adapted from the dissertation proposals of final-year Psychosocial Studies students at the University of East London.*

Why do narrative analysis?

Epistemology

Narrative analysis does not only function as a method through which researchers explore how people remember, structure and story their experiences. It is also a process that can lead researchers to understanding the complexities of human selves, lives and relations. This means it is useful to illuminate both the individual experiences and social processes that shape these experiences. Narrative analysis provides the analyst with useful tools to integrate the individual details and complexity in the construction of stories rather than analysing these stories under predetermined categories (Andrews *et al.*, 2004).

Narrative research enables researchers to see multiple and sometimes contradictory layers of meaning, to reconstruct meanings through linking these layers, and to explore and understand more about individual and social processes. By working with narratives, researchers investigate multiple aspects in the construction and function of stories.

Questions to explore the multiple functions of stories (Riessman, 1993; Squire et al., 2008)

How are stories structured?

Who produces stories?

By what means (e.g. discursive, performative) are stories constructed?

What are the socio-historical contexts in which stories are produced and consumed?

How do stories work in these specific socio-historical contexts?

How are stories silenced and/or contested?

Approaches in narrative analysis differ on the core questions of 'why' and 'how' the stories under investigation are constructed and told. 'What' is told in stories is also important in the analysis. As I will describe in the following paragraphs, understanding the differences between epistemological approaches is the first step in narrative analysis as this will guide the narrative analyst in choosing the relevant questions to ask the data.

There are two key epistemological approaches to narrative analysis: the naturalist and the constructivist approaches (Gubrium & Holstein, 1997). 'Naturalist' approaches use rich descriptions of people in their natural habitats. For example, this approach is applicable to research that aims to explore interpersonal relations in specific conditions (e.g. trauma cases). 'Constructivist' approaches focus on how a sense of social order is created through talk and interaction. These are useful to consider how identities are constructed in various psychosocial contexts (e.g. in education, in families), for example.

Both naturalist and constructivist approaches are primarily concerned with people's lives and experiences. However, 'while the naturalist view is that the social world is in some sense "out there", an external reality available to be observed and described by the researcher, the constructivist view is that the social world is constantly "in the making"' (Elliott, 2005: 18). Therefore, understanding the production of the social world, which shapes narratives, is central in the constructivist approach.

The naturalistic and constructivist approaches ask different questions in the process of understanding narratives. Table 5.1 lists the questions that each approach asks while analysing narratives.

Table 5.1   Questions asked by the two approaches

Naturalist approach: focuses on 'what' questions	Constructivist approach: focuses on 'how' questions
What happened?	How do storytellers make sense of their experiences?
What experiences have people had?	How do storytellers talk about their experiences?
What did people do at that particular time? What does it mean to storytellers?	How do storytellers position themselves while telling stories about their lives? How are multiple stories told in the research context? How does interpersonal and/or social interaction shape the construction of stories?

The discursive positioning of storytellers and listeners is important in the constructivist approach. Davies and Harre (1990: 46) argue that it is through discursive practices that people position themselves. According to them, storytellers draw upon both cultural and personal resources in constructing the present moment in telling their stories. Narratives are constructed within a special conversation that includes both their cultural resources and the interaction between the people who are producing these narratives. A subject position incorporates both a conceptual repertoire and a location. Having once taken up a particular position as one's own, a person inevitably sees the world from that position, and in terms of the particular images, metaphors, storylines and concepts that are made relevant within the particular discursive practice in which they are positioned (Davies & Harre, 1990: 46). 'Positioning' and 'subject position', in contrast, permit individuals to think of themselves as a choosing subject, locating themselves in conversations according to those narrative forms with which they are familiar, and bringing to those narratives their own subjective histories through which they have learnt metaphors, characters and plot (Davies & Harre, 1990: 51). In narrative analysis, it is important to identify the positions from which storytellers construct their stories because these positions are keys to understanding how various elements are put together in response to the available cultural resources and interpersonal interactions.

Mishler (1995) draws a framework for understanding the variety of approaches in narrative analysis. He offers a typology based on three aspects of narratives:

representation, structure and contextual features. In this typology, Mishler (1995) argues that some of the approaches focus on how the narrative represents the order of actual event/episode. These approaches particularly aim to explore the tension between the actual temporal order of events and the order in which these events are retold. Other approaches may be more interested in the structure or form of the narrative. These approaches aim to understand how a story is put together. The third category of approaches focus on the cultural, social, psychological and interactional contexts in which narratives are produced, told and consumed. While providing this typology for narrative analysis, Mishler (1995) emphasises his concern that there is no single 'best' way to analyse narratives, that narrative researchers need to pursue their own approaches while being open to explore what they may learn from other approaches.

The following section discusses how to do narrative analysis. It aims to provide descriptions of some ways in which narrative research is conducted, and describes commonly used analytical models. These models are shaped by the epistemological approaches to narratives summarised in Mishler's (1995) typology.

'Narratives do not speak for themselves or have unanalysed merit; they require interpretation when used as data in social research'. (Riessman, 2005: 2)

How to do narrative analysis

Narrative analysis considers how the narrator, the leading character of the told story, makes meaning of her/his life and/or experiences while telling their story. The analyst makes a systematic interpretation of these meaning-making processes by considering various aspects of the story being told.

Narrative analysis considers the structure, content and context of narratives. While it is possible to analyse only one of these aspects, applications of narrative analysis often integrate all of them. This is because it is important to understand the narrative process through which meaning is created and mediated as whole. For example, when narrative analysts choose to analyse the content of narratives, they describe the structure and context as well, because the ways, time and context in which stories are told shape their content.

As we have seen, narrative analysis refers to a family of methods. Each technique interprets texts that have in common a storied form (Riessman, 2008: 11). Models of narrative analysis offer different focuses and questions to analysts. Each model is shaped by different yet connected theoretical discussions. Table 5.2 illustrates some narrative analysis models.

Depending on the research questions and collected data, multiple models can be combined so as to capture multiple layers in the construction of narratives (e.g. Frost, 2009b). It should be noted that there are no strict guidelines that dictate to narrative researchers how to apply these analytical models. Depending on the interpretation of the model and specific research context, researchers apply each model in varied ways.

Table 5.2   Modes of narrative analysis

Models of narrative analysis	Focus of analysis
Structural model (Labov, 1972)	The structure of stories The ways in which in which stories are told
Thematic model (Riessman, 2008)	The content of stories The themes around which stories are told
Interactional/performative model (Riessman, 1993; Mishler, 1995; Denzin, 2001)	The contextual features that shape the construction of narratives How the meaning is collaboratively created through interaction between storytellers and listeners

The following sections will first briefly discuss the data-gathering and preparation processes in narrative research. Then they will summarise some of the main analytical models and basic guidelines that can help narrative analysts to constitute their own analytical path in working with narratives.

Sampling and recruitment

In common with other qualitative research approaches, sampling criteria are set by the researcher. The characteristics of research participants should be relevant to the research questions and aims. The number of participants in narrative research practice varies depending on the research topic. For example, for their research on young athletes' perceptions of self-ageing, Phoenix and Sparkes (2008) set the criteria as age and involvement in team or individual sports, and selected 22 people.

It should be noted that narrative methods are not appropriate for research conducted with a large number of respondents. The construction of rich, detailed narratives within the research context is the key to a good narrative analysis. Therefore, the number of participants is not a major concern. Narrative researchers often tend to interview each participant multiple times so as to capture the changes in the meaning-making processes in narratives. For example, in some oral history

Problem-based question

Consider yourself a narrative researcher who plans research to explore experiences of divorce among middle-aged men in London.
What will be your criteria for the selection of participants?
How many participants will you recruit for this research?
What is the best way to approach possible participants?

projects, narrative researchers work with five participants. They conduct multiple interviews with these participants over five years.

Decisions about sampling and recruitment are not limited to setting criteria about how research participants will be selected. The initial contacts and conversations about participation in research before the actual interview also need care. Possible participants may be approached either by researchers themselves or through gatekeepers. At this initial stage, it is explained clearly to potential participants, who are interested in being part of the research, what the research is about, what method(s) will be used to collect and analyse data, and how they are expected to contribute to answer the research question(s).

Ethics

Ethical considerations need extra care in narrative research in which the research process itself is integrated into the analysis. Similar to other social science research practice, researchers should follow the ethical guidelines of the university and places where they recruit participants and conduct research. Confidentiality statements and information sheets should include detailed information about research questions and aims as well as the rights of participants. You need to get approval from the ethics board of your university before you start interviewing participants. The written consent of participants should be secured.

As narrative research focuses on stories about people's lives and selves, confidentiality is of particular importance. Participants should be assured that personal identifiers will be removed or changed from the written data and presentations of analysis. Sharing transcripts, analysis and publications with research participants is common practice in narrative research. It is part of the conversation between researchers and participants in the co-construction of narratives.

Researchers have obligations and responsibilities in considering the effects of the research both on the participants and wider communities. Narrative research is no exception. Critical and systematic reflexivity about all layers of the research process, and the revelation of power relations between researchers and participants in analysis and presentations are part of these responsibilities.

Gathering data: narrative interviewing

Narrative researchers from various disciplines analyse narratives that are elicited from a wide range of sources. However, interviews are central to much research in social sciences. Over the past two decades, there has been a proliferation of discussions about the variety of approaches to interviewing methods and how to analyse interviews (see Elliott, 2005: 18). The link between in-depth interviewing and narratives has been part of these discussions. Similar to semi-structured interviews, narrative interviewing uses open, non-leading questions. Narrative interviews give priority to the elicitation of participants' stories with minimum intervention from interviewers.

In his book *Research Interviewing: Context and Narrative* (1986), Mishler (1986: 54–55) argues that interviews go beyond participants' responses to interviewers' questions within research contexts. Rather, the interview might be defined as a game, which is constituted over a complex interaction of responses. This accumulative process turns into collaborative meaning-making rather than simply imposing or receiving the interviewer's framework of meanings. Therefore, interviewing and the analysis of interviews require 'close attentiveness to what interviewers and respondents say to each other, and how they say it' (1986: 76). Interviews that view the interviewing as a participatory site in which meaning is co-produced by participants and interviewers are defined as 'narrative interviews' (Mishler, 1986).

Questions to be asked

Developing an interview schedule is one of the first steps in narrative interviewing. Although narratives can emerge in every kind of conversation, even in answers to yes/no questions, certain open-ended questions are more suitable to receive narrative responses. The narrative interview can begin with an open invitation: 'Tell me about your life …' or 'Tell me what happened … and then what happened.' This particular phrasing is less restrictive than a question such as 'When did this event happen?' Narrative interviews can involve more topic-orientated, open-ended questions such as 'How did you decide to go for further education?' or 'Tell me about your relationship with your parents.'

As Elliott (2005: 28–29) discusses, unlike the common expectation that narratives emerge in the context of interviews naturally, there are situations when researchers fail to get narratives from respondents. This is usually caused by problems with the effectiveness of questions. These should be simple and straightforward. Listening to participants' responses is the key in narrative interviewing. Sometimes even a very open-ended question may not help to produce narratives; events may be summarised and given little significance. Further questions that aim to encourage the participant to unpack the layers of the story should be asked in interviews.

Interview interaction

Emerson and Frosh (2004: 26) argue that the power between the interviewer and participants should be balanced well in interview practice. While interviewing places the interviewer in a powerful position to ask questions, this should not disempower participants. They have the right to choose how they are going to answer the questions, what they are going to tell the interviewer.

Mishler (1986: 118–119) argues that empowering respondents through re-structuring the interviewer–interviewee relationship is an important part of the interview design, to 'encourage respondents to find and speak in their own "voices"'. The respondents are likely to tell stories when the balance of power is shifted between interviewers and interviewees. One of the components of restructuring this relationship is asking less restrictive, open-ended questions. The other component is interviewers being attentive listeners.

Narratives can easily be suppressed if interviewers interrupt accounts that might develop into narratives, if interviewers do not respond to a response, or they appear not to be listening to interviewees. Narratives can be elicited in interviews where interviewers allow interviewees to continue telling until they indicate that they have finished answering. Attentive listening in narrative interviews includes discerning interviewees' silences in their responses to questions. These silences can give interviewers important clues about what or what not to ask in interview conversations.

Interviewers should be aware of the fact that interviewees have their own agendas and understanding of the interview interaction, that they cannot control this interaction. We should remember that the aim is to invite participants to tell their stories in their own way, to express their own views, which may be different from others' views. Interviewers' role in the interview relationship is neither to judge nor to approve any story and/or personality of the respondent. Instead, they should focus attention on and give non-judgemental validation of participants' stories (Bloom, 1998: 18). This validation is not limited to respecting participants' ways of telling stories; encouraging participants to collaborate in interviews is part of the interviewer's role.

Narrative interviewing provides a space for researchers to use the idea of co-construction of the meaning in a creative way. Contemporary researchers go beyond the classical question–answer interview style and expand the interview conversations by using other tools such as visual material (e.g. videos, artwork produced by participants, photographs taken by participants or participants' responses to others' photographs).

Transcribing

The transcription of interviews is part of narrative analysis. As Riessman (1993) states, the choices of what to include, how to structure and present the transcribed text 'have serious implications for how a reader will understand the narrative' (1993: 12). The act of transcription is an interpretive practice that is shaped by the assumptions of the researcher (Mishler, 1991). The transcription of interviews is carried out in multiple rounds. Riessman (1993: 56) advises to begin with a 'rough transcription'. This is a first draft of the entire interview, and includes all the words and other main features of the conversation such as crying, laughing and pauses. The interview can be re-transcribed to add the shorter pauses, false starts, emphases and utterances such as 'uhm'. Researchers also utilise fieldnotes about the interview interactions so as to include the interactional details into transcriptions. These notes are very useful in the transcription and analysis process as they help the researcher to locate the narrative sections in the whole interview (see Frost, 2009b).

Example

Example interview schedule

This is the schedule that I used in my research on the construction of sexuality in the narratives of educated young women. I interviewed young women aged between 18 and 25 with university education. One of my aims was to explore the generational differences in telling sexual stories. Therefore, I also interviewed the mothers of younger participants. I asked the same questions to both groups.

Introduction

In this section, I introduced my research, what I aimed to explore in this research, how participants would contribute to the research, what I would do to take care of confidentiality matters. I explained to participants their rights. I clarified that I was open to listen to everything they wanted to tell me; that I was not there to judge them for what they would tell me. Having considered the sensitivity of the research topic (sexual experiences), this clarification was necessary to open up the space for a collaborative interview. I also told the participants that I was ready to answer their questions if they had any.

Questions

Can you tell me about yourself, your life, your family, your friends?
Can you remember your initial conversations about sexuality? Who did you talk to? What did you talk about?
Can you tell me the story of your first period?
Can you tell me about your relationships and sexual experiences? Anything that *you* want to tell me?
[To younger participants] What kind of conversation do you have with your mother about sexual matters?
[To mothers] What kind of conversation do you have with your daughter about sexual matters?

Closure

Is there anything else that you want to talk about? I'd love to listen to you.

Reflexivity and positioning of the researcher in narrative analysis

The positioning of researchers, both in interview conversations and in the analytical process, is particularly important in understanding, analysing and presenting narratives. Ruthellen Josselson (2004: 3–5) defines two distinct positions for narrative analysts. The first is characterised by a willingness to listen and understand meaning in its given form. The analysts in this category aim to present the narratives of storytellers as they are told and highlight meanings that are present in the participants' story. By contrast, the second position focuses on decoding the meaning while analysing narratives. According to Josselson (2004: 16), this second position recognises the relativity of all narratives. In this approach, the researcher may seek to understand the interrelations of various voices and positions depicted in a narrative, beyond the connections made by the narrator. In such a framework, the narrative analyst's aim is not re-present the stories of participants as they are told but to offer a different reading of them. While presenting their analysis, narrative analysts clearly distinguish their own voice from that of the participant. For example, while storytellers are recounting their experiences in a story, researchers may be more interested in the conflicting cultural discourses behind the presentation of that story.

The integration of critical and systematic reflexivity in narrative analysis is a way for researchers to position themselves. Reflexivity as a research practice means examination of research decisions such as theoretical assumptions, selection of participants, interview schedules, interviewing, analysing the data and presentation of analysis, as well as the relationship between the researcher and participants. Reflexivity underlines the role of the researcher in the constitution of narratives.

Example (from PQR analysis)
Integrating the analyst's position into analysis

In my first reading of Liz's interview transcript, I thought that she did not talk about her body except the lines where she described the baby as a part of her body. Later, I realised that she implicitly talks about her body in between the lines where she tells about the tiring routine of looking after a child. However, even if she implies her body, this is the body of the mother. There might be a few reasons to explain why her body is missing in her narrative. One of them might be the core of the interview, which is her emotional experience of motherhood. Since she focuses on the emotions she might skip the embodied experience.

The other one I can think of is related to my own expectation, which is shaped by my research interests. I work on social construction of sexuality. Therefore the connection between the body and sexuality is one of the first themes I had in mind in analysing data. Probably because of this I found her not telling much about her own body interesting. However, since she voices storylines within motherhood discourse, which portrays mothers as 'asexual', it is not surprising not to hear anything about her own body.

Example

Data analysis

Basic steps in analysing narratives

1. Situating the epistemological approach

Situating the methodological approach is the first and one of the most important steps in the analysis of narratives. This first step will influence the choice of the analytical model as well as the analytical position of the researcher. Research questions and the theoretical framework of the research can help the researcher in his/her decision about whether they are going to situate their analysis within a naturalist or constructivist approach to narratives. As discussed above, these two approaches differ in their understanding of how meaning is created in narratives.

2. Selecting the analytical model(s) to be used

The next step is to decide which analytical model or models will be used in analysing narrative data. Different models of narrative analysis are interested in different features of the narratives and they ask different questions while analysing narratives. Decisions on using singular or plural models in analysing the narratives are informed by the epistemological approach that shapes the research design.

3. Selecting narratives to be analysed

Selecting narratives in the data is important. Even in applications that aim to analyse the data as a whole instead of selecting parts of it, particular narratives can be put under close scrutiny for analytical purposes. The selection can be made by first breaking down the text into segments (sentences and paragraphs), as suggested by Hiles and Cermák (2008: 153). Then segments can each be considered as a self-contained episode in telling a story, as they constitute the micro units of analysis. The selection of these units is determined by the researcher's analytical strategy.

4. Analysing narratives

The clear and systematic application of one or multiple analytical models is essential in narrative analysis practice. It does not matter which method or methods are employed in generating insight into the structure or function, content, context and impacts of narratives (Willig, 2008: 133). So how do researchers choose? Narrative analysts are aware that the stories located in data are also varied. Storytellers often do not follow structured lines in telling their stories. This variety leaves the analyst with questions concerning the choice of the best analytical model that can preserve and respect the content, meaning and context of stories within which they are constructed.

Structural model

The structural model proposed by Labov and Waletzky (1967/1997) closely examines how the narrative is formed, how different elements in this structure function in personal experience narratives. This model treats personal narratives as a text,

Table 5.3 Basic steps in analysing narratives

Step	Activity
1. Situating the epistemological approach	Decision on using naturalist or constructivist approach
2. Selecting the analytical model	Decision on using one or more models of narrative analysis: • structural • thematic • performative
3. Selecting narratives to be analysed	Breaking the narrative into segments/units of analysis
4. Analysing narratives	Application of analytical models so as to explore the multiple layers of meaning

Problem-based question

Researcher B designed a research project that aims to understand how immigrant women's experiences in further education in the UK influence their processes of self-construction. The researcher aims to explore the interconnected psychological, social and political factors that shape the experiences of these women in education. Her research draws on in-depth interviews with immigrant women from X country living in London. She selected a group of participants by their age and current status in education. She planned to interview participants twice over the course of a year. She structured her interview schedule with a focus on the participants' experiences in education, how they make sense of these experiences and how they relate these experiences to their experiences of immigration.

Consider yourself as researcher B.
What will be the epistemological approach that you will use to situate this research? (Consider the research questions.)
Which analytical model or models will you use in your analysis?

which functions as a representation of past events in the form of a story (Patterson, 2008: 23). The focus of analysis in the structural model is on the way an event is told in a story text.

Labov (1972: 362–363) developed his model on the assumption that stories of events contain narrative clauses. These clauses have a beginning, a middle and an end. But there are other elements of narrative structure found in more fully developed narrative clauses. He developed a six-part model to be used in analysing the structure of narratives (Table 5.4).

Table 5.4 The elements of story text in Labov's model

1. Abstract (A):	There are one or two clauses that summarise the story When the whole story is heard it can be seen that the abstract does encapsulate the point of the story
2. Orientation (O):	Orientation clauses function to provide a setting in which the events of the story are told
3. Complicating action (CA):	Complicating action clauses relate the events of the story These clauses usually represent time in a linear way with a chronological order following the 'then, and then' structure They may relate a series of events
4. Result (R):	These are the clauses that tell the listener how the story ends
5. Evaluation (E):	The evaluation clauses present the narrator's perspective on the events They mediate the 'point' of the story Labov (1972) identifies three main types of evaluation in story texts: 1. *External:* these are the clauses in which the narrator steps outside the complicating action and tells the listener the point 2. *Embedded:* these are the clauses in which the narrator tells the listener how they felt at the time, without interrupting the flow of the story 3. *Evaluative*: these clauses report actions that reveal emotions as a part of the story
6. Coda (C):	These clauses link the past world of the story to the present world of the storytelling They function 'to "sign off" the story and offer the floor to the listener' (Patterson, 2008: 27)

Analysts can use the 'question method' for the categorisation of clauses in narrative that can be assigned to one element in Labov's model. This is based on the idea that narratives provide a series of answers to the underlying questions that all narratives address. Thus the function of clauses in narratives is to answer different questions (Patterson, 2008: 25). Table 5.5 shows the questions that could be used to identify each element in a story.

Strict use of the structural model has the danger of decontextualising narratives by paying little attention to the broader historical, socio-cultural and institutional narratives as well as to the interactional factors that shape the context of the narration (Riessman, 2008). Labov focuses on the narrative as a straightforward representation of past events in a story. The narrative text to be analysed is a naturally produced monologue in his approach rather than being co-constructed in interview conversations. These narratives are likely to be produced in research interviews within which the interviewer has a minimal role and the interviewee sticks to the point. This idealised, controlled context is rarely the case in interview experiences. However, the structural model provides the analyst with a detailed method that can be utilised as a good starting point in analysing transcripts of spoken narratives produced in various contexts. It can be used to identify important narratives in a

Table 5.5 Questions that could be used to identify each element in a story

Elements	Questions
Abstract	What was this about?
Orientation	Who is the story about, when did it happen, What happened, where did it happen?
Complicating action	Then what happened?
Evaluation	So what?
Result	What finally happened?
Coda	This element does not answer any particular question It functions to sign off the narrative as it returns to the present time of the telling

transcript. Mishler (1995) argues that the model proposed by Labov and Waletzky is not only interested in the structural sequence of event but also in the evaluative function of the narrative content. This model aims to make clear the meaning of those events and experiences told in the narratives.

Presentation of narratives analysed by the structural model usually follows the same principle of focusing on the 'core narrative' in a story. Analysts usually present the details of their application of the six-part model to a selected story using a table, and give detailed descriptions of their structural analysis under each element of the structure defined in the Labovian model.

Table 5.6 Example of Labov's narrative analysis model

I saw him on the bus	Abstract
yesterday, months after the argument we had.	Orientation
I was on my way back home, reading a funny magazine.	Orientation
Then my phone rang. I was trying to find it in the depths of my bag. Then he touched my shoulder.	Complicating action
I was like 'Oh my god! I haven't seen him for ages …'. I really miss him, you know, he was my best friend.	Evaluation
We chat for ten–fifteen minutes then it was my stop.	Complicating action
He apologised for what happened between us just before I got off. I promised to keep in touch.	Result
But I know, Nothing will be the same	Coda

Thematic model (Riessman, 2008)

This model focuses on the content of a narrative: 'what' is said more than 'how' it is said, the 'told' rather than the aspects of 'telling' (Riessman, 2008: 54). The content of the told story is at the centre of thematic analysis. There is minimal attention to structures selected by the narrator to tell her/his story, function or contextual details of the stories. The thematic model can be applied to a wide range of narrative text, including narratives produced in interviews and written documents.

The analyst can start the thematic analysis by the open coding of data. This means building a set of themes by looking for patterns and meaning produced in the data, labelling and grouping them in connection with the theoretical framework of the research. In practice analysts utilise both the ideas and themes from their conceptual framework and 'new' themes in data while conducting thematic narrative analysis.

The steps in the categorical content analysis described by Lieblich *et al.* (1998) can be used in the process of thematic analysis. The categorical content analysis focuses on thematic similarities and differences between narratives generated in interviews. The analytical approach of Lieblich *et al.* (1998: 112–113) involves breaking the text into smaller units of content.

The thematic model is useful for theorising across a number of cases, finding common and different thematic elements between the narratives of different

Table 5.7 Four stages in the application of the thematic model

1. Selection of the subtext/segments
All the relevant sections of the transcript relevant to the research question are marked and assembled to create a new file or subtext. For example, if the research question involves healthcare, all the sections about various aspects of healthcare should be marked for analysis. Usually the selected subtexts are treated independently from the total context of the narrative. However, in practice, narrative researchers include contextual details in their interpretation (see Riley & Hawe, 2005; Phoenix & Sparkes, 2008).

2. Definition of thematic categories
Themes or perspectives are identified across the selected subtext. These can be in the form of words, sentences or groups of sentences. These categories can be predefined by the theory. Another method can be reading the selected subtexts multiple times and defining the themes that emerge from these readings. There is no limit to the number or form of thematic categories. The decisions on the number of categories depend on the analyst's perspective. Some analysts work with many, subtle categories that retain the richness of the narrative, which will require meticulous work on the identification and analysis of categories. Some analysts, on the other hand, work with a small number of broad categories, which require less work.

3. Sorting the material into categories
Separate sentences and utterances across the narrative texts are assigned to relevant categories. In this way, different parts of narratives will be grouped under the defined thematic categories.

4. Drawing conclusions
The narrative content collected in each thematic category can be used to describe the meanings in the content of the narrative text.

research participants. One of the limitations of using this model is to do with the meaning reported in narratives. It is not possible to know that all the participants in a research context mean the same thing although the analyst groups their narratives into a similar thematic category. The narrative analyst can tackle this problem by making nuanced, well-illustrated descriptions of the thematic categories, including the contextual details of the interviews.

Presentation of thematic analysis is usually structured by the thematic categories used in analysis. The description of categories, and similarities and differences between different narratives are illustrated by the case studies and small sketches.

An example of thematic narrative analysis is applied by Phoenix and Sparkes (2008). Their study explores young athletes' perceptions of self-ageing. In their analysis, the researchers sought connections across narrative segments and themes in interviews with 22 young athletes (2008: 214). They aimed to identify patterns and meanings constructed both within and between the stories, which helped them to develop conceptual categories of the self, namely the 'sporting self', the 'settled self' and the 'reflective self'. While developing the categories, the researchers also analysed the structural and contextual elements that constituted the narratives.

Example

Interactional-performative model (Riessman, 1993; Mishler, 1995; Denzin, 2001)

The focus of analysis in this model is storytelling as a co-construction in which narrator and listener (the interviewer and audience in a broader sense) collaboratively create meaning. This model also pays attention to thematic content and narrative structures, but goes beyond a structural analysis. It requires close reading of contexts, including the influence of researcher, audience, setting and social circumstances on the constitution and performance of the narrative. Storytelling is seen as performance by an individual with a history, who involves, persuades and moves the audience through language and gesture, both 'doing' and 'telling' (Riessman, 2008).

The interactional-performative model understands stories as composed and received in interactional, historical, institutional and discursive contexts (Riessman, 2008: 105–106). As social products, stories not only tell listener(s) about individuals, but also about society and culture in which they are constituted and performed. The interactional context of interviews is particularly important in this model. Mishler defines interview interaction as 'a dialogic process, a complex sequence of exchanges through which interviewer and interviewee negotiate some degree of agreement on what they will talk about, and how' (1999: xvi). The analysis of interview conversations as one of the contextual layers provides the analyst with the necessary tool to understand how the interview moment facilitates or obstructs the way respondents make sense of their lives.

Denzin (2001: 24–25) defines the interview as an active site where meaning is created and performed. Indeed, the interview produces a site where the meanings are contextual and improvised in a conversational performance. This performance further crafts the interview as a narrative device, which allows persons who are so inclined to tell their stories as part of an ongoing dialogic conversation. So the interview process does not simply work as an information-gathering exercise, but also as a performance in which both the teller and the listener participate so as to transform information into a shared experience.

Close reading of data is essential in applying interactional-performative analysis. The analyst can ask several questions about the co-construction of narratives; these will help them to reveal multiple elements in the construction of narratives. Interactional-performative analysis deals with questions such as those listed in the following box.

Questions to ask in the application of the interactional-performative model

- How is a story co-constructed?
- How does the interaction between storyteller and listener, and their historical and cultural location shape this co-construction process?
- Why was the narrative constructed and told in that way?
- How does the narrator position him/herself in relation to the audience, and vice versa?
- How does this positioning influence the construction and interpretation of the story?
- How does the storyteller talk about the characters in the story and her/his relationship with these characters?
- How do these relational characters, including the narrator her/himself influence the construction and performance of the story?
- How does the presence of audience (interviewers, listeners, readers) shape the construction and the performance of the story?

The process of analysis can be constructed as a conversation between the analyst and the narrative. The analyst can ask these questions and other relevant ones to gather data, build her/his interpretation on the responses and ask further questions to make the analysis more detailed. By asking these questions, the analyst may focus on one or more features, such as the characters and their positioning in a story, the circumstances of performance, the enactment of dialogue between characters, and audience (listener and reader) response to the performance.

The model requires transcripts that present all conversational details of the interview interaction. This should include all participants in the conversation and unspoken features of interaction. The transcript should not only be seen as a vehicle for content: it must tell the analyst the story of the interview conversation. The unspoken is a very important element in the analysis. Some researchers use video tapes to record interviews in order not to skip the unspoken parts of the interaction. As mentioned above, fieldnotes on the details of the interview conversation can also be included in the transcripts. As Riessman (2002) reminds us, it is misleading to focus only on the transcripts that have been constructed from the interviews. The multiplicity of voices in the narrative performances should be part of the analysis in this model. While telling our stories, we do not speak from a single position. As we draw on available storylines, public discourses and others' stories, our position changes continuously in connection with the discursive resources. For example, while telling about her experiences, the research participant may start by voicing the dominant public discourse of the necessity of full-time motherhood. The participant may answer another interview question in a voice critical of the same dominant discourse to say that working mothers can also be as attentive as full-time mothers.

The interactional-performative model is suitable for detailed studies of identity construction and for studies of communication practices, as it analyses the positioning of the narrator and her/his interaction with the audience in narrative performance. Narrative researchers working with the interactional-performative model use creative ways to present their analysis. As the analyst follows the narrative closely in analysis, the presentation usually aims to demonstrate this close relationship. It usually takes the form of a narrative, which tells the audience the story of the interaction-performance. In addition to extracts from transcripts, details of cultural and historical contexts that shape the narrative, as well as the details of dialogic performance, are presented as part of the analysis.

Example of interactional-performative analysis

Aida: Later, I started to go to classical music concerts at the weekends. It was like a blossoming for me. [...] you know how it is ... I felt relieved outside home by these outings. I hadn't had any problems with my family until then. The problems started with these concerts. To that point, I was [err], compared to my sister, more modest, more respectful to parents, more serious whereas she was loose, lazy, and unsuccessful [...].

Example

Questions	Analysis
• How is a story co-constructed? How does the interaction between the storyteller and listener, their historical and cultural location shape this co-construction process?	Aida was a vivid storyteller with a highly analytical voice, which was shaped by the feminist perspective that Aida and I shared throughout the interview. She constructed stories on her analysis of gender discourses and her position(s) in connection to these discourses. She presented herself as a 'performer' so as to describe her discursive movements within the gender regulations constantly shaping her as a young woman.
• How does the narrator position him/herself in relation to the audience, and vice versa?	Aida was aware of the availability of multiple positions for her in the gender-power networks in which she was raised. In telling her stories, she refers to the dominant and marginal storylines uncovering the links between gender and sexuality in contemporary Turkey.

In this particular interview excerpt, she tells me about the tensions she experiences in leaving her 'good girl' position in search of a space of freedom outside the regulations of home.

By the phrase 'you know how it is …' Aida also positions the interviewer as someone with similar experiences in the same culture who will understand what she means. |
| • How does the storyteller talk about the characters in the story and her/his relationship with these characters? How do these relational characters, including the narrator her/himself influence the construction and performance of the story? | Aida portrays her sister and herself as representatives of two storylines located in the dominant discourses of gender. While describing herself as a 'good' girl who is 'modest' and 'serious', she positions her sister as a 'bad' girl who is 'loose' and 'lazy'. |

Pluralist approach to analytical models

While mapping out the contemporary models of narrative analysis, Riessman (2005) underlines the considerable variation in the definition of narratives and narrative analytical methods, which are often shaped by the disciplines of the researchers. Although it is possible to identify some models, according to Riessman, 'in practice, different approaches can be combined; they are not mutually exclusive and, as with all typologies, boundaries are fuzzy' (2005: 2).

In practice, a combination of analytical methods is common among narrative researchers as this can work as a methodological tool to analyse the multiple aspects of data. Narrative researchers aim to explore the multiple layers of meaning that are constructed and presented in narratives. Combining various analytical models is a way to explore structural, linguistic and contextual aspects of the narratives that can enrich the multilayered analysis. This approach usually draws on the strengths offered by each analytical model to uncover the layers of meaning in narratives. In addition, using *multiple* methods for data analysis is more likely to make the findings and analysis grounded and, as a result, they are more likely to be valid (Mello, 2002: 235).

Narrative researchers who analyse narratives with a pluralistic approach usually start their analysis with structural or thematic models and expand their analysis by revealing multiple layers in the construction and performance of narratives. In mapping out these layers, researchers apply various versions of interactional-performative analysis in order to analyse the historical, cultural and discursive circumstances in which narratives are constructed and function. The role of interviewer and/or researcher in the collaborative production of narratives in research contexts is one of the elements explored through the pluralistic approaches. This exploration includes the positioning of the storyteller and researcher in telling, listening to and analysing narratives.

In the following research example box you will find the summary of Nollaig Frost's research about the transition to second-time motherhood, which was conducted using a pluralistic approach to narrative analysis.

Frost, N. (2009). 'Do you know what I mean?': the use of a pluralistic narrative analysis approach in the interpretation of an interview', *Qualitative Research*, 9(1), pp. 9–29

Aim of the research

Frost's research aimed to explore women's experiences of transition to second-time motherhood through participants' maternal narratives. The researcher chose to use narrative analysis in her research so as to understand how stories are functional for storytellers to make sense of changes in their sense of self and in their social relationships at times of incoherence in events and the individual's sense of identity. Through the narrative analysis, she aimed to understand the ways in which the participants made sense of the changes in their identity as they became mothers to two children (2009b: 14). Unlike other psychology research about motherhood, which tends to medicalise this process, Frost aimed to privilege the voices of mothers in understanding the experiences of motherhood.

Participants

The participants in the research were British, white, middle-class women who lived in London and were professionally employed. Participants were recruited when they were six months pregnant with their second child. All of the participants were in stable relationships with the father of their children.

Research Example

Research Example

Methods

The research draws on interview data collected over the course of a year. Frost carried out three or four semi-structured interviews with each research participant and gathered accounts of their experiences of second-time motherhood. The interview questions were constituted around participants' 'hopes, fears, expectations and, as appropriate, realities of being mothers in the past, present and future of their transition to second-time motherhood' (2009b: 14).

Frost carefully positioned herself as an interviewer as she, too, was a British, middle-class, white, professional woman with two children. She avoided imposing her own story of motherhood, but was open to the questions of participants about her experiences. Rather than strictly drawing on her interview schedule, Frost followed the participant's story in each interview closely.

Analytical approach

Frost (2009b) employed a pluralistic approach to analysing the narratives elicited in interviews that she conducted. Her aim in using this approach was to understand the multidimensional meaning of the narrative by adding texture to the interpretation of it rather than verifying meanings (2009b: 10). Frost uses a combination of structural and linguistic models from a critical analytical perspective that take account of the context, the interaction between narrator and interviewer, and the unspoken interactions and nuances in the narration of stories. In her application, she selects different narratives from the same interview and analyses the structural or linguistic features of each narrative. She conducts her analysis by applying the same analytical model to different pieces of the interview and employs different models of narrative analysis to the same selected data. Since Frost works with a critical perspective, she adds another layer to her structural analysis by providing the details of interview interaction, which creates a specific context for the production of the narratives analysed.

Frost employed her narrative approach in a flexible way. She followed the structure and content of stories within each interview while making decisions about the model she was going to apply to each piece of data. For example, if there were stories with clear temporal order, Frost used Labov's model for the initial analysis of these stories. If there was a part of the interview that sounded like a narrative without a temporal order, she used linguistic or performative models for the initial analysis. Frost used a systematic technique to build the layers in her analysis. Following her initial analysis of different pieces, she revisited the interview transcript, her fieldnotes and written observations, to understand the positioning of the participants as storytellers, the location of the particular story within the whole interview as well as the interactional features that constituted the story as it was.

By her systematic, pluralistic approach to narrative analysis, Frost explored the complexity and diversity of participants' narratives about second-time motherhood. Her approach was also useful in the recognition of multiple ways in which women might express their feelings about and experiences of motherhood.

Reflection on Practice

I was very excited at the idea of being a part of the Pluralism in Qualitative Research Project. Reading the same data from different analytical approaches has always been a very interesting idea for me. I thought that this would be an excellent opportunity to contribute to a very rich methodological approach. I was also a little bit nervous, for this was the first time I met a 'participant' in a transcript as a researcher/ analyst. I had analysed various types of material before, but I had not analysed an interview that I had not conducted myself. My approach to narratives includes uncovering the layers in their construction. These are multiple interrelated contextual layers that constitute the narratives that we analyse.

Similarly, my focus was on the way narratives were constructed in the PQR interview. The interview was about the participant's experiences of second-time motherhood. I focused on multiple stories in the interview, on different aspects of motherhood, and applied narrative analysis to understand some of the layers in the construction of these stories. I used a mixture of thematic and performative models in a flexible way. One of the steps in my analysis was to identify the positions that the participant inhabited and utilised in constructing and communicating her stories of motherhood. Eventually, the positions of the participant and her movements between – sometimes contradictory – positions became central in my analysis to understanding the ways in which she made sense of her experiences.

I briefly mentioned the interaction between the participant and researcher in my analysis, but I made a decision and did not integrate the interview context into it. I thought that I needed more than the transcript to analyse the interview process. The timing and phrasing of the questions and responses of the participant revealed a positive interview interaction. However, I did not feel confident enough to make a further reading of the interview conversation. Instead, I focused on the stories of motherhood that the participant constituted in the interview, and structured the analysis in a standard way – around themes.

Reflection on Practice

> It was very interesting to read the analysis of other analysts who used different qualitative approaches, particularly to find out how we all selected similar parts of the interview transcript to analyse. This experience made me think further about the meanings created in stories as well as my role as an analyst in this meaning-making process.

Chapter summary

- Narrative analysis is an umbrella term, which refers to multiple approaches and analytical models, and that takes the story itself as the unit of analysis.
- The roots of narrative analysis can traced back to the humanist and post-structuralist traditions that aim to understand narratives. While humanists approach narratives from a person-centred, holistic perspective, post-structuralist approaches are more concerned with the meaning created in narratives.
- Narratives are forms through which people make sense of their experiences and mediate the meanings they give to these experiences.
- While personalised over time, narratives are not created by individuals independently. They are constructed by drawing on a number of available resources.
- Narrative research enables researchers to see multiple and sometimes contradictory layers of meaning, to reconstruct meanings through linking these layers, and to explore and understand the interrelations between individual and social processes.
- There are two main epistemological approaches that shape the understanding of narratives: 'naturalist' approaches use rich descriptions of people in their natural habitats, whereas 'constructivist' approaches focus on how a sense of social order is created through talk and interaction.
- Narrative analysis makes a systematic interpretation of meaning-making processes in narratives. Unlike other qualitative research approaches, narrative research does not offer strict rules about the nature and mode of investigation.
- Close attentiveness to research relations, contextual details in the construction of narratives and interview conversations is the main principle in conducting narrative analysis.
- Analytical models in narrative analysis differ from each other by their focus of analysis. The focus of analysis in the structural model is on the way an event is told in a story text. In contrast, the thematic model focuses on what is said in narratives. The interactional-performative model, on the other hand, places collaborative meaning-making processes at the centre of narrative analysis.

- There are no strict instructions on how and where to use each model. These decisions are shaped within the specific context of research. There are many studies in which combinations of analytical models are used as a methodological tool to analyse the multiple aspects of narratives.

Further reading

Chamberlayne, P., Bornat, J. & Wengraf, T. (eds). (2000) *The Turn to Biographical Methods in Social Science: Comparative Issues and Examples.* London: Routledge.
This book provides illustrations of using biographical/narrative methods in research practice. It highlights the interdisciplinary character of narrative techniques and perspectives.

Clandinin, J.D. (ed.) (2007) *Handbook of Narrative Inquiry: Mapping a Methodology.* Thousand Oaks, CA: Sage Publications.
This book is useful for further methodological discussions about narrative inquiry in psychology.

Gergen, M. (2001) *Feminist Reconstructions in Psychology: Narrative, Gender and Performance.* London: Sage.
This book includes feminist arguments on the role of epistemological positions, research ethics and relations in the construction of narratives.

Jones, R.L. (2004) 'That's very rude, I shouldn't be telling you that': older women talking about sex. In Bamberg, M. & Andrews, M. (eds) *Considering Counter Narratives: Narrating, Resisting, Making Sense.* Amsterdam/Philadelphia: John Benjamins.
This article discusses the role of cultural storylines in the constitution and performance of sexual narratives among older people. The argument on the interconnections between dominant and counter-storylines explains the role of positioning in narratives.

Lee, R.M. & Renzetti, C.M. (1990) The problems of researching sensitive topics. *American Behavioral Scientist,* 33(5), 510–528.
This article poses questions about the ethics and politics of researching sensitive topics such as sexuality, abuse and illness. It is useful for narrative research as it includes a very interesting argument on the individual differences in the collaborative meaning-making in research contexts.

Tamboukou, M. (2008) A Foucauldian approach to narratives. In Andrews, M., Squire, C. & Tamboukou, M. (eds) *Doing Narrative Research.* London: Sage.
This chapter describes a different approach to narrative analysis that is shaped by the methodological perspective of Michel Foucault. This approach aims to analyse narratives by locating them in the specific social and historical contexts in which they are produced.

PART 2
Combining Core Approaches

Part Contents

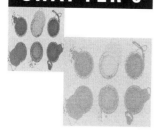

CHAPTER 6

Pragmatics of Pluralistic Qualitative Research

Sevasti-Melissa Nolas

Introduction

This chapter is about conducting pluralistic qualitative research in psychology. In the previous chapters we have looked at a selection of research approaches that tend to be used separately for qualitative research in psychology. In this chapter the focus will be on combining these different approaches. Combining approaches in research is not unproblematic and, as such, it is important to reflect on the appropriateness of doing so, as well as the possibilities and limitations of combining different approaches. Many of the headings in this chapter will be familiar to readers as the chapter covers a range of issues involved in doing qualitative research in psychology. However, each section is written with the issues that pluralistic research raises in mind. The chapter begins with a short introduction to the background and history of pluralism in qualitative research in psychology. It continues with a discussion of the ontological and epistemological issues raised by combining different approaches. It then provides a detailed description of the practicalities of combining approaches, including research design, data collection and analysis. The ethical concerns that are raised while attending to the practicalities of a pluralistic approach are also addressed. The chapter provides several empirical examples of pluralistic qualitative research in psychology throughout, as well as reflections on practice.

Background: pluralistic approaches in psychology

The term pluralism in psychological research has been used to denote the mixing of qualitative and quantitative research methods (Todd et al., 2004; Barker & Pistrang, 2005). In this book we develop an approach to pluralism that concentrates on qualitative research traditions in psychology. What we are proposing is the combination of different qualitative approaches in the same piece of research or research programme. We also suggest that a pluralistic approach can extend our understanding of a phenomenon being researched by offering a range of readings and interpretations. There is a small but growing literature in psychology, especially in applied settings (see the section entitled 'When is a pluralistic approach useful?', page 134), that follows a pluralistic research approach and in doing so suggests that the multi-ontological characteristics (Mark & Snowden, 2006; Mason, 2006) of such settings are best engaged with through multiple conceptual lenses.

Mixing research methods and research strategies has been on the rise for some time (Bryman, 2006). In the last 15 years, what we refer to as *pluralism* has been approached using a range of conceptual labels. Kellner (1995, cited in Kincheloe, 2001: 682) refers to *multiperspectival* research intended to develop a variety of ways of seeing and interpreting social realities, and illuminating the multiple dimensions and consequences of the text. The older concept of *bricolage* (Denzin & Lincoln, 2000, drawing on Levi-Strauss's 1962/1966 work) has been used to connote a 'heterogeneous repertoire' of thought that makes do with whatever materials or tools are to hand (Levi-Strauss, 1962: 17). In research, bricolage is often used as a metaphor connoting the use of a range methods or analytical tools aimed at solving a practical problem. Bricolage calls into question disciplinary boundaries since it challenges singular and reductionist approaches to understanding the complexity of the social world (Kincheloe, 2001: 680). As such, it is concerned with multiple methods of inquiry as well as with 'diverse theoretical and philosophical notions of the various elements encountered in the research act' (Kincheloe, 2001: 682). Dicks, Soyinka and Coffey (2006), for instance, refer to multimodal research. This approach looks at combining a range of different data modes in a single research project, and the authors have argued that different media 'afford' different kinds of meaning modalities.

In a study that looked at the rationale and practice of mixing quantitative and qualitative research methods in a range of social science disciplines including psychology, Bryman (2006) found that, in practice, researchers combine methods in order to enhance or complement an existing quantitative or qualitative strategy or the findings of a particular strategy, to triangulate research approaches in order to corroborate findings, and to expand the breadth and range of inquiry. Meanwhile, Mason (2006) argues for a 'qualitatively driven' approach to mixing methods as a way of thinking outside the box, creatively engaging with the tensions of conceptual dichotomies (e.g. structure–agency, macro–micro), from a constructionist position, and of enhancing and extending the logic of qualitative explanation.

Ontology of the approach

The theories and methods we use contain explicit and implicit ontological assumptions. Ontology refers to the assumptions we hold about the nature of the social world and the groups and individuals that participate in it. Common ontologies in psychology and the social sciences include positivism, realism, pragmatism, social constructionism, and postmodernism. These ontologies create a common language and set of assumptions for those that work within them. They also determine what sorts of theories and methods might be used and hold different assumptions about the nature of being/personhood. In this section we look at the philosophical assumptions of the pluralist approach that we are presenting in this book.

Postmodernism

The pluralistic qualitative approach is underpinned by a postmodernist philosophy of science. Postmodernism reached psychology and the social sciences in the 1980s following the publication of Jean-Francois Lyotard's (1984) *The Postmodern Condition: A Report on Knowledge*. As a general orientation it is a response to the simultaneous shrinking and expansion of the world due to increased information and communication technologies, the decline of heavy industry and the advent of service and knowledge economies, at least in the westernised world. These social changes have implications for the way in which we understand ourselves and others, and how we relate to one another. As such, postmodernism is concerned with issues around language, discourse, identity and culture. In particular, it challenges, and in some cases rejects, modernist ideas about the person as a fixed entity with a whole and stable identity. Postmodernism is interested in the processes of becoming, and views these processes as multiple, fluctuating and fragmented (as opposed to unitary, stable and cohesive). Postmodernism also attends to the ambiguities, contradictions, disruptions and tension of the lived experience, as well as at times intervening to create them. Pluralistic qualitative research in psychology engages with the postmodernist project in bringing together epistemological approaches that are usually considered to be in opposition to and incompatible with one another (this is called 'incommensurability'), and explores the dissonances (and congruities) that are created by such combinations.

Reflexivity

The challenges posed by postmodernism raise issues for the role of the researcher. No longer the central and only voice in research, we need a way to account for our own engagement and interaction with our research, people, places and circumstances. The practice of reflexivity is key. Reflexivity has developed out of a number of critical approaches in psychology, most notably feminism. Reflexivity refers to the practice of situating oneself in the research context and analysing the implications of one's subjectivity both in the context of and in relation to the research being carried out. It is an awareness of, a sensitivity to and engagement with the social and cultural embeddedness of our theories, methods and research questions, as well as a way of checking and critiquing one's assumptions about the research. Pluralistic qualitative research in psychology engages with reflexivity on two levels. The first is the same as in a mono-method approach where the researcher engages with their assumptions, their motivation for the study, and their gender, socio-cultural and economic positioning vis-à-vis the research they are conducting. The second level of reflexivity is in the combination of approaches, and the engagement in the tension and incongruities they create.

Context

Context is another important aspect of the pluralistic qualitative approach. Context can refer to the built environment, to the social relationship near and far, the symbolic and material resources available to people, and the different levels of meaning that can be created in conversation. Context has always played a key role in ecological and social approaches to psychology (Lewin, 1951; Bronfenbrenner, 1979). In some approaches (both quantitative and qualitative) researchers have tended towards a priori definitions of contexts and contextual variables, with the aim of investigating how context mediates or moderates outcomes. Other approaches (predominantly qualitative) have treated context as emerging through the meanings that people ascribe to their contexts through their interactions with each other. The pluralistic approach presented in this book stresses the importance of context in shaping our understanding. The call to take context seriously in psychology is a call to reconnect knowledge to the human sources that created it (Jovchelovitch, 2007). From a pluralistic perspective it also means acknowledging that those human sources, and the knowledge they produce, are diverse in their worldviews, making context multilayered and multilevelled.

Images of organisations (Morgan, 1997)

Morgan's bestselling book on organisations analyses the different *metaphors* that organisational theorists and practitioners have drawn on over the years in order to understand organisational life. These metaphors include organisations as machines, organisms, brains, cultures, political systems, psychic prisons, complex adaptive systems and instruments of domination. Read as a whole, the book provides an example of a pluralistic approach to understanding organisational realities, and to making sense of experiences of working and participating in different organisations.

Example

Practical aspects of pluralistic qualitative research

This section provides advice and guidance on conducting pluralistic qualitative research in psychology. What does a pluralistic research project look like? There are both similarities and differences between working with a single method or a pluralistic approach. Like other qualitative research approaches, a pluralistic approach would require the researcher to follow familiar guidelines for good practice in qualitative research (Henwood & Pidgeon, 1992; Elliott *et al.*, 1999; Bauer & Gaskell, 2000). Such guidelines would include ensuring that there is a clear rationale for the theories and methods being used, that the researcher demonstrates reflexivity and documents their research process in an accessible manner. Guidelines also suggest that theorising is grounded in examples and thick description. Being open to the element of surprise is also suggested, as is purposefully looking for challenging and contradictory examples that might help the researcher tell a different story about the phenomenon under investigation (see Chapter 2 for more details). Researchers are also asked to think about their participants and audiences as thinking-acting-feeling beings that can, and often do, respond to research about them (Angrosino & Mays de Pérez, 2003). Finally, guidelines ask the researcher to consider other contexts in which their theories might apply, as well as the relevance of their findings to real-world situations.

Table 6.1 Guidelines for good practice in qualitative research as discussed by three different sets of authors

*Henwood & Pidgeon (1992)	*Elliott *et al.* (1999)	Bauer & Gaskell (2000)
Importance of fit Integration of theory	Coherence Clarity of research aims	'Corpus construction'
Reflexivity	Owning one's perspective	Triangulation Reflexivity
Documentations	Providing credibility checks Grounding examples Situating sample	Procedural clarity Thick description
Theoretical sampling Negative case studies		Surprise value
Sensitivity to negotiated reality	Resonating with readers	Communicative validation
Transferability		External viability

* In Willig (2000).

You will notice that, whereas different authors write about the guidelines using different language, many of these guidelines refer to similar processes and outcomes. For instance, 'thick description', a term originally coined by philosopher Gilbert Ryle and popularised by the anthropologist Clifford Geertz, refers to the 'piled-up structures of inference and implication' (Geertz, 1973: 7), the symbols and meanings of culture, that a researcher tries to understand. Bauer and Gaskell (2000: 366) use it to remind researchers that findings should be reported with detailed descriptions of situations, events and experiences, to increase the relevance of the evidence and give the audience confidence in the interpretations. This meaning is similar to Elliott *et al.*'s (1999) advice about grounding the research in examples.

Unlike single-method approaches, pluralism relies on *combining* approaches. Existing advice does not provide any guidelines for quality when it comes to combining approaches and, as such, the rest of this section will focus on the practicalities of combining qualitative approaches. Some of the headings below will already be familiar to students and researchers from the previous chapters, as well as from their other reading. This section will focus attention on the issue of combining in each of the research stages. The key issue we are concerned with might be referred to as the 'interfacing' between different approaches (to borrow a term from computing), and the coherence that one achieves in doing so.

The focus on 'interfacing' draws attention to the links, relationships and 'meshing' between different data, methods and approaches, without seeking to assimilate, subsume or privilege any one approach over another (Mason, 2006: 20). Pluralism in research can occur on a number of levels (e.g. theoretical, methodological, empirical), and we refrain from prescribing the level or moment that a pluralistic approach should be taken. As with any other research approach we would expect students and researchers to ask themselves what it is they are trying to achieve and whether a pluralistic approach is the most appropriate one to take for the aims and objectives of the study. In the pluralistic research approach there is a conceptual tool that we draw on to support the research process. Following Marshall and Rossman (1989), research can be thought of as a series of decision making points. In terms of supporting your decision making there is one tool that is important for pluralistic qualitative research and that is the tool of 'dialectical' thinking (Marks, 2006; Mason, 2006). **Dialectics** is a very old philosophy. Socrates referred to it as **'maieutics'**, a metaphor for giving birth to ideas, where he employed a question–answer style of communication, asking probing questions of his students to enable them to arrive at their own answers. Dialectical thinking holds different ideas in mind, and in relation to one another, enabling one to explore complementarities, tensions and contradictions between ideas.

Students will be most familiar with dialectical argumentation when writing essays. The formulation of thesis–antithesis–synthesis is the basis of dialectical thinking. Pluralistic research is about keeping a number of dialogues going at the same time and in a systematic way. In this respect, the term **polyvocality** (Chandler, 2002) captures the outcome of dialectics in the plural. Polyvocality refers to the shifting of narrative voice, the person telling a story, from person to person, thus providing different points of view of the same event (Chandler, 2002: 191). When these different points of view are put into conversation with one another, we have what in cognitive and computing sciences has been referred to as **'multilogue'**, a conversation between three or more participants (Ginzburg & Fernández, 2005) – think of your experience of being on social networking sites such as Facebook, or mailing lists; these are conversations between more than two people at the same time.

Literature review, research question and design

Research serves a number of functions, such as developing new theories and methodologies with which to understand the world, but also developing a better understanding of certain phenomena. Researchers, depending on their interests, will follow a number of strategies in setting up their research. Some will be more interested in developing a theory or methods; others will want to know more about a phenomenon and will be less concerned with the development of theory and methods. These different interests also result in different types of literature that students and other researchers come across in scientific databases (such as Web of Science or Psychinfo). You will notice that some of this literature asks more pragmatic, or 'factual', questions, while other literature is interested in pushing the boundaries of our theoretical understanding of the social world.

Taking a hypothetical example of research on children's views and experience of social exclusion, a literature search might produce both types of literature. In the first instance, you might find articles that deal with 'fact', producing findings that tell us that children in X area reported the following views and experiences of social exclusion. This sort of research is realist in orientation. The focus is often on what is previously known about a subject, and then how the piece of research that is being reported supports, contradicts or develops what is already known. Other articles you might find will be interested in social facts for the purpose of developing a theoretical understanding of people and the social world. Articles here will be written from a specific theoretical vantage point (see previous chapters) and will use associated conceptual language to analyse and report on children's discursive constructions of social exclusion, their stories and experiences of social exclusion. The interest here is both in what we learn about children's views and experiences of social exclusion and in what those views and experiences teach us about a particular theory.

In a review we might find both types of article, as well as a range of theoretical articles. A pluralistic literature review would seek to appreciate and synthesise the literature in a number of different ways. We want to look at that literature that foregrounds the empirical findings, but we also want to look at the literature that has been specifically approached from different theoretical perspectives. A pluralistic literature review would then synthesise the different domains of knowledge. It might read something like this:

> Research in the general area of children's social exclusion suggests that … A study carried out using Foucauldian discourse analysis highlights that … By comparison narrative approaches to children's social exclusion have been instructive in shaping our understanding of … From a grounded theory perspective we find that actually … Finally, interpretative phenomenological analyses share some similarities with the previous approaches … There is a tension between X and Y approach that raises interesting questions about children's exclusion in the context of …

Of course, each review will differ depending on what previous research has been conducted. The point is that, in a pluralistic approach, we are continuously comparing and contrasting different views and perspectives, asking what they add to our understanding of children's social exclusion, and where the tensions are between approaches. It is worth noting that we are not suggesting that every piece of research take a pluralistic approach. Once you review your literature you may well find that the range of theoretical approaches is absent. In this case it may be more sensible to research a topic using a different theoretical perspective and then compare your findings and analysis with existing approaches. Similarly, you might find a broad agreement in the literature about children's experiences of exclusion irrespective of theoretical perspective. A pluralistic approach to qualitative research in psychology is most likely to be productive when a number of different theoretical perspectives result in tensions about what we know or how we interpret our phenomenon.

Research question

Research often starts with a personal interest or motivation, and a literature review helps to formulate that interest as a research problem and to create a research question. Research questions in pluralistic qualitative research might emerge out of the tensions between different theoretical perspectives. In pluralistic qualitative research we are not necessarily looking to resolve the tensions, but instead, we aim to constructively explore them. What do they tell us about the phenomenon we are interested in? What do they tell us about the people, groups and processes? How do the contradictions point us to new areas of research? How have researchers' roles and identities impacted on the study outcomes? In pluralistic qualitative research the question is very important and should be your main guide (Mason, 2006). This is also true of mixed-method research (Barker & Pistrang, 2005), and there, as in pluralistic qualitative research, the research question acts as a compass and map while you explore different perspectives.

Study design

Once you have reviewed the literature, decided that a pluralistic research approach is suitable and settled on a research question, the next step is to think about how you might go about designing your pluralistic study. A piece of pluralistic research might be one that combines different methods within a single study or across the same research programme (see Barker & Pistrang, 2005). The research design will be informed by the research question. As such, we would need to think what type of question we are asking and design a study appropriate to answering that question. For example, if you were interested in what a particular cultural activity (e.g. a village festival) meant to people, you might design a study that used both interviews and participant observation. Such a design would enable you to ask questions about the sort of stories that people tell about that activity and their participation in it, how they position themselves and other participants, and what meanings they give to the activity and their participation. It would also enable you to observe people's interactions during the cultural activity, what they do on their own (e.g. walking around) and with others (e.g. talking, eating, drinking) and when. Your study might then draw on a combination of grounded theory and narrative analysis. Grounded theory would enable you to analyse actions, interactions and the process by which the activity is enacted by participants. Narrative analysis would enable you to develop a better understanding of their stories, and the meanings and interpretations given to the activity.

There are a few other concepts that have been written about that you might find useful to think about for your research. For example, Dick, Soyinka and Coffey (2006) talk about 'multimodal' research to describe (ethnographic) research that draws on a number of different data modalities such as text, image and sound. Their approach has been to draw on the language of semiotics (theory of signs) in order to provide a conceptual framework that treats what we traditionally call 'data' as different pieces of meaning that can be produced by a range of different media (text, visual, sound, touch, smell) (think of a puzzle where each piece is produced using different material – wood, stone, paper – but still depicts parts of the puzzle's picture). This enables them to bring together a range of meaningful pieces with each of these pieces (or modes) affording a distinctive semiotic potential, as well as cross-overs in meaning, to the overall research project (2006: 87–88).

The point of a piece of pluralistic research is not to cover all bases and so to uncover an 'objective' reality. As Kellner (1995) argues in his formulation of 'multiperspectival' studies, different vantage points help us to avoid one-sided reductionism (cited in Kincheloe, 2001: 682). The puzzle is always missing some pieces. The aim of a pluralistic research approach is to elicit and explore creative tensions, irreducible and irresolvable complexities between different modes, or pieces in the puzzle. In this process, having an overarching framework for the research is very important. A framework here is not necessarily a theory, although it can be. It is a set of ideas that can bring together the many different parts and levels of the research into some sort of coherent whole. For example, Charlotte Burck's research on the experiences of bilingualism and their implications for family therapy used three different analytical lenses to look at her data (grounded theory, narrative and discourse analysis). Her overall study, however, was framed with a social constructionist philosophy and her research design was framed using a social constructionist version of grounded theory. She argued that grounded theory was 'particularly appropriate for discovery-oriented research in areas which are under-theorized' (Burck, 2005: 244). I would add that the discovery-orientation of grounded theory makes it more open-ended than her other approaches, and so in combination makes for a good foundation from which to draw on other approaches for particular aspects of the data analysis.

Participant recruitment

Pluralistic qualitative research does not necessarily require a different approach to participant recruitment or data collection. As in singular approaches to qualitative research, sampling will be purposive to the research question. Researchers might use a snowballing method (Bauer & Gaskell, 2000) to recruit more participants once the parameters of the sample have been established. Such parameters can be defined by asking what or who the research is about, and what or who are likely to be key actors in that particular context.

There are some particular recruitment issues that do need to be considered, however, when working with a pluralistic approach. Depending on your project you might want to interview a number of different participants from different groups who are connected to whatever it is you are interested in. This is often the case in evaluations where a number of different people might be involved in delivering and/or participating in a programme, project and/or intervention. These are people who form a heterogeneous group and who might not otherwise have any relationship to each other. They are related in terms of their interest and/or involvement in a particular activity. In pluralist research, **communities of interest** might be one way of characterising an otherwise heterogeneous sample. Similarly, if you are doing participant observation or document analysis (e.g. policy documents), you might want to think about 'moments of interest' (Hosein, 2002) in terms of selecting events to attend or reports to analyse. Working with people from the same group is less challenging in terms of making sense of your sample and would follow conventional sampling methods in qualitative research.

Data elicitation

Pluralistic qualitative research does not necessarily require a different approach to data collection either. There are a number of publications addressing different types of data collection methods (Kvale, 1996; Denzin & Lincoln, 2000; Willig, 2000). While it is beyond the scope of this chapter to outline all the advice given in these various publications, some key ideas for thinking about qualitative research methods in psychology are outlined. What these ideas have in common is an emphasis on the naturalistic dimensions of data collection in contrast, for instance, with quantitative data collection methods, which are often dealt with in a much more technocratic manner. As such, Kvale (1996) suggests that interviews are best conceptualised as conversations, the outcome of which is a co-production of meaning between interviewer and interviewee. Gaskell (2000: 46) suggests that focus groups possibly provide a more genuine form of social interaction and communication than the in-depth interviews, as participants talk to one another, respond and react to each others' points of view and experience as they might do in any other group setting. Hammersley and Atkinson (1995: 2) suggest that ethnography, with its method of participant observation, 'bears a close resemblance to the routine ways in which people make sense of the world in everyday life'. Included in this resemblance is, as the term suggests, the ability to take both observational and more involved stances towards an event, community or situation, and to reflect on the meanings being produced therein, as well as one's stance in accessing those meanings (e.g. through experience or through observation).

However, once again there are a number of issues to consider in terms of 'combining' the different qualitative approaches. Working pluralistically, it may be that you end up with a combination of unstructured conversational interviews (this is quite common in ethnographic research in anthropology and sociology), and semi-structured and/or narrative interviews if you are working with more text-based approaches. For example, imagine that for good reason you think that combining an interpretative phenomenological approach with a narrative analysis would be insightful on experiences of illness. You decide to interview a group of women suffering from a chronic illness. You would need to decide before the interview which approach to interviewing you were going to adopt because interviewing the same women twice using a slightly different interviewing style would not be ethical, practical or methodologically sound. It so happens that the interviewing styles for an IPA or NA interview are quite similar: they both try to elicit experiences. If this weren't the case and you were, for example, interested in themes and narratives, you might want to approach the interview beginning with the open-ended invitation to discuss a certain topic (Jovchelovitch & Bauer, 2000) and then, once the interviewee has exhausted that topic, you could move into a more semi-structured form of interviewing where your discussion centres around different topics (providing these have not already been covered by the interviewee). As a 'rule of thumb' my suggestion would be to start as open-ended as possible, and use prompts and follow-up questions to elicit answers to specific questions. In this way you can avoid imposing your meaning and views of the research topic onto the participant, who might have a completely different take on the issue.

You can use your research question and interest to guide your use of different data elicitation methods. It is sometimes helpful to think of data elicitation methods as channels for expression. It doesn't matter what channel you use to express meaning so long as the research questions and topics stay the same across the different forms of expression. For example, while researching children's experiences of a health intervention in schools, a colleague decided that she would ask the children to respond to her question about their experiences of the intervention using whatever medium they preferred (e.g. interviews, drawing, photographs, film) (Deighton, personal communication). The resulting data can be considered as different expressions on the same topic. Self-directed methods (Singh, 2003; 2004) empower participants to determine the boundaries of what they feel comfortable sharing with the researcher within the parameters of a given topic, as well as to direct the conversation in ways that are meaningful to them. For instance, Singh (2003; 2004) asked mothers and fathers of children with ADHD to select up to ten images from a range of magazines, which they felt captured or spoke to their thoughts and feelings about Ritalin and other psychostimulant treatments (ADHD medication). The images became a starting point and guide for conversation with parents, who thus directed the interviews through their choice of images (see the research example on page 25 of Chapter 2).

Data transcription and analysis

Approaches to transcription would conform to the method – for example, say you were doing a Potter and Wetherell-type DA, which requires a very detailed transcription. Rather than create a number of transcriptions to suit your different analytical lenses, you might create the DA transcript, as it's the most detailed, and use the same transcript for narrative or interpretative phenomenological analysis.

The actual process of analysis can be managed with the use of qualitative software packages such as Atlas/ti or *NVivo*. In these packages you might create different analyses projects for each of your analytic approaches. If you are doing the analysis by hand, think of working with Word documents and your computers' filing system to create different folders and files for your different analyses.

Researchers often talk about 'passes' in their analysis (the first pass at the analysis, second pass, etc.). In the pluralistic research model, each of your passes would represent a different analytical approach to looking at the data – like swapping your reading glasses for your sunglasses and then for a pair of goggles.

While you are analysing you may find that it's not that easy to stick to one 'lens'. You can shift between lenses as you work – just make sure that you create a system for yourself to enable you to track these shifts. For example, if you were working by hand you could code all your discursive analysis in green and your grounded theory analysis in orange. In a software package you could either create a 'memo' for yourself or move between your different project folders.

Research groups

Working in a pluralistic way raises a number of questions. As a lone researcher does it mean that every researcher needs to be skilled in every qualitative approach? There is a tendency for researchers to have a preferred theoretical/methodological orientation from which they work and in which they are experts. We will see in the next section that such specialisation can be constraining in an applied research setting. For this reason at least, familiarity with a couple of qualitative research approaches can only be a good thing.

Pluralism in qualitative research (Frost, 2009a)

The PQR project is an example of a piece of research that explicitly aims to investigate the application of different research approaches to the same piece of data. Frost assembled a team of researchers to analyse the same interview on the topic of second-time motherhood. The interview was analysed using grounded theory, interpretative phenomenological analysis, Foucauldian discourse analysis and narrative analysis. Researchers worked independently on their analyses and then met to discuss and bring together their different interpretations. Another aspect of the approach was to explore the role that subjectivity played in the different analytical approaches, and how that contributed to the interpretation of the data.

Example

However, the bigger challenge arises with the volume of work that a pluralistic approach might entail. A small sample of interviews or focus groups is manageable for a lone researcher. However, as the sample size grows it can become increasingly challenging for one person to work pluralistically on their own. For a much larger sample, pluralistic research works well when the research is done in groups. Below we explore both options.

The pluralistic approach and the lone researcher

Practically speaking, working as a pluralistic researcher you will need to have a good understanding of the basic tenets of each of the approaches that you decide to use in your analysis, as well as some experience of analysing data with these approaches. At a conceptual level your main tool will be to think in terms of links and relationships between the different approaches. What do comparisons between approaches tell you? Where are the tensions? This is a quite different way of working to that of the sole-method approach. The commitment is not to one individual approach (e.g. narrative) but to the combination of different approaches and their relationship to one another. Additionally, and in terms of practising and demonstrating reflexivity, the pluralistic researcher is encouraged to keep a diary outlining their experience of and insights to working in a pluralistic way.

The pluralistic approach and working in groups

The pluralistic approach lends itself well to working in groups, and there are different ways to organise such a research group. For instance, it could be that the group consists of researchers each with expertise in different approaches. The data collected could then be analysed by each researcher using their particular research approach. Bringing the data together would be done through group meetings where each researcher reports on their findings. Much of the interpretation that would be done individually about the tensions between each approach would then be done in conversation with the group. There are a couple of roles that need to be fulfilled when working in a group. The first is a coordinator role, one researcher who, a bit like the conductor in an orchestra, helps to bring the different analyses and their insights together in an overarching narrative. The greatest challenge for the coordinator is to guide the formation of the analysis into a narrative without imposing their own voice on it. The coordinator seeks to ensure that all the researchers' voices are heard and that the participants' voices do not get drowned out by those of the researchers. At the same time, they become another part of the research themselves, as they bring their own interpretations to the work already carried out.

The other role is that of documenter. This is a researcher who collects, captures and reflects back the group's conversations, interpretations and decisions. This role fulfils the requirements of reflexivity in a pluralistic approach. Informal interviews with colleagues can be a useful way of eliciting reflection as well as recording meetings. Both can be analysed formally, time permitting, to track the development of thinking in the project. As with the coordinator's role, similar challenges in managing subjectivity and interpretation are found here.

When is a pluralistic approach useful?

Traditionally in research we are taught to work with single concepts, to test their explanatory possibilities and limitations on the data, and evaluate and develop the concepts accordingly. In applied settings, however, things are different. Practitioners, rather than working with single concepts, work with multiple concepts in order to make sense of and act on the reality that is presented to them. This process of making sense and acting on reality has been described in a number of ways, one of which is bricolage (see also Chapter 1). Schön, who has written about a range of applied contexts, tells us that 'in real-world practice, problems do not present themselves to the practitioner as givens. They must be constructed from the material of problematic situations which are puzzling, troubling and uncertain' (Schön, 1983: 39). Bricolage has been used to describe the process of turning something that makes no sense into something meaningful. Orr calls it 'the reflective use of what is at hand – things, understandings, facts – to accomplish a defined goal' (Orr, 1996: 11). As such, pluralistic approaches to research that provide a range of concepts are most useful in applied (research) settings, where often a single concept will not suffice.

Informing practice

An early example of pluralistic research in clinical practice comes from systemic family therapy. Charlotte Burck (2004; 2005) has conducted a study on the experience of living in two (or more) languages (bilingualism). Her choice of a pluralistic qualitative approach to research is multifaceted. On the one hand, her research is rooted in systemic family therapy, which recognises the family as a multilevel system. A single methodological approach could not adequately capture the different levels of experience in such a system. In addition to this, Burck argues that a great deal of emphasis in systemic family therapy focuses on measuring outcomes. Unfortunately outcomes do not capture the process, subjective experience and meaning of change, and say little about the application of findings to practice – two issues that also interest therapists. As such, Burck turned her attention to process research, and specifically qualitative research for looking at process (2005: 238–239). Embarking on her study, Burck found that while the application of qualitative research methods in family therapy had been fruitful, she had found it hard 'to find a comparison of different methodologies in the qualitative research literature, and what they accomplish with the same research material' (2005: 240).

Burck's study provides an excellent example for comparing the possibilities and limitations of different qualitative methods used together on the same data. Burck chose to use grounded theory, discourse and narrative analyses. Grounded theory (Glaser & Strauss, 1967) analysis provided a first step in identifying concepts and categories, and allowed Burck to analyse the contexts in which these concepts and categories were salient for her interviewees. Discourse analysis helped Burck explore the ways in which the concepts and categories that emerged in the grounded theory analysis were discussed by her interviewees. In particular, she worked with key discursive psychology themes of discourse, power and subjectivity, exploring where they intersected with one another, and critically evaluating how individuals positioned themselves and were positioned in and through language (2005: 251). Finally, Burck conducted a narrative analysis of her interview transcripts which, following the approach's focus on experience and self-presentation, allowed her to look at how individuals whose experiences are embedded in more than one language construct their identities, and especially the ways in which they managed their different senses of self (2005: 252).

Experiences of living life in more than one language (Burck, 2004; 2005)

Burck's study of bilingualism is an example of the use of multiple analytical tools (grounded theory, discourse and narrative analysis) with which to explore the experience of living in more than one language. Burck's study addresses a gap in the psychotherapy literature, which had neglected bilingual and multilingual experiences. Her grounded theory analysis provided her with initial categories characterising bilingual experience of language. Discourse analysis helped her scrutinise the ways in which interviewees used different categories (e.g. 'natural') in order to position themselves in a wider context. Finally, narrative analysis informed her analysis of the way in which interviewees presented themselves and made sense of their experiences over time.

Example

Evaluating practice

This example of pluralistic research is also from the world of psychological therapy, but this time looking at the evaluation of therapy. In psychological therapy, as in other areas of clinical practice, there has been an increased focus on the evaluation of therapy. These debates are usually framed in terms of the outcomes of therapy (what works for whom?) and the process of therapy (how does it work?). Qualitative research is particularly suited to answering the how does it work or what does it mean type of questions. The work of Georgaca and Avdi (2009) and Avdi (2008) represents a very interesting example of the use of the pluralistic approach to answer these sorts of questions for counselling and psychotherapy.

The authors have conducted a systematic review of what they call 'language-based analyses' (McLeod, 2001) of counselling and psychotherapy, and examined the usefulness of language-based analysis for evaluating psychotherapy. In their review, they look at the different aspects of psychotherapy that have been evaluated using either narrative, discourse or conversation analysis, and reflect on the implications of this research for the understanding and practice of psychotherapy (McLeod, 2001: 234). While their review does not set out to promote pluralistic qualitative research in psychotherapy, in including studies from a variety of qualitative approaches the authors are able to demonstrate a nuanced and textured understanding of the client and their problems, the therapeutic process and the role of the therapist. Furthermore, the authors engage with both the commonalities and differences of the different analytic approaches used in the evaluation of psychotherapy. They argue that, while these approaches focus on meaning and the constructive function of language, there is considerable divergence in terms of their underlying theory, analytical focus and methodology. They also note that language-based analyses have an affinity with psychotherapy of a postmodernist or constructionist orientation, and that sometimes this results in the tendency of language-based studies to concentrate on such psychotherapeutic approaches at the expense of other therapy approaches. They suggest that sometimes, because of this affinity, studies can adopt a less critical perspective. The authors also note that these language-based studies can be placed along a continuum of studies, from those that fully accept psychotherapeutic assumptions to those that are more questioning or deconstructive. Those that accept assumptions aim to illustrate the linguistic and interpersonal processes through which these are produced and utilised in actual sessions. Those that are more critical explore psychotherapy as 'a social institution that actively promotes modern subjectivity and its associated ways of life and critically examine the interactional discursive processes that constitute the therapeutic institution' (McLeod, 2001: 235). These are useful distinctions of which researchers can be mindful when conducting pluralistic qualitative research.

Georgaca and Avdi (2009) conclude that language-based analysis can be used as a clinical assessment tool with which to support problem formulation and to judge therapeutic change, in a way that is grounded in the client's language and meanings, and not in researcher-defined categories. They also argue that language-

---

Systematic review of qualitative research in psychotherapy (Avdi, 2008; Georgaca & Avdi, 2009)

Georgaca and Avdi have conducted a systematic review of qualitative research methods used to assess different aspects of psychotherapy. Their review draws together studies using conversation, discourse and narrative analysis for looking at the way in which the clients formulate their problems, how the therapeutic process develops and the therapist impacts on the therapeutic process. Georgaca and Avdi's engagement with the challenges of bringing together diverse qualitative research methods results in a useful typology for identified psycho-therapeutic research on a continuum that can be critical or embracing of therapeutic assumptions.

Example

based analysis can be used 'to examine the micro-processes through which psychotherapy is accomplished in practice, and in this way highlight actual therapist skills and therapeutic processes' (Georgaca & Avdi, 2009: 243). Finally, they also suggest that language-based analysis can provide an opportunity for the profession to question its assumptions and practices.

Designing interventions

The third area of applied psychology that has recently discussed pluralism is critical health psychology. Critical health psychology developed out of the limitations of mainstream health psychology with its exclusive focus on the individual and its use of the biomedical model to explain health and illness. Critical health psychology tries to redress this balance by focusing on a number of other factors beyond the individual as a biological being. Marks *et al.* (2005), for instance, provide us with an 'onion' model in which health and illness are conceptualised as having one core and five contextual levels. In this framework individual demographics (e.g. age, sex and hereditary factors) are but one of a number of factors influencing health processes and outcomes. Other important contexts include lifestyle, social community influences, living and working conditions, and cultural/historical conditions such as socio-economic, political and environmental factors. Their model can be said to represent a pluralistic conceptualisation of health and illness in which different contexts overlap and contribute, in different measures, to individual and population health.

Hepworth (2006) argues that as critical health psychology has developed, pluralism in relation to the inclusion of theories and methods has become central. Pluralism in critical health psychology refers to the different philosophical orientations and the practical concerns of the field, especially in terms of relational, contextual and rights-based approaches to understanding and working in a critical way. In critical health psychology, rather than using one model for explaining health behaviour, for instance, health psychologists draw on a number of available concepts to help them address the different contextual levels that impact on health and illness. Here pluralism refers to the conceptual resources that are available to the critical health psychologist in the field as they engage with global health challenges (Hepworth, 2006: 338–339).

As a tool for working in a pluralistic way the critical health psychologist David Marks introduces the concept of 'dialects' in order to work creatively with the 'diverse and conflicting views … about the direction and shape of the field [of critical health psychology]' (Marks, 2002, cited in Marks, 2006: 369). Marks argues that each of the contextual levels that impact on health will require different kinds of analyses for understanding health experiences at each level. This is because what might provide a meaningful explanation or result in a useful practice at one level of experience may not be constructive or valuable at another level. Marks also suggests that pluralism supports the promotion of 'a more theoretically complex version of health psychology that includes a diverse range of perspectives rather than a single, fixed point of view' (2006: 369). He warns against approaches that promote a single method, theory or level of health determinant, which can lack ecological validity, and risk being too narrow and of little salience beyond their initial context (Marks, 2006: 369).

Ethical considerations

Ethical issues are not restricted to the design stage of a study but occur throughout the entire research process (Kvale, 1996). As with mono-method approaches to research, so too in pluralistic qualitative research there are a number of ethical considerations that the researcher needs to engage in. Kvale (1996: 119–120) proposes five ethical questions that a researcher should ask before conducting a study.

The first question relates to the benefits of the study. A piece of research should not only contribute to advancing our knowledge of a topic but should also contribute to enhancing the human condition. Kvale urges us to think about the direct and indirect benefits of our studies – for example, whether our participants will be the immediate beneficiaries of the study, or whether it is the group of people represented by our participants, or whether benefits will be realised in the form of general knowledge of the human condition. In the context of pluralistic research, the issue of who benefits needs to be asked in the plural (e.g. who are the beneficiaries?). The 'human condition' ceases to be a unitary, homogeneous goal and is instead understood as a fusion of overlapping but often competing interests. In this respect, the researcher who works within a pluralistic framework needs to consider the implications of such heterogeneity for their work. Being aware of and discussing the different actors (both human and non-human, e.g. technology) and their interests, so far as these are themselves visible, is one of way of engaging in ethical questions about who benefits. It is also worth thinking about the decision-making processes in the research in relation to the different stakeholders involved and how these research decisions (dis)empower different groups.

The second and third questions relate to informed consent and confidentiality. Here we are asked to think about the logistics of informed consent such as whether we are forming an oral or written contract with our participants, who is best suited to give consent (e.g. in the case of children), and how much information about our research we are to give in advance of an interview or focus group. In terms of confidentiality we are asked to consider the importance of anonymity, who else might have access to our research material, how the identity of the participants will be disguised and whether there are any legal implications involved in protecting a subject's anonymity (e.g. again in the case of children, contemporary researchers are having to weigh up these issues in relation to safeguarding and child protection concerns). Informed consent and confidentiality are the most explicit part of the research contract that we enter into with our research participants. In the context of pluralistic research, informed consent and confidentiality need to be considered in terms of the possibility of a number researchers being involved in conducting the research. In this instance consent is being given to an entire research team and not just a lone researcher, all of whom will have access to and quite possibly be involved in analysing the data. The same applies in terms of confidentiality and anonymity where the information that is provided by research participants in a research context is likely to be shared and discussed among a group of researchers. Furthermore, in terms of informed consent, it should be made explicit to research participants that a pluralistic research project endeavours to analyse research data from a number of different perspectives that will have different analytical aims and objectives.

The fourth question posed by Kvale refers to the consequences of our study. Consequences can be thought about as immediate consequences to participants, such as participants being harmed by participation in the study. In such cases careful consideration is necessary in order to determine whether the harms outweigh the benefits. Research on topics of a sensitive or potentially upsetting nature can sometimes leave research participants feeling vulnerable or exposed. While every effort is made to avoid creating such feelings in the first place – for instance, by allowing an interviewee to take ownership of their interview and direct the conversation thus avoiding upsetting topics if they choose to – it is not always possible to know how people will react to a given topic of conversation. In such cases, being able to direct participants to other sources of advice or support (if necessary) is important. A piece of pluralistic qualitative research would follow the same advice in terms of mitigating the potential negative impact of research on participants. A piece of research can also have more general consequences. This is especially the case when it comes to the publication of a piece of research. In particular, it is important to think about the impact that such publication might have on the participants and the groups they represent, especially when the researchers' interpretations differ, challenge or contradict those of the research participants. In the context of pluralistic qualitative research such considerations are all the more acute as the research can potentially represent a number of different perspectives, and present a range of differently, theoretically informed interpretations.

The fifth and final question we are asked to consider relates to the researcher's role in the study. Here we engage with issues relating to scientific quality and the independence of the research, both in relation to research sponsors and the researcher maintaining a critical stance towards their topic and participants. In the context of pluralistic qualitative research, an additional dimension relating to quality that needs to be considered is the soundness of the reasons given for taking a pluralistic approach in the first place, and a discussion of the complementarities, tensions and contradictions that may emerge in combining different theoretical traditions.

Kvale's advice regarding ethics may be enhanced by thinking about positive ethics. Positive approaches to ethics refer to thinking about the ways in which psychologists can do better in helping those they work with or study (Knapp & VandeCreek, 2006: 10). Positive ethics promotes an understanding and appreciation of traditionally marginalised groups in order to address issues around non-discrimination (Knapp & VandeCreek, 2006: 12). It also strives to maximise the 'subject's' participation in the development of research, and asks psychologists to treat participants as 'moral agents' with intrinsic worth and helpful perspectives, instead of simply the means by which investigators can reach their research goals (Fisher, 2000b, cited in Knapp & VandeCreek, 2006: 13). This approach to non-discrimination has long been practised in critical psychology (see Hook, 2004), which focuses on the consequences of power and its asymmetries, on individuals and groups. In a pluralistic research context, such an approach would extend to include the participant's view as a possible conceptual framework, or worldview, alongside that of the analyst. Positive ethics further focuses on psychologists' striving for excellence in competency, and espouses the enhancement of the quality of relationships between psychologists and those they work with. This suggests that continued professional training and updating of knowledge and skills is an ethical duty as much as a professional necessity. Working pluralistically as a sole researcher this means keeping abreast of developments in a number of relevant fields of knowledge and contributing to a range of scholarly communities. Finally, positive ethics treats confidentiality as a process of striving to enhance trust throughout the research process. This suggests that thinking and acting ethically is an ongoing process that goes beyond the one-off contractual transaction involved in signing consent forms at the beginning of our study.

My own experience of pluralistic research was my doctoral work (see the reflection on practice box, page 37, Chapter 2), although at the time I had yet to meet Nollaig and the other authors in this book and had not yet come across the term 'pluralism' in this context. The thesis was an example of pluralistic research on a theoretical and methodological level. Methodologically I used a range of data collection methods (interviews, focus groups, audiovisual compositions, documents and news articles) and included a number of perspectives in the study (young people, youth workers and project workers, managers, policy community and researchers). At the time I was involved in evaluating one aspect of a national youth inclusion programme in the UK, namely young people's views and experiences of participating in this particular programme (Humphreys, Nolas & Olmos, 2006). We used participatory video with the young people and collected a number of 'audiovisual' compositions that the young people made about their communities and aspirations, and views and experiences of the youth inclusion programme. We also ran focus groups in which young people reflected on and interpreted their work. I was given permission to use the data for my thesis and I could have confined myself to a secondary analysis of the young people's audiovisual compositions and focus groups. However, two things motivated me to look at the research

Reflection on Practice

context slightly differently. As an evaluator I had come into contact with a number of other relevant actors in the field (e.g. youth workers, project coordinators, service managers, civil servants and other researchers), as well as the young people. I had also been doing a good deal of reading on youth inclusion at a policy level, as well as looking at academic research in this area. As such, if I wanted to study youth inclusion I didn't feel that I should confine myself to young people's views and experiences alone. I would have to situate these views and experiences, and relate them to the contexts in which they occurred. This meant including a number of other actors' perspectives in my research. I interviewed youth workers, I selected a number of relevant policy documents relating directly to the programme being evaluated as well as to the policy context from which the programme emerged, and collected copious amount of fieldnotes about my time spent as an evaluator. I ended up with what I have since discovered that Bella Dicks and colleagues (2006) refer to as a multimodal ethnography. My research materials comprised documents, interview transcripts, focus group transcripts, audiovisual compositions and fieldnotes. At the time there was little discussion around the implications of working pluralistically (or multimodally) that I was aware of, and one of my main challenges was working out how to manage the range of perspectives and research materials I had collected. Here two things were useful. The first was an ontological framing of the research that allowed for plurality. Here the work of postmodernist thinkers such as Deleuze and Guattari (1987) was useful. The second was an epistemological approach that worked from the bottom up. The ethnographic approach, heavily indebted to grounded theory, that is developed by Emerson, Fretz and Shaw (1995) was my second tool for managing plurality. Together these two helped me to 'hold' (in the psychoanalytic meaning of the word) the creative tensions and dialogue (Mason, 2006) that working pluralistically represents. Deleuze and Guattari provide a unifying, non-linear and non-reductionist philosophy for thinking about the dynamics of everyday life. The emphasis on dynamics between multiple, interacting parts, the emphasis on processes and interactions, and the emergent nature of change also helped me to hold the different levels and perspectives in my data in mind. Ethnography/grounded theory allowed me to document and make sense of what emerged from those dynamics.

Chapter summary

In this chapter we have focused on the practical issues raised by combining different approaches to qualitative research in psychology.

- The ontological and epistemological underpinnings of combining approaches were discussed. Postmodernism, reflexivity and context were identified as key components of the ontology. The epistemological orientation of a pluralistic approach was discussed in terms of the 'interfacing' of different approaches and the role played by dialectical thought and the tensions produced by it. It was argued that researchers needed to reflect carefully on whether their particular study would benefit from a combined approach and that not all research projects would be suitable.
- The discussion of the practical aspects of pluralistic qualitative research in psychology was preceded by an overview of some commonly agreed guidelines for ensuring the quality of research in qualitative research in psychology. These included the provision of a clear rationale for the theories and methods being used, the practice of reflexivity, the accessible and transparent documentation of the research process and the possible application of findings to different contexts. Guidelines also recommend that theorising is grounded in examples, and that it is open to surprise and challenged by 'negative' cases. Finally, researchers are also asked to consider their participants and audiences not as a naive subjects but as experts of their own social realities.
- The chapter looked at the practical aspects of a pluralistic approach in terms of reviewing the literature, creating research questions, designing a study, and collecting and analysing data. Working in groups, as one way of conducting pluralistic qualitative research in psychology, was also discussed. In this chapter we have also looked at the practical applications of a pluralistic approach in different applied contexts. We saw how a pluralistic approach can be used to inform and evaluate clinical practice, as well as how thinking pluralistically might inform the design of social interventions.
- The chapter closed with a look at ethical considerations.

CASE STUDY

A small team of researchers with expertise in the psychology of old age were commissioned by the council to look at the options for supporting healthy elderly people's independent living. There is a particular residence in the area that seemed to have a good model of support and the council wanted to find out more about this model of support and whether it is feasible for them to replicate it across the area. The team of researchers proposed to explore residents' experiences of living in this particular residence. One of the researchers conducted the literature review looking at what had been written about 'old age' in psychology and about 'independent living' in old age. The other researcher interviewed the 15 residents. These interviews were long, almost two hours or more in some cases. The residents told the researchers a number of anecdotes and stories about their lives, how they had come to live at the residence, how they occupied themselves, what they thought of other people's views of 'old age'; in fact they challenged a number of conceptions of 'old age' throughout these interviews. Once the interviews were transcribed, a third researcher analysed them using a thematic analysis. The analysis concentrated on general impressions of living in the retirement community, reasons for moving to the retirement community, positive and negative aspects of living there, and any changes or improvements that the residents felt would make the community a better place to live in.

- What do you think about the researchers' decision to only interview the residents of the retirement community? Is a system of support made up only of those people that are being supported?
- What do you think about the researchers' decision to analyse the findings using thematic analysis only? What other types of 'talk' did their data include? What other methods might the researchers have used?
- How was the team organised in this research? How could the team be organised to reflect a more pluralistic approach?
- Imagine that you had been asked by the council to carry out this research. How would you redesign it as a piece of pluralistic qualitative research?

Problem-based questions

Below are a series of questions that are designed to help you engage with the chapter's contents and think about your own research.

1. What would you say are the advantages and disadvantages of taking a pluralistic approach to qualitative research in psychology?
2. Why is reflexivity important in the research process?
3. What is your view on the debate regarding the combining of different ontological approaches?
4. Monologue, dialogue, polyvocality. What do these terms mean and how do they relate to the pluralist project?
5. What would you say are the similarities and differences between a mono-method approach to literature reviewing and a pluralistic approach?
6. Why is the emphasis on combining methods in a coherent way so important?
7. What is the role of dialogical thinking and polyvocality in pluralistic qualitative research?

Further reading and research studies

Burck, C. (2005) Comparing qualitative research methodologies for systemic research: the use of grounded theory, discourse analysis and narrative analysis. *Journal of Family Therapy*, 27, 237–262.
A research example of using three different analytical approaches, in the study of bilingualism/multilingualism. The article provides a succinct overview of the three approaches, giving examples of the different analyses and interpretations of the experiences of people who live their lives in more than one language.

Fiske, D.W. & Shweder, R.A. (1986) *Metatheory in Social Science: Pluralisms and Subjectivities.* Chicago, IL: Chicago University Press.
An edited volume with contributions from a number of leading social scientists from psychology and related disciplines. The chapters explore different conceptual frameworks and their consequences for the study of human behaviour.

Georgaca, E. & Avdi, E. (2009) Evaluating the talking cure: the contribution of narrative, discourse, and conversation analysis to psychotherapy assessment. *Qualitative Research in Psychology*, 6(3), 233–247.
A different research example where the authors look at the range of studies that evaluate psychotherapy from the perspectives of narrative, discourse and conversation analysis. They conduct a systematic review of these studies and look at the usefulness of each analytical approach for assessing the value of psychotherapy.

Kincheloe, J.L. (2001) Describing the bricolage: conceptualizing a new rigor in qualitative research. *Qualitative Inquiry*, 7(6), 679–692.
This is a theoretical article in which the author looks at the possibilities offered by the concept of bricolage for describing interdisciplinary research. The author explores the dialectical relationships that pluralism and interdisciplinarity entail.

Marks, D.F. (2006) The case for a pluralist health psychology. *Journal of Health Psychology*, 11(3), 367–372.
The article explores the potential for a pluralistic health psychology that involves and brings into dialogue the various interests and concerns of health psychologists. Pluralism here refers to the different levels used to contextualise health, as well as to the research methodologies employed to understand how different contexts influence health. A pluralistic approach is viewed as enabling dialogue and change in the discipline of health psychology.

McLeod, J. (2001) *Qualitative Research in Counselling and Psychotherapy.* London: Sage.
An excellent and concise book on the different research approaches (grounded theory, conversation, narrative and discourse analysis) that can be used to conduct qualitative research in counselling and psychotherapy.

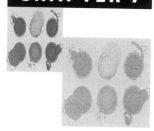

CHAPTER 7

Interpreting Data Pluralistically

Nollaig Frost

Introduction

This chapter is about how the process of interpretation is carried out in qualitative research, and particularly in pluralistic qualitative research. It presents some of the challenges to the pluralistic interpretation of data and highlights the ways in which new insights to meanings can be brought to the close examination of text and other data. As with the other chapters, this chapter will illustrate all that is talked about using real-life research examples and include problem-based questions that aim to provoke you to consider your own use of pluralistic approaches to data interpretation. Interpreting data pluralistically can mean using different methods of data analysis and interpretation, different data sources or different researchers to access meaning within data. These approaches aim to minimise the imposition of researcher bias and assumption by drawing on different paradigms, epistemologies and ontologies to view the phenomenon in different ways. This can be particularly useful when studying topics where realities are changing for the individual, or experiences that researchers are not familiar with are being described. In order to transform the data the qualitative researcher needs to consider possible meanings in the data, the context in which the data have been elicited and gathered, and their own role in the process. This means applying systematic techniques of data analysis and being aware of personal pre-existing views and suppositions. The combination of these processes is the process of interpretation.

A history of interpretation

The interpretative approach to research in psychology is a relatively new one. Early psychologists were more concerned to understand relationships between external stimuli and associated internal sensations experienced by human beings than to gain insight to individual experience. There was an emphasis on identifying laws of cause and effect that explained human interaction with the world in generalised terms. Investigations that sought to establish such laws and understandings followed traditional scientific objective and positivist approaches. Psychologists were not concerned with the roles of context, social meaning, historical understandings, or researcher assumptions and impact because they believed that what they were investigating was not affected by such issues. The focus of qualitative research is often on human behaviour and interaction with the social world. Instead of seeing the researcher as outside the research, qualitative researchers see themselves as very much part of the research process.

This approach means that qualitative researchers have to acknowledge their role in interpreting all aspects of the research throughout the process. This ranges from understanding why they make decisions about research questions, through to how they transform the data gathered, to its final presentation to the interested audience. One theory of interpretation is 'hermeneutics'. This philosophy seeks to gain insight to the 'lifeworld' of individuals. The lifeworld is understood to be the system of meanings with which they make sense of their experiences (Husserl, 1977). Access to the lifeworld can be sought either by asking individuals to recollect experiences (the hermeneutics of meaning-recollection) or by inquiring into what lies behind the phenomenon being recounted (hermeneutics of suspicion). The hermeneutics of meaning-recollection approach takes the accounts of individuals for analysis in order to extract close descriptions of their experience. These are checked with the individual and then relayed as an outcome of the research. The hermeneutics of suspicion approach aims to look behind the data that participants provide, to gain some understanding of how they make sense of their experience.

Hermeneutics offers one approach to interpreting data and underlies phenomenological approaches to understanding lived experience such as interpretative phenomenological analysis (see Chapter 3). There is also an increasing engagement with *questions* of interpretation by qualitative researchers as they seek to move away from the systematic capture and re-presentation of themes in data (Willig, 2008). Questions centre on theories and practices of data elicitation, gathering and analysis by those seeking to challenge existing norms within psychology. For example, feminist researchers seek new ways of conducting research that will give voice to those who have previously been unheard. Psychoanalytic thinkers call for the research to be both grounded in data and driven by theory in a binocular approach (e.g. Frosh & Saville Young, 2008).

Ontology

Ontology asks what is real, and it is therefore very important to understand your position on this when making interpretations of other people's experience. The interpretation of accounts of experience brings with it questions about how we define and perceive experience and how we set out to gain insight to it. This is the process of interpretation and, in qualitative research, it often has the aim of increasing our understanding of human interaction with the world. Epistemologically, interpretation can be founded on principles that range from critical realism (the world is made of fixed entities to which the actor brings their unique perspective) through to social constructionism (unique realities are created by individuals through their interactions with others). Whatever underlies the researcher position and the method being brought to the data transformation, the interpretation process involves questioning and mediation of the participant, their intentionality, their accounts of experience and the meaning of the experience to them.

Social constructionism is an ontological position, which means that interpreters view what can be known about experience as created by individuals through their interaction with the world and others in it. Hermeneutics enables their accounts to be regarded as recollection or representation. Some researchers refine these two broad positions and (e.g. Eatough & Smith, 2008) outline 'levels of interpretation' (2008: 189) that range from 'empathic-descriptive' to 'critical-hermeneutic'. The view of the world that you bring to the research as a qualitative researcher becomes even more important when you consider how and what you regard as 'reality'. Is it something that you believe is created through interaction with others? Through language? Are there some things that are fixed and real, and others that change? Often called 'reflexivity', the researcher's awareness of what they bring to the research and how they engage with the process of data interpretation means the researcher must turn a critical gaze on to themselves (Finlay, 2003). Reflexivity can take many forms, some of which are listed in Table 7.1.

Table 7.1 Forms of Reflexivity

Finlay (2003): four types of reflexivity
Reflexivity as introspection
Reflexivity as intersubjective reflection
Reflexivity as social critique
Reflexivity as ironic deconstruction
See Finlay (2003) for more detail.

Wilkinson (1988): three types of reflexivity
Personal reflexivity
Functional reflexivity
Disciplinary reflexivity
See Gough (2003b) and Wilkinson (1988) for more detail.

Macbeth (2001): two types of reflexivity and a third
Positional reflexivity
Textual reflexivity
Garfinkel's constitutive reflexivity
See Macbeth (2001) for more detail.

It is also important to remember the potential for power that interpretation of other people's accounts of experiences can provide, and to consider your ontological position in relation to this. Interpretation of one person's account of experience by another can suggest that a greater understanding of an individual can be acquired by another person than by the individual themselves. Participants providing accounts of their experiences may not be aware of the process that they bring to their behaviour, nor of the role that they play in their lifeworld. This highlights the importance of the qualitative researcher making explicit their way of seeing the world and seeking to avoid imposing their understanding of it on to the experiences of others.

Pluralistic interpretation provides a way to minimise the imposition of any one ontological position. It aims to illuminate what is real for others while minimising the impact of the researcher and their lifeworld.

Problem-based question

You have been commissioned by the owners of a chain of care homes to investigate how older people with early stages of Alzheimer's make the transition from living independently in their own home to being cared for in a nursing home. The research commissioners are interested in this research because their numbers of new admissions have been declining and they are concerned to find out why. How will you investigate this and what epistemological frameworks will you employ in the data interpretation?

Why interpret data pluralistically?

Psychologists set out to explore and understand the world around them and the behaviour of human beings within it. In conducting their research into this they have to construct a route through the data they collect, to look for possible meanings within the data. The outcome of this journey is inevitably going to be a researcher's interpretation of other people's experience. It will be derived from the systematic analysis and reflexive engagement of the researcher with their participants' accounts of their experiences. Some researchers have argued that all research is interpretative, including statistical analysis (e.g. Bauer & Gaskell, 2000). Others (e.g. Hammersley, 2008) have criticised the subjective and non-generalisable nature of interpretation that is made explicit in qualitative research.

So, one reason to interpret data pluralistically is to seek to minimise the bias arising from the use of one researcher or one method. By combining methods of analysis we can combine ontologies and epistemologies, allowing for fewer assumptions to be brought by the researcher to understandings of what is real. This is relevant to many areas of qualitative research that look at other people's unique perspectives of themselves, their world and their relationship with it, but can be especially useful when inquiring into topics where reality is not universally agreed. These might be topics such as people's experiences of religiosity, spirituality or the paranormal, for example.

Pluralistic interpretation also allows for flexibility in its approach to research by building up multi-perspective layers of insight. Each layer can be more or less relevant to understanding someone else's reality at different moments or to different people seeking to understand other people's reality. This might be especially useful when reality changes – as it may do, for example, for those having extreme emotions about an experience or for those with mental illness.

Pluralistic interpretation allows for a more holistic view of other people's experience. It can provide insight that cannot be gained using one method alone. This might be useful to understand the complexity of experiences such as motherhood or bereavement.

Arguably, a pluralistic interpretation approach is valuable in longitudinal studies in which there may be cause to return to interviews conducted earlier or to gain an overview of data gathered over time. It may be useful to re-analyse data collected by other people or at another period to understand changing trends in topics such as emigration or education choices.

Problem-based question

Some friends of yours are considering counselling as a career. They are not psychologists and simply want to make money from providing counselling. Who would you advise them to talk to find out more about the field, the training needed and the amount of money to be made from it? What should they think about when analysing the accounts they gather?

How to interpret data pluralistically

Whether you have reached this part of the book by reading it through chapter by chapter or whether you have turned directly to this point in a quest to know more about pluralistic interpretation, it will not surprise you to know that there is no one set of rules or guidelines about how to do it! As in the interpretation of data using mono-method approaches, the challenges and the attraction of qualitative research can be in knowing that what you bring to the research is as important as the data you gather for it. It is essential that the research outcomes can be trusted and taken seriously, and this is only achievable by knowing (and showing) that your research has been rigorously conducted. This means ensuring that the interpretation process is clear, systematic and as transparent as possible.

When considering pluralistic approaches to interpretation we can think about using multiple researchers, multiple methods and multiple data sources. In this section, we consider these different approaches to interpretative pluralism, how pluralistic interpretation has been done and the issues that have arisen for those that have done it.

Pluralistic interpretation across methods

Using different methods of data analysis to interpret data usually means involving several researchers. Commonly, qualitative researchers are trained in one method and become expert in its use. As part of qualitative research methods learning, all researchers are encouraged to develop practices that make explicit as much of what they bring to the research as possible. Working as part of a team of researchers – each of whom may be employing a different method of analysis – provides another source of reflexive practice, as researchers can discuss their experience of the research process with each other. This may be particularly useful when the researchers are interpreting the data as it allows them to focus on their role in this and not simply on the method of analysis they are employing.

Working pluralistically with several researchers allows for differences within and between analysts' written and spoken descriptions of the analysis to be made clearer. Following up the data analysis with individual interviews with the analysts can also show how personal biographies influence the choice of method. In a PQR study, we found that analysis of the analysts' relationship with the research artefacts shows that, when working with a written transcript of an interview conducted by someone else, interview context and narrator demographics are created by analysts (Frost *et al.*, 2010).

Each of these insights to the impact of the researcher on the analysis process is valuable in opening up the process of bringing meaning to data and, taken together, they represent a powerful tool for potentially accessing more insight to how meaning can be made of data. This approach can also serve to highlight differences and contradictions in the findings that emerge from the analysis, as well as to generate complementarity by providing a multi-perspective insight.

Using different methods to analyse data means that different ways of looking at the data are being brought to the process. One method might look for themes occurring within it, while another may look at how language is being used in it. The way that what is found is interpreted will reflect what has been looked for. This means, for example, that themes might be identified and then used to describe a person's understanding of a relationship they have, or the discourse that a person draws on to describe themselves might be identified and used to develop a picture of how they position themselves in a particular role. Both of these meanings might be found within the same piece of data, and simply emerge in response to how data are analysed and by whom. Pluralistic interpretation allows for these meanings to be taken separately or combined to construct a picture of a person. The example box presents an instance of the pluralistic analysis of one woman's (Mary's) description of becoming a mother. Grounded theory analysis revealed a theme of this woman's description of herself in a gendered relationship; discourse analysis highlighted some ways in which she positioned herself as a good mother by drawing on accepted discourses of motherhood.

It is interesting to note that different researchers using different methods to make interpretations of data often arrive at findings that are in broad agreement. Studies (e.g. Frost *et al.*, 2011) show that analysts working separately choose to focus on more or less the same sections of text within interview transcripts. Pluralistic interpretation allows for the illumination of different meanings and for each to be taken singly to address specific research questions, or for all to be taken together to

Example of pluralistic analysis

Text from interview transcript

'I didn't believe that anyone else was capable of looking after her. I don't think that I was supercapable I just mean that you know who else would know her routine and know what she meant when she cried and you know how could she possibly be happy with other people looking after her. I found that really hard to get my head around ...'

A grounded theory (GT) analyst interprets this as illustrating a theme of 'traditional gendered roles'. The analyst describes how Mary regards women and men as different in their nurturing capacity and that, while her capacity provides a strong bond with her child, it also means that she is compelled to be the primary carer.

To the analyst, this suggests that Mary sees herself as a mother, as someone who is able to be more loving, nurturing and affectionate towards her child in a way that her husband cannot be. Her words imply that she feels this is a fundamental difference between men and women, not just between her and her husband.

A discourse analyst (DA) interprets this as illustrating that this woman sees herself as having a special and unique relationship with her child that is based in part on knowledge about her child that no one else can have because of the biological link between them and the care that she is therefore able to offer her child. The existence of this relationship positions her as a mother and the best person to care for her child.

Taken together, these interpretations of the data present a picture of a woman who describes her traditional approach to mothering, which enables her to be the primary caregiver to her child because she feels that no one else could know her child like she does (GT), and who feels that she is the only person that can have this relationship with her child (DA).

While each interpretation, taken alone, is useful in providing insight to the narrator's experience of being a mother, taken together they allow for a more holistic view of the emotional landscape provoked by the strength of the bond, as well as its nature and the purpose it may serve for this mother.

provide a multi-dimensional insight to one person's experience. The findings that emerge from the approach provide a variety of ways to understand (and therefore develop strategies to address) behaviours and experiences.

To evaluate the evidence produced using the pluralistic approach, allowance must be made for the range of epistemological positions underlying it (Madill *et al.*, 2000). The inclusion of methods such as grounded theory, which contain both positivist and interpretative elements (Charmaz & Henwood, 2008), alongside approaches such as discourse analysis, which seeks individual realities through their construction with language, means that evidence of the rigour of the research needs to be based on criteria other than reliability, generalisability and objectivity (Yardley & Bishop, 2008). Pluralistic research expects each researcher to make transparent their relationship to the research artefacts and their interpretation and transformation of the data so that reassurance of credibility applicable to the epistemological variety of this approach can be provided. Additional quality checks on each type of analysis as well as on the synthesised use of them might include triangulation, paper trails and cross-comparison between researchers (e.g. Yardley & Bishop, 2008).

By using multiple methods, the pluralistic approach heightens opportunities for transparency of data transformation processes by focusing on both the individual use of each technique and the findings reached from their combined use. This approach highlights further research usefulness and potential for impact, which in themselves are further quality checks for qualitative research. Pluralistic interpretation allows qualitative researchers to move beyond the constraints imposed by the use of just one epistemological or ontological position. An epistemologically agnostic stance can be taken in order to try to access as much meaning as possible in data.

Pluralistic interpretation within a method

The example above provides insight to individuals through examination of their accounts of their experience using incoherent epistemologies, represented by the use of different methods. Using the same method to examine data allows for epistemological coherence and can reveal divergent as well as convergent findings. A particularly apt approach to pluralistic analysis is the phenomenological psychological approach. Its aptness lies in its fundamental aim to draw out the human meaning of experience using empirical data. Where it distinguishes itself from other qualitative approaches, such as the discursive approach, is in its focus on the person's experience 'in its appearing' (King *et al.*, 2008: 81). It strictly puts aside all reference to reality, makes no judgement on whether the person's account of their experience is in accord with reality or not, and points to the field of awareness of the research as key.

The setting aside of reality is the epoche or bracketing within which phenomenological research takes place, and gives rise to differences in practice across the approach. At one end of the spectrum the requirement to work within the epoche means the researcher must put aside all presuppositions including their prior experience, knowledge of it and interpretation of it in order to access the lived experience itself. At the other end of the spectrum, the researcher will be actively incorporating assumptions and expectations into the research process. The different value that researchers place on the importance of bracketing allows for diversity in how the approach is employed. It prioritises the place and role of interpretation in the process, while highlighting the impact of the researcher. We shall consider this in more detail in the next section.

One form of this approach within phenomenology is 'dialogical phenomenology', developed over the past 20 years in Seattle University (e.g. Halling & Leifer, 1991; Halling, Kunz & Rowe, 1994). It draws on the use of 'reflective conversation' (Halling et al., 1994: 111) between researchers to conduct the work of the research process. The reflective conversations bridge objectivity and subjectivity in a 'search for a level of understanding that will be beneficial to the community as well as illuminating in a theoretical sense' (1994: 111). In practice both data and researchers are transformed as the phenomenon under inquiry becomes alive and is more readily analysed.

A recent example of a group phenomenological approach is the work carried out by King et al. (2008). The team members carried out a phenomenological analysis of an interview about an individual's experiences of mistrust. Each analyst conducted a qualitative analysis of the interview transcript, being told only 'that the analysis should be descriptive (i.e. not offering an explanatory or causal account) and focused on mistrust' (2008: 84) in order to obtain the variants of the phenomenological approach. Each member then presented a summary of their analysis to the group and a statement of the convergent analysis was produced (see the 'Analysis' section of King et al., 2008, for the full version of this). Following the group meeting the individual researchers each wrote up their analysis in two parts: consensual analysis and individual analysis (the first being the parts of the analysis that fitted with the group's reading and the second representing that which was excluded from the group's reading of the data). Each consensual analysis was sent to all members of the group, who amended their own consensual analysis accordingly. The individual analyses were written up by another researcher, following paired consultation between the researchers.

The thorough and detailed way in which this study was conducted allows a useful evaluation of its benefits and challenges. The consensual analyses allowed a rich insight into the world of the participant (while acknowledging that they remain partial and emergent). The divergences reflect differences in phenomenological commitment and enable multiple interpretations, which raise epistemological issues of presentation and inclusion, and questions of coherence of the research methods and aims. The group members identified issues around discursive construction by one member and acceptance of reflection of the participant's own reality in her account by two others. The group members differed among themselves about the usefulness of these divergences and did not work through the differences collaboratively until they reached an 'integrated account' (King et al., 2008: 97) as proposed in the dialogical phenomenological approach. Apart from questioning pragmatic challenges of time to devote to this group process, the researchers raised the question as to whether the very stimulation of intriguing and intangible questions is a sufficiently important part of the research process to warrant its approach. They asked whether the high degree of consensual analysis is enough for that to be the privileged component of the process. Their individual divergences (around the participant's use of metaphor, the co-production of the findings and the embodied empathy) added opportunity for contextualisation and reflection on the process that may not otherwise have occurred. (For a full description of this study, see King *et al.*, 2008.)

Another way of thinking about within-method pluralistic interpretation is for one person to employ one method in a number of different ways (e.g. Frost, 2009b). A multi-dimensional understanding of a phenomenon can be obtained by drawing on strengths offered by different models of the same data analysis technique. The text guides the form of analysis employed, so that an initial understanding of the account is gradually enriched by systematic exploration of the text until a new story emerges.

I used different models of narrative analysis to explore women's descriptions of the transition to becoming a mother to a second child. I wanted to understand as much as possible about the women's hopes, fears, fantasies, expectations and realities during this time from the transcripts of semi-structured interviews I conducted with them (Frost, 2006). It was important to privilege the women's voices as far as possible so that other stories did not become imposed on theirs and this flexible use of narrative analysis seemed to offer one way to do this. I used models of narrative analysis that variously focused on the structure of the stories (Labov, 1972), the linguistics of the stories (Gee, 1991) and the performative function of the stories (Riessmann, 1993). I also adopted a critical narrative approach (Emerson & Frosh, 2004) to consider my own role in the process.

In practice, I often started with Labov's model as a way to initially identify stories that fitted the conventional structure of 'beginning, middle and end'. Once identified, I looked at the context in which they appeared in the interview transcripts by considering not only what had come before and after them, but also what role I had played in encouraging, limiting or guiding the telling of the story. This process often led to identification of other less conventionally structured stories such as narratives of emotions, or narratives that meandered across the interviews with frequently changing endings as events unfolded and were recounted. One outcome of this approach was to learn much more about my role in the research process, as well as about the experiences that the women recounted, because I had to focus on each approach I took as well as the decisions I made about taking it.

The objective in using different methodological perspectives to the interview text was to extract as much meaning as possible from it. The methods were each grounded in narrative analysis, and their application followed models proposed by researchers from the fields of linguistics, sociology and psychology. I adopted this approach because I sought to gain insight to many dimensions of individual experience that included expectations, realities, hopes, fears and fantasies. After each phase of analysis, I moved to another to extract further meaning from the text.

In order for there to be confidence in each of the findings made using different approaches it is essential that the interpretation process employed by each is as clear and transparent as possible. This can be achieved by including sufficient data to show the reader what steps have been taken in the analysis process, by describing how decisions about selecting sections of text to examine in detail were reached and by including careful discussion of theories brought to the understanding of findings made. It is important to verify to the reader whether you are prioritising the use of one method over another and, if so, why. Similarly, if your aim is to be guided by the text in your use of each method, this should be stated with a clear description of how this process has unfolded.

The example described above drew on several narrative analysis techniques and combined the findings arrived at by using each approach. Each finding on its own was reached using a systematic and rigorous process, and so offered paths to further research. For example, after applying Labov's model, questions about the content of the clearly definable stories that appeared in Mary's interview text could be pursued. After applying Gee's (1991) approach, questions about what further aspects of her life were dictated by gendered beliefs, and where she gathered and formed these beliefs, were asked. Detailed transcription to show linguistic features, such as pauses, led to questions about the influence of culture and discourses on Mary's view of herself as a mother. By considering my role in the process of interpreting the data, I included assumptions, biases and suppositions brought to the interpretation through my role as an interviewer. These included issues arising from being a woman interviewing another woman, a mother interviewing a mother, and a psychologist interviewing a non-psychologist. As far as I was able, I sought to understand the power imbalances that such differences can lead to, such as leading the interview, identifying sections of text to analyse and overlooking the participant's meaning by not recognising times when I might have been imposing my own.

Of course, we cannot always be aware of all the ways in which our engagement with the research process has impacted on it. By the very nature of acting with unconscious motivations we are unable to make explicit all that we may want to. Knowing that we have an audience interested in what we bring to the research can itself inform what we choose to bring to our own and the audience's awareness. However, by taking all the steps we can to illuminate what we can about our role in the process, and by applying that to the ways in which we have employed models of the systematic analysis of data, we can be confident that we are presenting findings that have emerged from a sound and high-quality research process.

Reflexivity in pluralistic interpretation

As this chapter has shown, working pluralistically, either across or within methods, or with a team of researchers, provides good opportunities to heighten the transparency and raise the quality of the research process by illuminating the role of the researchers in it. The importance of the researcher role to the whole process is emphasised by many qualitative researchers, through consideration of critical approaches (e.g. Emerson & Frosh, 2004), subjectivity (e.g. Wetherell, 2008) and reflexivity (e.g. Finlay, 2003; Finlay & Gough, 2003). Subjectivity and reflexivity in qualitative research are terms used to illustrate the co-constructive role of the qualitative researcher in the research process. Both terms and concepts are widely used in qualitative research in recognition of its turning away from positivism, and of the impossibility of the qualitative approach representing a search for absolute knowledge (Frosh & Saville Young, 2008: 111). Similarly, both terms present challenges in findings ways to describe an individual's inner world or a relationship. The challenges range from seeking to make concrete an abstract concept that is based on what is in part unknowable to an individual and in part on what is to be presented to an unknown audience, to finding ways to present this meaningfully in words or other forms. The importance of doing so, is paramount in order to enable the reader of the research to gain insight to the relationship that the researchers have formed with the data, how this may have differed and impacted on the data transformation across method and researcher, and to evaluate the quality of the research process.

A widely used way of raising awareness of the researcher impact is for researchers to keep field journals. In these they record their experiences, thoughts, ideas, hunches and any other aspects of the research process that arise for them. The journals are usually regarded as confidential, in order to facilitate free expression within them and for the maximum advantage of their creation to be gained. The idea is that, by using field journals, fewer of their own personal experiences and their influences are brought by the researchers to the research process. This is also a role in discussing the experiences of aspects of the process with study supervisors. These journals also serve to aid recall of the process for the researcher, so for example when they are transcribing an interview they may use their journal to aid their recollection of how they were feeling when the participant was narrating a particular event to them. Awareness of personal feelings can help to illuminate the subjective aspects of interpretation in the data transformation process.

The journals are sometimes used (with permission) to study the role of the researcher (e.g. Frost et al., 2010). They provide a very personal insight to what the researcher was experiencing as they systematically analysed the data, and allow for consideration of how this may have impacted on the final presentation of the research. Working pluralistically enables a number of field journals to be studied. By assigning one member of a team to a group co-ordinator role (see Chapter 6, on the pragmatics of pluralistic qualitative research) an overview of the reflexive practices and experiences can be gained. Through group discussion of this, careful insight to why people have made some of the decisions in the research can enhance its transparency.

Another way of accessing the experience of the researcher is to simply ask them! Semi-structured interviews can be used to ask researchers about their experiences of the process. This might highlight aspects that they were unable or unwilling to write down; it may provoke further reflection, and it may illuminate contradictions between what is written and what is said. Combining the two ways of eliciting data allows for a complex insight to the reflexive process.

Challenges to researcher impact and its evaluation lie partly in finding appropriate ways and places to present it in the research write-up. Many researchers choose to add a paragraph at the end of their carefully written report that presents information about themselves, and a brief reflection on how their relationship with the study has impacted on their data transformation and the research process. While this is perfectly acceptable (and even encouraged) in many student dissertations, when working pluralistically there is scope to consider the impact of reflexive practice more broadly. You might want to include it from the outset of the write-up by presenting the group discussions that, for example, may have led to the formulation (and usually re-formulation) of the research question. You might want to include the different researchers' voices throughout the report (much as we have tried to do in this book using the 'Reflections on Practice' feature). You might want to be adventurous and include a DVD that presents the researchers discussing their reflexive awareness.

In a study that the PQR team conducted we found differences in the way researchers wrote about their use of their chosen methods. On paper they were usually very formal, employing the accepted language of research to describe systematic application of models of analysis. They sometimes suggested different methods that they would have liked to employ, and highlighted some of the advantages and limitations that they perceived with their choice of method. During the interviews, however, it became clear that the choice of method was sometimes simply down to the researcher having been trained in it because it was a method that was the specialism of their PhD supervisor or a preferred lecturer at university. Interviews can also highlight the influence that personal biography has on the use of methods by different researchers, with those who prefer organised thinking employing more structured methods and attempting to present the data in organised categories. This approach may penetrate into the researcher's view of the data, whereby those descriptions of experience that do not fit neatly are regarded as troublesome and 'messy'. It may be that what comes across as an authoritative voice on paper is exposed as a personal frustration in interview!

Use of language and style of writing will vary across researchers, quite often depending on the level of experience they have. This too can lead to an erroneous portrayal of researcher impact. We found that those with more experience wrote the research in a more tentative voice than those with less experience. Also, the accepted style of writing perpetuated by journal editors (Willig, 2008) meant that a more positivistic slant came across than was intended in some writing about researcher impact. Closer questioning of this phenomenon also highlighted cultural differences and expectations with regards to how to write, and how open to be when describing personal experiences for an audience.

Awareness of some of these aspects of researcher impact will give rise to a heightened awareness of how your relationship with your study will have made a

I used an interpretative pluralistic approach to analyse interview transcripts gathered from seven women during their transition to second-time motherhood (Frost, 2006; 2009b). I chose to do this because I was left with several questions about whether other people would have arrived at the same findings as me if they had used the same model of narrative analysis and whether different researchers using different methods would have arrived at different findings in the data. My approach to eliciting and gathering the data had been very much focused on gathering stories from participants, and for this reason I chose to stay with the identification and examination of stories within the data set, but I wanted to look at them in as many different ways as I could in order to access as much meaning as I could within them. This seemed like a respectful approach to take to those participants who had given up their time and spoken of painful and meaningful times and events in their lives in the name of furthering understanding about them. I was also very much aware that my interest in investigating this phenomenon arose from my personal experiences of motherhood and I was keen to find ways to minimise the imposition of my story on to theirs.

In order to carry out this pluralistic approach, one of the major challenges I found was to trust my hunches and ideas, and to follow them through the data. This may have been about how I found myself listening to the interview (Becker, 1999) or how I chose a method with which to analyse it. Often I applied several different models to the same section of data and obtained a multi-layered insight to meanings within it. All the time, though, I was aware that my heightened awareness was raising other questions for me: How did I select the stories? Was that saying more about me than about the narrators of them? Was I only drawn to the 'juicy' parts of the text and overlooking the accounts of the mundane aspects of day-to-day life as a mother? Was it only me that found these parts mundane? And so on.

By taking a pluralistic approach I found myself feeling liberated in that I was able to roam around in the data. It felt a little like being in a large field where the boundaries were represented by the theoretical, empirical, methodological and personal frameworks that I brought to it, but that the field was large enough for me to forget that the boundaries were there in the distance until I was brought up short against them.

This meant it felt unrestricted and full of opportunities to really seek to understand as much as possible of what people had chosen to tell me.

difference to it. Thinking about ways to present this will further enhance your research and the interpretation you bring to it.

Chapter summary

This chapter has considered issues surrounding the interpretation of data. They have centred on theoretical aspects of the process, such as hermeneutics and the theory of interpretation, and on how these have been applied, such as in the dialogical psychology approach. We have also considered the researcher's role in this process and discussed several ways in which reflexive practice can be developed. It has included examples to illustrate the pluralistic use of one method to analyse data, the pluralistic use of different methods and the employment of different researchers to analyse the same data.

It is difficult to be prescriptive about interpretation in qualitative research. The approach sets out to recognise the role of interaction and context in investigating human behaviour. At the same time qualitative research often has a purpose of changing or contributing to members of communities in a beneficial way. Even this aim is subjective in its inclusion of what is beneficial and what is change.

Therefore this chapter has presented different ways of thinking about data interpretation without prioritising any one of them. It is for you the researcher to think through how you will transform the data you gather and also, to be prepared to describe this to the readers of your research in a way that allows them to form their own critique of how you have reached the outcomes that you have.

Further reading

Alvesson, M. & Skoldberg, K. (2009) *Reflexive Methodology: New Vistas for Qualitative Research* (2nd edn). London: Sage Publications Ltd.
A detailed and up-to-date book that covers reflexivity in the research process, including methods, hermeneutics and critical theory. Also includes a chapter on applications (Chapter 9), and issues of language in discourse analysis, feminism and genealogy (Chapter 7).

Bolton, G. (2010) *Reflective Practice: Writing and Professional Development* (3rd edn). London: Sage Publications Ltd.
This book focuses on ways in which reflexive practice can be put into narrative form through 'reflective writing'. Useful when writing up, but also throughout the research process as it provokes awareness about how the process is being carried out and the data transformed by you.

Lyons, E. & Coyle, A. (2007) *Analysing Qualitative Data in Psychology.* London: Sage Publications Ltd.
This book's careful descriptions and illustrations of data interpretation by each of the four methods, plus its chapter on similarities and differences across and between the methods, makes this a useful source of information on issues of interpretation, both using single-method and pluralistic approaches.

CHAPTER 8

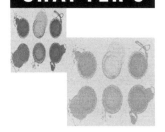

Writing Up Pluralistic Qualitative Research

Nollaig Frost

Introduction

This chapter is about writing up your research. The presentation of your work allows for the assessment of your study and your study's findings by others. Research is carried out to be disseminated. The qualitative research approach regards the writing-up of the work as part of the research process. It provides an opportunity for (and a challenge to) the researcher to reflect on their role in the research process, and to consider their relationship to it and to the topic under study. One aim of qualitative research is to ensure that voices that may otherwise be silent or obscured are heard. This means that ways of including the researchers' voices in the presentation of the work have to be found. At the same time the voices of the participants and all others involved in the research also have to be heard. The write-up must also convey the rationale for the study, the research questions it is addressing, its methodological approach and analysis techniques, the ways in which the data have been transformed and the implications of its findings. The context and setting of the study are also important in enabling the reader to review it fully.

Qualitative research writing uses both content and style to convey an effect to its reader. The reader should be provided with enough detail to be able to form her/his own critique of the study and of the way in which it was carried out. Although still the most common form of disseminating qualitative research, it is not always presented using the written word. Computer technology means that video links to interviews and data are possible. Performance techniques allow the portrayal of the emotional impacts of the topic and its study.

In this chapter we discuss the evolution of the qualitative research write-up, and the ways in which single-method and pluralistic qualitative research can be presented. We focus on writing style and content.

Background/history

Since the seventeenth century, writing has been divided into scientific and literary writing (Richardson, 2000: 925). Broadly speaking, scientific writing presents facts and objectivity, while fiction is associated with subjectivity and rhetoric.

Quantitative research reporting presents details of the inquiry and portrays the researcher as a witness to it. Scientific studies are described, and evidence for their results presented, for assessment and replication. This style of research reporting has dominated the field of psychology. With the emergence of qualitative approaches come questions about how to include subjective experience and the researcher's role in the research write-up. The questions have led to new styles of research writing and the use of different genres of writing, such as 'creative non-fiction' (Caulley, 2008) and 'Grab' (Glaser, 1978). Both seek to enthral the reader and enliven qualitative research writing: 'Grab' by presenting 'interesting and memorable' material that clearly links the study to theoretical concepts (Gilgun, 2005); 'creative non-fiction' by using fiction techniques to write non-fiction that remains close to the study data.

The qualitative research write-up is a method of inquiry itself (Janesick, 2000). It allows the researcher to examine and consider their relationship with the topic, and to show the audience how this has shaped and influenced the research. By illustrating the co-construction of the research through the involvement of participants and researchers the reader is invited to contribute further to the process through the openness of the relationship formed with them.

To address the issues of co-construction and reader involvement, qualitative research write-ups are increasingly moving away from simply adding a section on researcher reflexivity at the end. The interweaving of researcher and participant voices, and the inclusion of anecdotes, poetry and metaphors, work to bring the research context to the reader. Interactive forms of research writing invite feedback from the reader and extend the research process (Grbich, 2007). Fuller pictures of the data-gathering process can be developed through video links and transcripts of data.

Understanding writing as both a product and a process (Colyar, 2009) allows insight to the meaning and use of other linguistic features, such as silence and non-words, in the representation of research. Van Manen (1990) proposes that in order for the text to achieve a certain effect on its reader it can be important to leave some things unsaid. If a researcher is unable to access the language and concepts referred to by the participants, the inclusion of direct quotes from them can play an important role. Participants' silence about topics or experiences can be more telling to a researcher than attempts to elicit responses from them (Van Manen, 1990: 113). For the researcher as author, the inclusion of non-words that symbolise memory joggers, unvocalised meanings and cues to recall for her in drafts and rewrites can be an important part of the research process (Colyar, 2009). Although usually edited out in the final presentation their inclusion in the draft leaves their mark on the final style and content of the research write-up.

Why write up?

Your reasons for writing up your research will always include sharing the information you have gleaned from the experience. The reasons for sharing your research and the audience it is going to be shared with will vary. Students usually have to write up their work to present as a final-year project or a dissertation in pursuit of a degree. In addition to demonstrating what research you have carried out and how you conducted it, you will have to demonstrate that you have met the criteria for the report's structure and presentation. You may view writing up as a continuation of the research process, but the pressures of deadlines can mean that the submission of a final product dominates over the process of creating it.

The good news is that you can use this tension between process and product to enhance the quality of your project. By using the writing process as a way of informing yourself further about the study you can write an insightful and reflexive project that is bound to earn you higher marks than a qualitative project that pays scant regard to anything other than facts and statements. Writing up qualitative research openly and reflexively allows the author to pursue processes of 'showing', 'telling' and 'knowing' a topic and its study through discovery and analysis of the data they have collected. Writing up the research advances and develops the research process that has been conducted. It fixes thoughts and actions on paper and distributes them to interested audiences.

Through high-quality writing up the researcher provides the reader with relevant information in sufficient detail to enable them to understand and review the research process. The audience is well placed to consider the findings and their implications, and to consider how the research has addressed the research questions asked. If your readers find your research write-up interesting and review your study as rigorous, you will have achieved your purpose of writing up the research to disseminate new findings, and insight to how they have been reached.

Problem-based question

Writing up your research for assessment (at university or by journal editors) usually requires you to meet a set of criteria. These might be to write within certain word limits, to include certain aspects of the research or to present the work in a certain format. Imagine you have been told to submit your final-year project 'according to all the usual criteria'. What might these be? Make a list of the key sections you think make a good piece of written-up research and then, beside each, write the possible challenges to meeting it.

How to write-up qualitative research

Introduction

Qualitative research write-ups are affected by what is expected of them – that is, why they are being written and the audience they are being written for. The write-up expects to continue the research process and to invite the reader to become involved in the process. Qualitative research writing shows the decisions, the data and the people involved in the study, and enables the reader to form their own view of the inquiry. Reports are commonly written in the first person to underpin the co-constructive approach to the process and to acknowledge the researcher subjectivity in it. They can be written up in a variety of structures, ranging from the traditional 'Aim, Method, Findings, Discussion' structure to narratives, short stories and poems.

In the following section we present some practical ways of writing and of writing up qualitative research by examining single and pluralistic qualitative research write-ups, as process and as product.

Problem-based question

You wish to study the ways in which three different newspapers reported the earthquake in Christchurch, New Zealand. You are interested in how the language used differs across newspapers. What are the important decisions that you had to make in conducting this inquiry and how will you present these in your write-up? How will you decide which sections of newspaper text to use in the write-up?

General features of writing up qualitative research

Writing reflexively, writing reflexivity

Writing reflexively is about using the writing process to reflect on what you are writing about. Writing up a research study reflexively is an opportunity to reflect on the topic and on your study of the topic. Although it is a term that conjures up images of still waters and periods of reflective calm, writing reflexively is a dynamic and fast-moving process leading to insights and understandings about how and why you reached the findings that you did in your research study. There may be some conscious realisations about yourself and your relationship to the topic. There may also be unconscious impacts on the study of the topic that you will be unaware of.

Dissertations and final-year projects commonly address reflexivity in a subsection somewhere towards the end of the write-up. This 'reflexivity section' usually talks about why you selected this topic and how you gained further insight to it during the research process. This approach to incorporating reflexivity in the research write-up often feels frustrating to both writer and reader. It has a 'last-minute' feel to it, like something that has been tacked on just before handing in the write-up. It fails to capture your immersion in the work and the intensity of your relationship with it.

The challenges of writing reflexively and of writing about self-reflexivity can range from finding words to convey feelings, through to concerns about exposing personal experiences, to uncertainty about where to include reflexivity in research write-ups.

Example of writing reflexivity into your research

I began this research because of my personal interest in the abuse of women by men. It was something I had felt had dominated my life as a child and now I wanted to use this research to find out more about how women coped. I quickly realised that it was going to be difficult to detach my own experience from those that were being recounted to me during the interviews, and found myself turning more and more to psychological theory for explanations and understandings of what I was being told. This resulted in my first interpretations being very dry and depersonalised. It seemed that both my voice and those of the participants had been lost and an 'expert view' derived from other psychologists was being imposed on personal unique experiences. I realised that, as the interviewer, I had felt caught between feeling like there was an opportunity for the participants to be empowered by telling their stories and feeling that they were relying on me to bring change to their situation. (I had decided to be open about my personal interest in this topic.) I believed that what they wanted from me was action rather than words, and this meant that at times I felt disempowered and useless in the face of harrowing accounts of abuse. I strove throughout the research process to draw on the support offered by my supervisor and colleagues to remain grounded in the participants' words rather than stray any more into their lives.

Keeping a reflexive journal

One of the challenges to writing reflexively arises from crafting a piece of text that conveys your personal involvement in the research process in a way that readers can appreciate and with which you feel comfortable. Writing reflexively differs from writing practically because you are seeking to fix on paper your thoughts, feelings and experiences. When writing reflexively for a research study write-up, you are challenged to convey these components in a way that demonstrates their relevance – to the study and to the reader's understanding of your relationship to the study.

One way to assist you in this process is to keep a confidential reflexive journal from the start of the research process. In this journal you can write down thoughts and feelings as they occur and in a way that you feel comfortable with. There will be key points in the process at which you will want to fill in your journal. These might include the beginning of the study when you are trying to decide what topic you want to study, after meetings with your project supervisor, before and after interviews (or other forms of data collection), during the data analysis and in the writing-up period. There may well be other times when you will want to record personal thoughts and experiences. These might include 'eureka moments' when you have a flash of insight to your study, 'celebration moments' when you reach turning points in it and 'doldrum moments' when you feel you will never reach either of the former two points.

Although you are unlikely to use all that you write in your reflexive journal, keeping one aids your reflexive writing practice in many ways.

- Keeping a journal provides a record of the process. Although you will think you will never forget key experiences, information, events and insights to your research, you probably will as the process twists and turns towards the submission date.
- Keeping a reflexive journal will help you to separate out those feelings that arise from your personal experiences and those that arise from your participants' accounts of their experiences. This will be important throughout the research process, and particularly during the data analysis stage. If you are conducting the study as a member of a research team you will need to be able to convey some of your reflexivity to your co-researchers. If you are working with many methods of analysis you will want to be able to consider your impact on the application of each method and in the cross-analysis.
- Keeping a journal will also help you to become comfortable with writing about your self, your experiences and your role in research. Producing parts of your research write-up in the first person may be new to you. It may feel as though you are being 'unscientific' and risking losing marks. In fact, with practice in writing reflexively, you will gain sensitive insight to the study that you have conducted, and will enhance how it is perceived and understood by the majority of its readers.

Example from a reflexive journal

I find myself feeling very upset about Jane's story. The interview finished half an hour ago and I am on my way home. However, as I started to drive away from her house I felt tears welling up and after I had turned the corner I pulled over to consider all that she had told me. Her story had started off similarly to others in that she had planned to get married and have children with her long-term partner. However, within days of being married he had started to feel ill and after much confusion and delay her husband was diagnosed with cancer. Within a year of their marriage he had died. Obviously this is a story that most people would find sad but it has struck me hard and at the moment I do not know how I will return to her data in order to transcribe and analyse it.

Example

One week later

Jane and her story have been on my mind ever since last week's entry. I have been pondering its meaning to me. I realised that I had been struck by the apparent unfairness of the situation she found herself in. I ask questions such as 'How could they not have known beforehand?', 'If they had would they still have got married?', 'Is it possible that he had an inkling but didn't want to say?', and so on. I have to be very careful in the data analysis and interpretation phases that I do not set out to look for answers to these questions.

One week later: meeting with supervisor

I met with Dr Foster today and discussed with her the impact of Jane's interview. I explained that although I couldn't stop thinking about it and had a lot of questions about her experiences I was finding it impossible to actually return to the audio recording of the interview in order to start the data analysis. Dr Foster asked me what I thought were the preventative issues and, as I started to talk about the interview experience, I realised that I felt angry towards Jane for somehow getting herself into that heartbreaking situation. As we talked further it became clearer that this apparent anger was blocking my interaction with Jane's words. It was almost as if I could not bear to face the experience again. It leaves me with new questions, such as 'Is this how Jane felt when recounting her story to me during the interview?' and 'How might this have been manifest in the way she told her story?' I decided to start the analysis and take my initial interpretations to the next peer support study group.

Making space for reflexivity

Another challenge to writing reflexively is to find a place for it in your research write-up. Most undergraduate and postgraduate dissertations criteria expect reflexivity to be included in the final product but guidelines as to how to include it are few. On the one hand, this provides the author with subjective decisions to make about how to include themselves in their work. On the other hand, the lack of guidance can lead to uncertainty and concerns about how the inclusion of reflexivity is going to be evaluated by examiners.

Others provide a short introductory reflection on the topic or an appendix to describe their role in the study. Somehow the positioning and purposes of these sections can appear to serve to make the rest of the report more factual in style, as though the 'personal bit' has somehow been dealt with.

The comfort derived from these approaches to the inclusion of reflexivity usually arises from the ease with which examiners can find the 'reflexivity section' and evaluate it. Thoughtful inclusion of details of aspects of the study, such as decision-making processes, study context and its setting, can all form part of the reflexivity.

Writing with 'openness'

Particular challenges arise about how to present the decisions taken during the research process. The choice and use of qualitative method can be influenced by the researcher's biography. Inclusion of details about how aspects of the researcher's experience and choice have influenced their application of a particular technique of analysis can greatly enhance the reader's understanding of how the study was carried out.

To ascertain what kind of researcher you are, it may help to ask yourself questions such as those listed in the box below, to gain understanding of how your biography has led to your choice of method and to help you determine how you will write up.

What is your 'researcher biography'?

1. What is your history as a researcher?
2. How have you chosen your topic and its method of inquiry?
3. Do you like to work methodically and in a detailed fashion?
4. How confident are you about working creatively, and following hunches and ideas you have?
5. Do you use art and literature to understand the world around you? How do you like to bring these perspectives into your research?
6. How does your cultural background differ to that of those who may be reading, supervising and assessing your work? How will you address this in your write-up?
7. How systematic in the way you approach your work are you?
8. How has the teaching and training in qualitative research you have had influenced the way you carry it out?
9. What is your relationship with your project supervisor like? Have you discussed your choice of method with them?
10. How much time do you have to do this study? Are you the sort of person who will leave sufficient time to write it up, or are you someone who leaves things until the last minute?

Perhaps a useful way to prepare for this is to draw on the concept of 'openness' in the writing (Chenail, 1995). This can be regarded as a mixture of reflexivity, description and detail, and requires the author/researcher to present as much detail as possible (within the constraints of word limits and presentation style) of the research and the way it was carried out. This can be achieved by adopting a 'two study approach' (Chenail, 1995) in which the author/researcher considers both the research project and their study of that study.

This approach creates space to acknowledge the development of the method, and its application throughout the study and the impact of the researcher on its use. The resultant write-up includes details of the decisions the researcher made, and how and why they were reached. The researcher has several opportunities to examine the particulars of the steps taken during the study, from the formation of the research question, the selection of data elicitation settings and processes to the analysis of the data collected and presentation of the findings.

Chenail argues that this 'spirit of openness' (Chenail, 1995: 2) can be achieved by considering the 'other' in the process at all times. The other may be the intended audience for the write-up, the participants who took part in the study, and colleagues and peers who comment on and read the work. By communicating details and descriptions of the process of the study openly to the other, the spirit of openness engenders one of trust and of your work being considered trustworthy and rigorously conducted.

The conventional structure of research write-ups

The conventional approach to research write-ups is still found widely in qualitative research. The study is presented in sections that reflect broadly the order in which it was conducted. Certain facts and information are presented in each section. A typical structure might be as shown in Table 8.1.

Displaying data

In qualitative research it is essential to stay close to the data, therefore it is good practice to include as much raw data as possible in the write-up of the research. The 'openness' approach facilitates this by promoting explanation and description of decisions made at all points of the research and the analysis of the data. The data serve to restrain and ground the research process. Their inclusion in the report shows how the findings have been reached. The richness of the data becomes a feature of the write-up as the depth and complexity of meanings within it are revealed.

Enhancing the data feature can be achieved by developing a 'story' that creates a setting for it (where it was gathered), characters around it (from whom) and an action storyline (how it was elicited and gathered). These details provide the reader with the context of the study, which is further enriched by the interweaving of details about the researcher's decision-making processes during the research process. Care should be taken not to reduce the data unnecessarily and risk losing or changing its context. One way in which this can be addressed is to include interview or performance talk that came before and after it. Including the interviewer's words allows a fuller critique by the reader and enhances the openness of the write-up.

As discussed in the following section there are many ways in which the data can be displayed. Table 8.2 illustrates some of these.

Table 8.1 Typical structure of a research study write-up

Abstract	Typically a summary of the research study in up to 300 words. Presents its aims, methodology and some key findings. Suggests the implications of these findings and how they are discussed in the report.
Introduction	Presents a brief overview of the background to the study and what it is about. Explains why the topic is of interest and the way it has been studied.
Literature Review	Presents a critique of existing literature about the topic under study. Includes theoretical and empirical research studies. Evaluates and critiques studies and the approach taken to conduct them so that gaps, limitations and strengths are highlighted. Flows coherently to the statement of the study aims and research questions.
Study Design	Describes how the study was conducted. Usually includes subsections that present factual information.
Participants	How many, how and where recruited from, approach to sample selection (e.g. snowballing, purposive sampling, gatekeeping), details of individual participants.
Methodology	Rationale for adopting a qualitative approach and the technique of analysis to be employed. A discussion of why the method of analysis is most appropriate to the study. Inclusion of semi-structured interview schedule if relevant, of other forms of data elicitation if necessary. Brief outline of equipment used (e.g. audio data recorders). Brief discussion of how the data will be transcribed, if relevant.
Ethical Considerations	Describes the procedures required by the university and places of recruitment, refers reader to copies of consent forms, information sheets, confidentiality statements, debriefing sheets, letters of agreement, risk assessment forms, usually in an appendix. Opportunity to include statement of positive ethical considerations, such as how the study is likely to benefit the participants or the group that they represent.
Findings	Presentation of raw data, illustration of how it has been analysed and the outcomes of the analysis. Some discussion of how key findings were reached, to accompany the data display.
Discussion	Shows how the research questions have been addressed, the theoretical frameworks within which the findings can be interpreted, the strengths and limitations of the study, and implications for future research.
Reference list	All references cited in the text, listed in the appropriate style, usually Harvard but varying across universities and journals.

Using quotes

The challenge of displaying all the components of the research process with words has led to accusations of qualitative research reports being 'boring' (e.g. Richardson, 2000). Quotes enable participants' voices to be directly inserted into the write-up, but used to excess and without explanation also risk producing long lists that the

Table 8.2 Data display styles (after Chenail, 1995)

Style	Description
Natural	The data follow the shape of the phenomenon, e.g. sequences of talk in a therapy session
Most simple to most complex	Clear, short quotes or visual representations of the theme
First uncovered to last uncovered	Reflection of the researcher's journey through the data analysis process
Theory -guided	Data arrangements are guided by the theories the researcher draws on to understand the phenomenon
Narratively logical	Organised as a story with scenes linked by narrative; the links may be the researcher's voice or other voices that may otherwise be silenced
Most important to least important	The key findings are presented and discussed first, with lesser discoveries following
Dramatic presentation	The opposite of the above – the data are ordered to save the most important findings for presentation last
No particular order	Little explanation from the researcher so that the reader is invited to draw her/his own conclusions

reader does not see the point of. The importance of data display has to be balanced with the importance of the theoretical frameworks surrounding it. Enough data has to be accessible to the reader for them to understand and consider the theorising that comes from it. Lofland and Lofland (1995) suggest that showing more data than theory is good practice. This allows the reader/examiner/marker/editor to understand the process and to make suggestions for its improvement.

The most commonly used data for display are participant quotes. Chenail suggests that it is helpful to bear in mind ways of supporting the reader to stay with the data, and developing a repetitive template for the display of quotes might do this. Such a template might present a finding, followed by an introduction to an example quote that illustrates the finding, followed by further discussion of the finding, followed by a second example of the finding and further discussion, and so on (see Table 8.3).

Establishing a narrative pattern of data display such as this helps the reader to find their way through your paper and draws them in to the presentation's pace and style. In addition, the simplicity of this approach allows the complexity of the data to be illuminated. Simple questions are asked of the data and of the research process,

Table 8.3 Illustration of a pattern of presenting findings and examples (from Chenail, 1995) using data from a study by Frost (2006)

Section heading	Illustration
Present the finding	Gendered family roles
Introduce the first data example	In the example below Jane is highlighting her belief that she was the only person able to take care of her child
Display the first data example	*I also didn't really believe that anyone else was capable of looking after her*
Comment further on the first data example	This section of the text highlights the strong bond that this narrator has with her daughter and that no one knows her child like the mother
Make transition to second data example	Jane's strength of the bond is further emphasised with her words:
Display second data example	*I just mean that you know who else would know her routine and know what she meant when she cried and you know how could she possibly be happy with other people looking after her*
Comment further on the second data example	This illustrates the special knowledge about her child that Jane believes she has. As the child's mother, only she can understand her and bring her happiness in a way no one else can
Make transition to next data example	Her closing words illustrate how overwhelming this can be for Jane:
Third data example	*I can't get my head around it*

and complex answers revealed. Maintaining this balance can be the secret of success in both carrying out and presenting qualitative research.

Problem-based question

You have conducted a study of students' perceptions of Barack Obama. You carried out a grounded theory analysis of the accounts they provided by email, and a colleague conducted a discourse analysis of them. When you distributed a draft of the write-up to the participants, three of the students said that the discourse analysis did not accurately portray their views. They were happy with the grounded theory analysis. How will you incorporate this feedback into the write-up of the study?

Structuring pluralistic research write-ups

Writing up qualitative research that has been conducted pluralistically presents all the challenges and benefits of writing up single-method qualitative research. It requires the pluralistic researcher to find ways of including their voice among those of their participants and it acts as part of the inquiry process. In addition, the pluralistic researcher has to find ways to document a research process that has involved more iterations than some single-method approaches. The researcher/author has to position themselves among their team and seek to write in a way that incorporates fellow researchers and the voices that have emerged from their work. As with all qualitative research, there is no single way to do this. There are a number of ways in which multiple data, their interpretation and the reflexivities of the researchers involved can be displayed. Finding the way that is most appropriate for your study will be influenced by factors that include the audience for whom the research is being written, the context and conduct of the research study, and the personal biography of the researcher/author. Some pluralistic studies draw on all the researchers involved to directly contribute to the project write-up (e.g. Frost *et al.*, 2010). Others appoint a lead writer and contribute by making suggestions (e.g. Frost, Eatough *et al.*, forthcoming). What follows here is a consideration of some of the ways in which qualitative data can be included in qualitative research writing.

CASE STUDY

A class of 15 MSc Forensic Psychology students are asked to conduct a group study to investigate the question 'How do siblings of children who are given custodial sentences account for their sibling's crime?' The class is divided into three groups of five students. Each group is asked to gather qualitative data for analysis by three qualitative analysis techniques. The students are asked to work as a group to conduct the study, but to present the write-ups individually. Write-ups must include researcher reflexivity. The maximum word count is 7000 words.

One group decides that it will appoint one member of the group to carry out semi-structured interviews with children and three other members of the group to analyse the data using a chosen method of analysis. The fifth member of the group will cross-analyse the data findings gathered from the three analysts.

The challenge to each member of the group is to find a way to display the data and their interpretations. Group members must also decide how to incorporate descriptions of the analysis processes and the reflexivity brought to these by the other group researchers.

One member of the group presented her write-up within the word limit but included three appendices showing several quotes taken from each interview. Another member of the group presented the tables showing the themes from the cross-analysis with illustrative quotes. A third member included very few quotes but a CD was attached to the back of the dissertation with the full interviews recorded on it.

▶ To address the issues of reflexivity one member of the group wrote only about her experience of the analysis. Another member of the group described the reflexive position of each other member, as she saw it. A third member asked each member of the group to provide a paragraph describing their experience of the study for inclusion in her write-up.

Questions

1. What other forms of data display might have been used to enhance the dissertations?
2. How might focus groups have helped the group members to address the reflexivity of each researcher?
3. What ethical considerations need to be addressed by including recordings of full interviews?
4. What role might the fifth member of the group take up to enhance the data cross-analysis process?
5. How might the group members use each other to develop the rigour of the data analysis?

Using quotes

Pluralistic research writing presents the challenge of including interpretations reached using different methods. It will be important for the reader to see not only what each method's contribution to the study has been but how that contribution was made (Moran-Ellis *et al.*, 2006). Typically, the Findings section will provide the researcher with a variety of narratives and themes. Synthesis of the findings reached by single methods will develop new findings that will also need to be presented. The use of quotes to support and illustrate the themes and stories identified will be useful and bring the write-up to life. It might help to categorise your quotes into 'power' quotes, which compellingly illustrate themes, and 'proof' quotes, which provide additional support for each point made (Pratt, 2009). This approach will enable brief explanations and descriptions of the purpose of the quotes.

Some of the other components of the pluralistic research process can be displayed using quotes also. As illustrated throughout this book, the use of Reflections on Practice from the researchers involved can go a long way to personalising the research report, while also illustrating the reflexivity present in the process.

Quotes about the observations of researchers on the location and timing of the fieldwork for the study can invite the reader to place themselves in the researcher's or participants' shoes. Quotes from the project leader of a pluralistic team can bring yet another perspective to the research process, as can quotes from those involved in the different aspects of the study. Below is a quote from an interviewer who interviewed each researcher after they had completed their analysis, followed by a

Table 8.4 Example table showing four interpretations of the same piece of text

Text/power quote	Grounded theory	Interpretative phenomenological analysis	Foucauldian discourse analysis	Narrative analysis
'But the car crash was not really her or the disruptive effect on our life but more the emotional tidal wave that is suddenly no longer being the most important person in your life'	Describes emotional impact of becoming a mother for the first time Uses many transport metaphors to describe the intensity of the experience 'Car crash' describes emotional impact but is vague, which is later clarified when she tell us 'it is definitely the emotional side that is almost impossible to explain to anyone' (proof quote)	Describes emotional intensity of mother/child relationship Clarifies by saying 'it is definitely the emotional side that is almost impossible to explain to anyone' (proof quote)	Does not refer to this part of the text but identifies anxiety as a key discursive resource that is drawn upon to describe her experiences of new motherhood Much of the narrative describes ways in which she has sought to normalise and depathologise her anxiety through comparison, lack of target and asserting agency Other parts of the narrative describe ways in which anxiety manifests, including fear of separation and assuming sole responsibility for care of the child	Analysis is constructed by identifying multiple positions of the mother. These include rational, emotional and capable. Anxiety is present as result of the tensions between attempting to be a good enough mother and an other Seeks to make objective explanations of her anxiety possibly in order to contribute to the 'scientific' research she is involved in by being interviewed

quote from the researcher she is referring to. Taken together these quotes provide us with insight to each person's experience of this research process.

Interviewer: *I wonder also to what extent the causal language that I found in [the researcher's] analysis has something to do with the philosophy of science that is assumed in the method that he employed.*

Researcher: *Usually when I could not be entirely sure of the participant's meaning, I have used words and phrases such as 'It would seem/appear', 'this implies/*

suggests'. However, after reading back over the finished analysis I can already spot some examples of when I have not done this and used language and phrases drawn from my reading of the theory used to discuss the interpretations.

The inclusion of researcher quotes from pluralistic studies allows the reader to conduct his/her own analysis of researcher impact on the study. The PQR study found that the ways in which a researcher describes their experience of a research process when they are writing about it often differs from how they describe it when they talk about it (see Frost *et al.*, 2010, for further details). Conducting interviews with researchers allows a new insight to their experience, and the inclusion of quotes from the interviews can supplement the way they have written about their reflexivity.

Although frequently employed, the use of participant quotes alone is rarely as rich as the process itself. Their use in a traditional narrative research write-up is unlikely to transport the reader to the complex and multi-layered environment of this research process.

Graphic displays of data

Students are often told to include tables and graphs to break up wordy research projects, and this provides a straightforward way to complement and supplement lists of quotes. Often associated with numbers, tables and diagrams can be included in qualitative research writing by using them to present details of the participants or biographic details of the researchers involved in the project. They can also show the chain of evidence leading to the findings. Relationships between researchers can be presented graphically, and diagrams can also be used to illustrate the research process itself, such as Figure 8.1 used in the analysis of one interview by four researchers, one interviewer and two project coordinators.

With the use of computers, graphic displays of data can be embedded as links within the report. Readers can be invited to upload transcripts and other voluminous information. The proliferation of online journals promotes such innovative use of graphic display of data, and allows for asides and other voices in the research process to be included (see e.g. http://www.mamsie.bbk.ac.uk). CDs of sound and visual information to supplement the narrative presentation can also be included with written research.

Layering

One aim of the pluralistic approach to qualitative research is to allow access to layers of insight to the meanings within the data. This aim can be supported by adopting a layering approach to displaying the data. There are several forms layering can take, but they all share the goal of making it easier for the reader to see what the researchers have seen. In traditional narrative form layering can be the sequential presentation of different voices. These may be taken from different interviews with one person to show the changes in meaning of a participant's story over time, as shown in the Example Box on page 177.

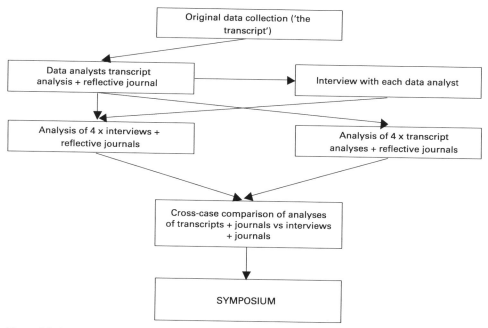

Figure 8.1 A process chart to illustrate a pluralistic study (taken from a PQR study)

Narratives can be constructed from the layering of the individual participant's perspectives on one phenomenon, as illustrated in the example box on page 178.

Layering can be developed into collages of data by displaying many voices on one phenomenon. A collection of comments from a participant can be displayed alongside comments from the researcher's journal and those of other people

Example narrative using participant quotes

There were many examples of the participants describing the differences in everyday life now that they had two children and not one. For some there were challenges of the simultaneous demands for attention that could arise, as this quote from Samantha illustrates:

> *Also I've learnt to deal with the sound of two of them crying at the same time and work out which one is the most urgent and which one is attention seeking. But you know to begin with it's just horrific so er so it's not been it's not been a terribly easy time.*

She describes the difficulties in having to figure out which child's cries are the most urgent and whether they might be seeking attention for a less important issue. Another mother described her way of dealing with this challenge as one in which she doesn't rush to the children when they cry and finds that often the situation resolves itself:

> *Well I mean, I can't possibly make it right for both of them and whatever I do I can't win so I usually just finish doing my make-up by which time one or both have stopped crying!*

involved in the study. Collages can be displayed graphically, as in Figure 8.2 taken from the PQR study.

A simpler collage (as in Figure 8.3) might reflect the different viewpoints of the analyst and another researcher on the team as voiced in a group discussion.

Recent work (Batten, 2009) has taken the concept of layering further to provide a bridge to polyvocal layering. The research example presented on page 180 describes the longitudinal qualitative case study of a health development programme in New Zealand.

Finally, collage lends itself well to presenting multimodal data. Photographs, written accounts and diaries can be presented as one data display using computer 'writing space' (Dicks *et al.*, 2006: 77). This helps to present completed work but also raises potential problems. These are fully discussed in the paper by Dicks *et al.* (2006), but in essence these centre on the integration of different meanings that can be afforded by different media. The authors suggest that different media forms can be fused into new 'multi-semiotic' modes (Dicks *et al.*, 2006) rather than viewed separately. This allows for development of ways of understanding what kinds of meanings are produced in multimodal ethnographic work, and so for new meanings in the data to emerge.

Layering can also be developed into pastiche. Pastiche combines different styles of data or imitates the styles and content of text. Commonly, fragments are displayed

Ok now about the exp the methodology itself um, what I wrote in the introduction so I am just repeating it so there's not much point but what I am trying to do is to get at the experience of people to account for what is going on for them and pause how do they make sense of what is going on for them so pause normally I would do it through interview obviously and this is obviously the first taste you get on this page not its not actually so on the next page is how to analyse and that is obviously the starting point in this project in the transcript. (Analyst in post-analysis interview)

"There are two possibilities for structuring the analysis.
(1) Sometimes a separate section is devoted to the analysis of each theme, followed by another section exploring their implications in relation to the existing literature.
(2) Alternatively, each theme is taken in turn, analysed and discussed in relation to the existing literature (Smith, Jarman & Osborn, 1999)." (Analyst write-up)

We are both equally knowledgeable in different areas of social research and so the usual, inevitable interview dynamics (the interviewer as expert, the interviewee as layperson) were a bit askew and I often felt silly when she was explaining the method to me. I also felt silly asking some of the questions and kept thinking 'Well, you should know that!' I find it really difficult trying to access what is essentially 'common knowledge' in terms of common methodological knowledge. (Interviewer's reflexive journal)

The document contains few personal references. It outlines each stage of the method as she used it with an example taken from the interview text accompanying the application of each stage. It contains a Table of Themes and a narrative account based on the table. (Group coordinator's cross-comparison of data)

Figure 8.2 Collage of interview quotes

and can be linked with a researcher's reflections. Pastiche can be useful to display pluralistic data interpretations when they reveal different voices or contradict each other. Inclusion and overlaying with the researchers' voices presents a powerful way to include pluralistic researcher reflexivity in the research write-up.

Analyst says:	Researcher says:
Er and it was I found it very straightforward the way that I did it because it was only one transcript and it was very light work I found because I've done 6 transcripts (ok ok) before and that was a lot heavier I found you're kind of sat there with masses of paper and not really knowing what to do (right) so this was kind of quite a lot easier and a lot less time consuming	Much easier than what she has done before, lighter workload, less time, very straightforward Reiterates in next narrative in interview 'fine', 'a refresher', 'practise to get back into swing of things'. Did exactly the same thing here as has done before

Figure 8.3 Example of a simpler collage

The study set out to investigate community members' perspectives of community participation in a health development programme (Batten, 2009). The programme aimed to increase members' intake of fruit and vegetables, with particular focus on certain groups within the community. Fruit trees and vegetable plants were handed out, and a community vegetable garden cultivated on public land. The research framework adopted postmodern and interpretative qualitative inquiry paradigms and sought to maintain congruence between the research components. The components included the longitudinal aspect of the study, interviews, participant observation, document collation, researcher conduct as a participant observer, and thematic analysis of the data. Attention was paid by the researcher to exploring health and participation in their broadest sense, and to attending to cultural issues in a participatory manner. The researcher sought to adopt a reflexive researcher position through regular analysis of the research progress.

In writing up the study she describes concerns about the limitations of presenting the work in the standard doctoral format and so devised new ways of presenting visual representations of multiple perspectives of events.

A word of caution about layering

The pluralistic approach seeks to maintain the wholeness of multiple perspectives through its production and multi-layered insight to a phenomenon. The reduction of the data to fragments challenges the achievement of this aim. To avoid fracturing the data and obscuring its meaning or context it is essential to keep in mind the data display as a whole so that the parts that constitute it are grown by their inclusion in it. This means reflexive consideration by the researcher of what to include, as well as careful thought as to how to present it. Stepping back from the pastiche during its creation as well as on its conclusion will enable the researcher to bring yet another perspective to the meanings it portrays.

Problem-based question

How would you display the data gathered for a case study of a mental health community group that conducted semi-structured interviews with the management committee and group members using IPA and narrative analysis?

Case studies

Case studies are useful pluralistic approaches that are most commonly used in health psychology and clinical psychology. They can provide a multi-perspectival examination of how and why patients experience treatments in the ways that they do, and develop detailed insight into contexts. Case studies can be used to investigate one individual, a group of people sharing the same issue, a specific treatment intervention, a specific clinic or one critical incident (Chamberlain, Camic & Yardley, 2004). 'Cases' are examined using pluralistic data sources and analysed using a variety of methods appropriate to the data gathered.

Ways of writing up case studies vary. Some researchers suggest adopting the conventional scientific structure to bring some order to them (Lincoln & Guba, 1985, cited in Robson, 2002: 511). Some may agree with this; others may actively seek to avoid the imposition of such order on 'democratic pluralism' (Lofland, 1971: 109).

Lincoln and Guba's suggestion is for a two-part structure to the write-up (Lincoln & Guba, 1985, cited in Robson, 2002). The first part focuses on the main question under inquiry. It explains the focus of the study and describes the setting in which it took place. This section includes a description of the data and their analysis, and discusses the findings. The second section is reflexive in nature and forms a methodological appendix to the write-up. Here the researcher's biography is presented, including training and experience, 'methodological predispositions' (Robson, 2002: 512) and any known assumptions or biases towards the topic or its setting. This section also includes description of the analysis techniques employed and the eventual study design (reflecting the changes and evolutions of the research process). The second section also addresses the ways in which trustworthiness was enhanced in the study. Decisions are reflected through the continual assessment and reassessment of each of these considerations throughout the life of the study and at different times in it, with particular respect paid to what was intended and what was implemented.

Problem-based question

You are conducting research into the transition of school children from primary to secondary school. You ask them to carry a camera with them to take photographs of anything they think is important. You ask them to also keep a daily diary for a month to provide accounts of their experiences. You will analyse the photographs using visual analysis and the diaries using discourse analysis. How will you display the data in your final-year project?

It was my 'job' to take the lead in writing up the work of the Pluralism in Qualitative Research (PQR) project when we finished its first phase in 2007. In my role as project leader, I had brought the team of seven researchers together and worked closely with them to support the data analyses processes. It seemed natural for me to take the lead in writing up the project. There were many outlets and forms of the early dissemination. I had to write a research report for the funders (Birkbeck, University of London) and a write-up for the national symposia (funded by the Qualitative Methods in Psychology Section of the British Psychological Society). As a team, one of our aims had always been to

Reflection on Practice

publish the work in respected academic journals, so I also prepared drafts of manuscripts.

Writing for each of these outlets had different requirements. There were practical differences between them. The funders of the project had to know certain information about how their money was used. As far as I knew they were not psychologists or qualitative researchers. The funders of the symposia, on the other hand, were expert qualitative researchers in psychology and were going to be using the account for publication in the Section Newsletter (Frost, 2008). Writing for the journals required meeting criteria requirements that ranged from word length to reference style. The editors and reviewers may or may not have been psychologists, but all had qualitative research expertise.

Each of these products promoted feelings of accountability, responsibility and vulnerability. I was concerned to get the 'facts' right. Would the funders question amounts spent? Would team members disagree with what I had written about how we reached findings? I rewrote each piece several times before passing it to team members (sometimes only one or two, sometimes all) for comment and amendment. I vacillated between striving for self-imposed deadlines to send it out to them and frustration at having to read it yet again for a final consideration. I had ambivalent feelings of ownership of the final product. Sometimes I felt protective of what I had created, and angry if others seemed to criticise it. At other times I never wanted to read it again and was happy to pass it on to the next person for review.

The process though continues to be one of exhilaration and excitement. I am still surprised at how lost in writing about this work I can become. I start out with bullet points written in orderly lists at first and then scribbled on scraps of paper, children's homework and notes for the milkman. I rarely refer to them again. Somehow even the process of writing them down cements them in my understanding and they morph on to the paper. I am always pleased when I do a check after the first draft that I have included all that I wanted to find that I have. What I rarely allow for is the extra that I have written, scribbled down and thought of as I have written.

Then it is a matter of how to say what I want to say. Bound by the aim of the piece and its final resting place (journal, newsletter, funder's desk) and my immersion in the study, I struggle along a continuum of the overly personal and the uncomfortably formal. I develop different identities as I write, all struggling for a place as learner, informer, participant, 'employee' and more. Part of writing, for me, is to find the correct place in the process for each of my identities. Sometimes that means leaving someone on the sidelines.

Chapter summary

- Writing up qualitative research is a process of creating a new reality about the topic under study. It draws the researcher as author into the process so that one study of the topic takes place alongside another study of the study.
- The final write-up is a consideration of both of these aspects, reached by examining and presenting your relationship with the topic and its examination. As the writing takes place it develops and informs the research process and its findings. In all qualitative research there is an emphasis on displaying the data in appropriate balance with the theory that informs their interpretation. This challenge is exacerbated in pluralistic qualitative research by drawing on data from several sources and more researchers carrying out its analyses. Details of context and voices of all those involved, participants and researchers, compete for inclusion as the authors struggle to develop a relationship based on openness with the reader.
- Openness means providing the reader with details and descriptions that enable her/him to form their own critique of the study. It means sharing decision-making processes with them so that they have insight into the research process. It means making the data the stars of the piece (Chenail, 1995).
- Innovative ways to do this have been developed for pluralistic studies. These include using words differently, developing poems, stories and performances out of them. Layering, pastiche and case studies are useful ways to present a lot of data while retaining the voices within them. Researchers have moved away from the written word and use computer technology to involve the reader even more in the process of the research.
- The requirements to meet the criteria laid down by universities for students, by editors for journals and by funders' expectations for reports can add an extra layer of necessity and challenge to the author/researcher.

Further reading

Golden Biddle, K. & Locke, K. (2007). *Composing Qualitative Research* (2nd edn). Los Angeles, London, New Delhi, Washington, DC: Sage Publications, Inc.
This is a short and readable book on all aspects of the style and practice of academic qualitative research writing.

Grbich, C. (2007) *Qualitative Data Analysis: An Introduction*. London: Sage Publications Ltd.
This book offers innovative and up-to-the-minute ways of presenting research, several of which are particularly appropriate to pluralistic work.

Robson, C. (2002) *Real World Research* (2nd edn). Oxford: Blackwell Publishing.
A long-standing and highly regarded textbook, full of useful information.

Wolcutt, H.F. (2009) *Writing Up Qualitative Research*. Los Angeles, London, New Delhi, Washington, DC: Sage Publications, Inc.
A useful and contemporary book from a frequently cited writer.

CHAPTER 9

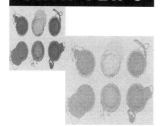

Looking Forward

Nollaig Frost

Introduction

This chapter will review some of the key points about the pluralistic approach to qualitative research that have been discussed in this book. Each chapter has presented techniques and arguments about methods, and all have included examples of how methods can be employed in the pursuit of learning more from data. In Part 1 the focus was on the use of qualitative methods singly. Through discussion and illustration of four methods, the plurality of each was highlighted. This provided a solid introduction to the presentation of a pluralistic approach in Part 2. Working with a pluralistic approach within methods, across methods and in a research team was considered. This chapter will discuss areas for future development of the pluralistic approach and how they might be taken forward so that the pluralistic approach is of use to psychologists. The chapter will consider some of the challenges to working pluralistically and will close with some reflections on the development of the pluralistic approach. It will consider how this approach is taking its place in contemporary qualitative research.

Pluralism in qualitative research

In the Introduction to the book (Chapter 1) we outlined how the establishment of qualitative research in psychology has led to the development of pluralistic approaches across qualitative methods. We discussed pragmatism, bricolage and multiperspectival analysis, and highlighted the development and decline of the 'paradigm wars' (Oakley, 1999). The next four chapters (Chapters 2–5) each centred on the techniques and employment of a method. These chapters each broadly followed the same structure in order to highlight the epistemological and ontological considerations associated with the method under discussion. In doing so most of the chapters demonstrated the plurality that is part of each method. In Chapter 2, Sevasti-Melissa Nolas presented several different forms and applications of grounded theory; in Chapter 4 Amanda Holt presented some discourse analysis approaches, including Foucauldian discourse analysis and discursive analysis; and in Chapter 5

Cigdem Esin discussed a range of narrative analysis approaches, including Labov's structural approach and Riessman's thematic approach. The relative youth of interpretative phenomenological analysis and its use in psychology (IPA was developed in the late 1990s – see, for example, Smith, 1999), means that to date it generally employs one approach. Pnina Shinebourne discusses this approach in Chapter 3. However the ways in which different researchers employ IPA can differ, depending on issues such as how they value the epoche (an essential aspect of the phenomenological philosophy). This plurality is discussed in Chapter 7 (also see King et al., 2006).

In Part 2 the book focused on issues around the employment of a pluralistic qualitative approach. In Chapter 6 Sevasti-Melissa Nolas considered the practical concerns associated with plurality in research. Although some overlap with conducting research alone or through the employment of one method is present, there are also some concerns that are peculiar to the adoption of a pluralistic approach. These include appropriate recruitment and allocation of roles to research team members, and careful consideration of how each method contributes to the ethical considerations of the study. In Chapter 7, Nollaig Frost considered the issues of pluralistic interpretation and analysis. This chapter emphasised the importance of the researchers and reflexive practice, and used existing studies of pluralism to illustrate some ways in which it can be employed. There is debate about the value and place of epistemological incoherence when combining methods (whether qualitatively orientated methods alone or qualitative and quantitatively orientated methods) and this chapter sought to show how some of these arguments are addressed or marginalised in the pursuit of knowing more about a phenomenon.

Finally, in Chapter 8, Nollaig Frost considered ways in which pluralistic studies can be written up and presented. The establishment of computer-based technology allows for a range of innovations to be brought to this. With the creativity inherent in qualitative research and in pluralistic qualitative research there is scope for all manner of ways of seeking to ensure that polyvocality is part of the final presentation. This chapter also emphasised that the writing-up process can be considered part of the research process itself, meaning that the research process can be explicitly or implicitly evolving through to (and sometimes beyond) its final engagement with its audience.

We believe that the pluralistic qualitative approach has much to offer research in psychology. It can allow for a more holistic view of the complexity of human experience to be gained. It can offer routes for the identity of the individual to be constructed in ways that are more salient to the complexity and flexibility of their identity. Rather than constructing identity through aspects derived by one analytic technique alone, the pluralistic approach allows for the possibilities of the individual being a constructivist and phenomenological and positivist and postmodern agent, depending on their context and situation. As with all research the appropriateness of the employment of the pluralistic approach will depend on the research question being asked and to some extent on the reasons behind it being asked. Mason (2006) has pointed out the value of qualitative thinking to topics of lived experience, and calls for its employment in mixed-method research. She also emphasises the necessity to maintain an open approach to the use of either or all approaches, in order to ensure that a range of research questions can continue to be asked as well as addressed in psychology. To some extent this can be seen as a continuation of Oakley's call for an end to the paradigm wars (1999) and Bryman's declaration of 'paradigm peace' (2006). We do not expect all research to be appropriate to a pluralistic qualitative approach, but can see clear strengths in its employment in some areas. These have been presented, discussed and highlighted throughout the book.

In this final chapter we will review when a pluralistic approach to qualitative research might be employed and present some of the challenges to its employment. Two of the most important of these are in the teaching of it to and use by students, and in the evaluation of research conducted pluralistically.

Uses of a pluralistic approach to qualitative research

When is a pluralistic approach useful?

We have discussed how the use of more than one qualitative method of analysis enables a multi-perspective insight to individual experience. This may employ the use of many methods to analyse one or more interview transcripts (e.g. see Chapter 7) or the use of one method in different ways to analyse several data artefacts (interviews or other forms of account). Working pluralistically may involve one researcher employing different methods sequentially or several researchers working simultaneously to analyse the same data. Given the time, analysis skills and other resources required to work pluralistically, it is important to consider the effort made to be worthwhile. Most qualitative methods expect to obtain rich insight into the complexity of phenomena of experiences, so why might you choose to use more than one method?

One reason is that each method brings its own ontology and epistemology to the technique that is employed. For example, one method may seek to understand how individual reality is created through the use of language (e.g. discourse analysis), while another method may seek to gain understanding of how individuals construct their reality through the stories they tell (e.g. narrative analysis). By combining the two methods the researcher can seek some understanding of how the language used in the stories told enable insight to the participants' understanding of the world they live in and the resources available to them from it.

The richness of this pluralistic approach offers insight to both the individual understanding of the external world and the context in which this understanding is formed. Analysis of the language used alone can inform the researcher of a great deal about the linguistic, cultural, political and other resources available to and drawn upon by a participant. By combining this with the way they use the language in storytelling, the researcher can begin to conceive how, and to some extent why, individual identity is formed. Use of language alone is useful to some research questions (e.g. How do women describe themselves as mothers?), while use of language in storytelling is useful to other research questions (e.g. How do women talk about themselves as mothers?).

Pluralistic approaches are advocated in the study of a range of topics, including reports of 'sense of presence' by those who have recently been bereaved (Steffen & Coyle, 2010). Here a lack of epistemological coherence among the analysis techniques can lead to a reduction in the likely imposition of supposed truth or reality on to participants' accounts of their experiences. The use of pluralism in the study of this topic promotes an openness to what is real to both participant and researchers. Mental illness is another area where the adoption of many epistemological claims to understand the complexity of experience is used. Here a pluralistic approach to understanding experience and behaviour can allow for a flexibility in the style and timing of interventions that can be made by professionals and an ongoing reframing of research questions can be achieved. Burck describes the usefulness of the combined use of grounded theory, discourse analysis and narrative analysis in a pilot study that investigated experiences of living life in more than one language (Burck, 2005). She applies this approach to systemic family therapy practice to highlight its usefulness in exploring research questions 'pertinent for the systemic field' (Burck, 2005: 237).

Pluralistic approaches to empirical research can be useful therefore when a flexibility is required in the research outcomes, or when it is particularly important to seek to avoid imposing a single 'truth' on to the data. Qualitative research goes a long way in addressing some of the rigidity of traditional empirical research that sets out to fix variables, answer research questions or test hypotheses, but it can also be susceptible to **methodolatry** (Curt, 1994), leading to the risk of entrenchment in a single-track approach defined by the sort of questions that can be asked and addressed by individual methods. In-depth insight may well be gained but there is also the risk of a restricted application.

Consider, for example, using qualitative research to gain insight to the experiences of those with mental illness, with a view to informing policy. Use of a single method will certainly help to identify themes and perhaps some connection between them. It may draw on a critical realist approach to further understanding of complex phenomena associated with individual experience of mental illness, or adopt a social constructionist approach to consider the creation of the participant's reality in the interaction. However, consider that by the very nature of mental illness, those who suffer it may have a fluctuating approach to their reality over short or long periods of time. The use of more than one method to analyse accounts gathered from participants can allow for differing epistemologies to be brought to the understanding of the data. Not only can the data be viewed in different ways, but the analysis outcomes can be combined, reviewed and addressed using different research questions, by different researchers (perhaps with different agendas) and at different points in time. The ongoing review of the pluralistic analysis of the data allows for the data corpus to be added to by the participants and the researchers as they bring a flexibility that allows for tailor-made policies that are perhaps more appropriate to the needs of those whose reality is uncertain and changing to be developed. Similarly, the lack of consensus about what is real can be applied to anomalous experiences such as the sense of presence of a deceased person sometimes experienced by those who have been bereaved (e.g. Steffen & Coyle, 2010).

Employing a pluralistic approach

In this book we have considered many ways in which a pluralistic approach can be employed. In Chapter 6, Sevasti-Melissa Nolas discussed some of the practical concerns in doing so. The chapter emphasised the need for clear research design, data collection and analysis, and consideration of ethical concerns. The need for clarity about what each researcher or method is bringing to the research was highlighted, and some of the issues of epistemological coherence and incoherence were discussed.

For this level of clarity to happen a great deal of work has to go on behind the scenes. The team members, or the lone researcher, have to take responsibility for practical issues such as those described below.

Recruiting a balanced team of experts in different methods

This requires decisions to be made about which methods are to be employed in the analysis and whether one or more analysts are going to employ them. There are choices to be made about how to distribute the data among the team, and how to supervise and assess the analyses conducted.

Setting (and resetting if necessary) deadlines for each phase of the research

This requires decisions about who will set the deadlines as well as what deadlines to set. Choices about whether to set blanket submission times for all the analyses to be carried out, and whether to conduct them sequentially or simultaneously, will have to be made.

Meeting deadlines

The group coordinator may well have different deadlines to those of the analysts. Decisions have to made about prioritising individuals' time as well as meeting deadlines imposed by university regulation, journal editors or funders.

Deciding how the analysis is going to be collated and presented

This decision is key to the worth of the study. If one person is going to cross-analyse and collate the analyses, there are choices to be made about whether and how they obtain feedback on this. If the decision is made that the presentation of the collated data interpretations is final, there are choices about whether group reviews should take place before reaching it. If the decision is made that more than one person will be responsible for collating the analyses, decisions about who these people should be and how they will work as a subgroup will have to be made.

Evaluating the research

The researcher(s) have to be confident that their research has been conducted rigorously and that its outcomes are trustworthy. All researchers involved in the process should be accountable to their analysis and interpretation, and able to show a transparency and reflexivity in the process that allows the others involved to form their own critique of the work. This applies equally to the collation of the analyses, and the ways in which the trustworthiness of the individual analyses are brought to the final presentation.

As well as the practical considerations there also need to be discussions and decisions about the theoretical implications of pluralistic research. These might be issues of how to combine differing epistemologies in a pluralistic interpretation, what ontological framework to employ and how to regard differences in findings.

Many of these decisions are just as relevant to single-method approaches to research but in a pluralistic approach might require more resources. Limitations of time, access to expertise, and sometimes money, can cause concern among researchers and supervisors about employing a pluralistic approach. The legitimacy and meaning of combining epistemologies that are incoherent can mean that researchers are wary of accepting findings made pluralistically. However, key reasons to carry out pluralistic research might include:

- setting out to investigate a topic with the aim of producing an outcome of interest to a wide audience (for example, investigating social services to reach findings that may be of interest to clients, policymakers and social workers)
- setting out to investigate a topic on which there is no agreed consensus (for example, reports about UFO sightings)
- getting to a point in your single-method analysis where you feel you can go no further but that you have not accessed as much as you can from the data.

Teaching pluralistic approaches to qualitative research

While there are no formalised guidelines for the teaching of qualitative research methods to undergraduate and other psychology students, this approach to research now receives attention to a greater or lesser degree in most psychology degree programmes. Choices about which methods to teach are commonly made on the basis of the qualitative methodological expertise within the department. Given the relative youth of qualitative research in psychology, the most widely taught methods seem to be the four we have covered in this book: discourse analysis, interpretative phenomenological analysis, grounded theory and narrative analysis. A brief informal survey of qualitative colleagues has highlighted that many doctoral students employ the qualitative method that their supervisor is a specialist in. Our research (Frost *et al.*, 2010) has highlighted the role of researcher biography in the employment of qualitative methods – for example, some researchers prefer a less structured approach and attribute this to having creative elements in their personality, while others lean towards a more detailed and structured approach that they attribute to wanting to have clear theoretical and other guidelines.

Given these institutional and personal preferences it would seem that there is a place for combining the expertise, biography and time of teaching staff to raise awareness of the benefits that each method can bring to gaining new meanings from data when used together. Timetables are always tight and qualitative research methods are often squeezed in. There is an argument that teaching a pluralistic approach (which can also include the mixed-method approach) will enable students greater breadth of insight to the role that qualitative research can play in gaining insight to other people's experience.

Evaluating pluralistic research

In common with bricolage and the pragmatic approach, the pluralistic approach can stand accused by some of diluting the intensity of findings reached by the use of one method alone. We would argue that, in contrast, a pluralistic approach can sometimes further enrich insight and provide a more holistic view of a phenomenon than can one method alone. The development of the research questions is key here (as with the use of a pragmatic approach – see Chapter 7) and researchers need to be clear who they are carrying out the research for as well as why it is being conducted. Pharmaceutical companies looking for the test results of a new drug are unlikely to wish for a pluralistic qualitative approach. Therapists wishing to understand more of the ways in which their counselling sessions can be of use to their clients may well see a benefit in viewing their accounts from many perspectives. Given the potential for pluralistic research to be seen as neither one approach nor another, the quest for the highest quality possible should be paramount to all pluralistic qualitative researchers (as it should be to all single-method qualitative researchers!). The good news is that the approach itself has many built-in opportunities to ensure this.

By using qualitative methods pluralistically all stages of the research process are affected by the assumptions they bring. The researcher argues that this can mean that ideas about the research questions, the data collection, the data analysis technique, and so on, may all be divergent in the pluralistic research process. In contrast to this view, however, mixed-method researchers have highlighted the benefits of differing perspectives and outcomes, such as for example the highlighting of gaps, the development of new research questions through contradictory findings and the opportunity for research to evolve in directions not present at the outset of the research (Bryman, 2006; 2007; Dicks *et al.*, 2006; Mason, 2006).

We would argue that this heightened opportunity for additional meanings to be made or further information to be accessed in the data using a pluralistic approach is possible only if every step is taken towards transparency and trustworthiness. As discussed in Chapter 8, such steps might include an open style of writing and the inclusion of as much raw data as possible. This is as you would expect in single-method qualitative research, too. With a pluralistic approach, however, you can extend this to include presentation of individual voices by asking each researcher to write about their analysis. You can conduct interviews with researchers after they have performed the analysis to find out how the way they talk about the findings might differ from the way they write about them. You can ask each researcher to make a statement about their research paradigm, and so on. Of course, having a team of researchers enables opportunities for spontaneous or formalised group discussions to be presented so that questions can be asked and issues raised and discussed. The use of different methods requires a clarity about the status of each in the research process. Moran-Ellis *et al.* have described different forms of triangulation that can be achieved by being clear about how each method is being employed (Moran-Ellis *et al.*, 2006). Dicks *et al.* have described how multi-modal approaches can enable a new semiotic to emerge from the research (Dicks *et al.*, 2006).

If working with many methods there are ways that each will bring to ensure its own trustworthiness. This is usually to do with carrying out a grounded systematic analysis to the full extent of its possibility (or to 'saturation', as in grounded theory) and in being clear about the way in which you are combining epistemologies.

Conclusions and reflections on the pluralistic approach

In this book we have presented and discussed ways of using qualitative methods in the pursuit of further knowledge. We have presented examples and arguments that show the benefits of adopting such an approach, and have also highlighted some of the challenges to its use. We think that pluralistic qualitative research has a place in contemporary psychology research, and can be of particular benefit to applied and interdisciplinary research. It is broadly pragmatic in that it sets out to address research questions as well as it can. It seeks to access as much meaning as possible in the data, while also striving to minimise the imposition of any one epistemology or ontology. This demands a rigorous approach to the research process from its initiation to its conclusion, and yet at the same time there are no prescribed ways of doing this. In common with other approaches to qualitative research its trustworthiness lies in the accountability of method and researchers. Historically, qualitative research in psychology has often taken a back seat to the objective empiricist approaches that have been derived from the early psychology experimentalists. We hope that some of the questions raised, addressed and left unanswered in this book mean that new researchers will use this approach, and highlight ways in which challenges, incoherences and incompatibilities can lead to new ways of exploring and gaining insight to human experience.

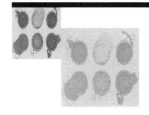

Glossary

C

Communities of interest: refers to people from different groups who come together or are brought together as the result of a shared interest. These communities may be temporary, for instance in the case of a project that is established to solve a particular problem or set up a particular structure or process. They may also be more long term, as in the case of a committee, advisory group or leisure grouping. Such communities are likely to be characterised by 'loose' membership. In other words, people come and go without any penalty or obligation. Communities of interest can be contrasted to communities of identity (shared identity among community members), communities of practice (where members carry out the same or similar role), or communities of place (where members dwell in the same physical location).

D

Dialectics: a form of argumentation where opposition is resolved through synthesis of the two conflicting positions. In psychology it represents an approach to understanding the world and human existence as fundamentally based on relationships between mind–body, self–other and individual–society. In philosophy, dialectics is most readily associated with the thinking of German philosopher Georg Hegel Marx. Social psychologist Ivana Marková has written extensively on dialogics in relation to psychology.

Discourse: the organisation of particular behaviours (or 'practices') and ways of talking about things that together work to construct a particular version of reality (that is, one particular *truth*). Discourses can be so dominant in particular cultures and at particular times that they become unquestioned and are taken for granted, which is problematic for particular groups who are marginalised by them.

E

Epistemology: asks questions about what knowledge is and how it is understood. It raises issues about how individuals regard truth, what they believe is real and how they develop their understanding of the world they inhabit.

Ethnography: an approach used to study the culture of a people. It relies on the researcher spending an extended period of time (called participant observation) with a given set of people. The time spent in the field is written up in fieldnotes and analysed by the researcher. In psychology ethnography has been used to study community responses to mental illness (Jodelet, 1991), death, bereavement and funeral rituals (Bradbury, 1999), family therapy (Gubrium, 1992), and therapeutic communities (Bloor, McKeganey & Fokert, 1988).

F

Foucauldian discourse: the Foucauldian notion of discourse is a concept beyond language, which describes interrelations between disciplines (bodies of knowledge in/ of particular domains, i.e. education, sexuality) and disciplinary practices (forms of social control and social possibility) (McHoul & Grace, 1998). The interaction between individual and society is configured through multiple discourses within specific historical contexts in Foucault's analysis.

H

Hermeneutics: the theory and practice of interpretation. Historically, hermeneutics developed from interpretations of biblical texts, but was subsequently established as a philosophical foundation for a more general theory of interpretation. According to Heidegger (1962), every interpretation is already contextualised in previous experience in a particular context. This is because human existence is fundamentally related to the world: human beings live in a particular historical, social and cultural context. From this perspective, understanding of events or objects in the world is always mediated and constrained by already existing knowledge. The voice that speaks from the text engages the interpreter in a conversation. The process can be envisaged as a 'dialogue between what we bring to the text and what the text brings to us' (Smith *et al.*, 2009: 26).

I

Idiography: a term that describes an in-depth focus on the particular, and commitment to detailed, finely textured analysis of actual life and lived experience.

M

Maieutics: literally means midwifery and 'giving birth to'. In philosophical terms it refers to the pedagogical process of helping students articulate their ideas and knowledge through the use of questions that elicit their views and experiences on a topic. Maieutics is about creating a dialogue between the teacher and the student, where each participant brings a different perspective to bear on a topic. In philosophy the approach is associated with Socrates and the 'Socratic dialogue'. More recently, Brazilian educator Paolo Freire placed maieutics at the centre of his critical pedagogy as a way of creating dialogue within marginalised and oppressed groups, thus enabling the groups to explore, reflect on and eventually take action to change their circumstances.

Methodolatry: a term coined by Curt (1994, cited in Willig & Stainton Rogers, 2008) to highlight researchers' greater interest in the way in which they carry out the research than in the topic that they are researching.

Multilogue: a term borrowed from computing to refer to conversations involving more than three people. It is used here to extend the notion of dialogue embedded in dialectics, by retaining the idea of a dialogue but extending it to include more than two people.

O

Ontology: the beliefs and assumptions that individuals hold about what exists in the world that they inhabit. It raises issues about what people believe is real and what they believe exists in the world.

P

Phenomenology: both a philosophical approach and a range of research methods concerned with how things appear to us in our experience and are perceived in our consciousness. The phenomenological method involves setting aside preconceived ideas and theories and letting ourselves experience the world. Phenomenological research in psychology draws on the philosophical approach in its 'focus on people's perceptions of the world in which they live and what it means to them' (Langdridge, 2007: 4). Although a number of diverse approaches have been developed, the focus on subjective experience of the world has remained a fundamental principle of all phenomenologically informed research methods, including IPA. (For a discussion of various phenomenological approaches in psychology, see Langdridge, 2007.)

Polyvocality: a term coined by Denzin and Lincoln (2000) to indicate the inclusion of many voices in the representation of the research. Researchers who strive to achieve polyvocality in their work will be aware of their own voices and the way they can change during the research process and be portrayed in writing up the study. They will wish to include the voices of the participants and seek to prioritise them over those of the researchers.

Positioning: an analytical tool that is widely used in discursive and narrative analysis in order to understand how individuals draw on specific discursive resources and relations while talking about their lives. It is part of the theoretical approach which argues that individuals locate themselves in specific 'subject positions' while having conversations.

These subject positions are informed by the social, cultural, linguistic, political and interpersonal resources available to individuals (Davies & Harre, 1990; Harre & van Langenhove, 1991). Positioning, as a methodological tool, helps researchers to explore how the subject position(s) chosen by individuals shape the ways in which they construct narratives in their interactions.

Purposive sampling: refers to a method of selecting participants because they have particular features or characteristics that will enable detailed exploration of the phenomena being studied.

R

Reflexivity: an awareness of the ways in which the researcher has devised the research question, elicited and gathered the data, analysed it and then presented the research to a wider audience. An important consideration in the understanding of how interpretations of the data were reached.

Reliability: a term used in quantitative research to indicate the consistency of measurement. The term is also applied to some qualitative research, particularly that which adopts a realist epistemology. In qualitative research, the evaluative criteria that are applied are more commonly transparency and trustworthiness.

Rhetorical devices: communication strategies (either verbal or non-verbal) that are used to achieve particular objectives (e.g. to justify one's actions or to claim the facticity of one's account).

Rigour: an evaluative term encapsulated within the trustworthiness of the research.

S

Snowballing: refers to a method of selecting a sample in which potential participants are asked whether they know of other people with relevant characteristics and experiences who might be approached. Snowball sampling is often used to find and recruit 'hidden

populations', groups not easily accessible to researchers through other sampling strategies.

Subject positions: the spaces that enable particular ways of being a subject, which are either 'opened up' or 'closed down' by the production of particular discourses (including their associated *discursive practices*). Some subject positions are particularly privileged, in that they enable access to resources and capital – others are not.

Subjectivity: the personal perspectives brought by individuals to the ways in which they view their world. This is as applicable to researchers' experience of the research process as it is to the data elicited and gathered from the research participants.

Symbolic interactionism: a theoretical and methodological approach to the study of social life and human relationships, originating from research emerging out of the University of Chicago at the turn of the twentieth century. It holds that reality is constructed through interactions between people and that people make sense of this reality through shared symbols and communal life. The symbolic interactionist tradition uses ethnographic methods for data collection.

T

Transparency: an important contribution to the trustworthiness of a research study. It seeks to ensure that everything that the researcher does is made clear to the reader. Steps taken, decisions made and all changes in the research process should be described in detail so that the reader can form her/his own critique of the appropriateness and rigour of the research process. This level of transparency is key to the formation of a judgement about the outcomes and implications of the study.

V

Validity: the extent to which research measures or reflects what it claims to. Most meaningfully used in research with a realist epistemology.

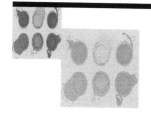

References

Abell, J., Stokoe, E. & Billig, M. (2000) Narrative and the discursive (re)production of events, in M. Andrews, S.D. Sclater, C. Squire & A. Treacher (eds) *Uses of Narrative*. New Jersey: Transition.

Alvesson, M. (2002) *Postmodernism and Social Research*. Buckingham: Open University Press.

Andrews, M. (2007) *Shaping History: Narratives of Political Change*. Cambridge: Cambridge University Press.

Andrews, M., Sclater, S. D., Rustin, M., Squire, C. & Treacher, A. (2000) *Introduction*, in M. Andrews, S.D. Sclater, C. Squire & A. Treacher (eds) *Lines of Narrative*. London: Routledge.

Andrews, M., Sclater, S. D., Squire, C. & Tamboukou, M. (2004) Narrative research, in C. Seale, G. Gobo, J.F. Gubrium & D. Silverman (eds) *Qualitative Research Practice*. London: Sage.

Andrews, M., Squire, C. & Tamboukou, M. (eds) (2008) *Doing Narrative Research*. London: Sage.

Angrosino, M.V. & Mays de Pérez, K.A. (2003) Rethinking observation: from method to context, in N.K. Denzin & Y.S. Lincoln (eds) *Collecting and Interpreting Qualitative Materials* (2nd edn). Thousand Oaks, CA: Sage.

Arribas-Ayllon, M. & Walkerdine, V. (2007) Foucauldian discourse analysis, in C. Willig & W. Stainton-Rogers (eds) *Handbook of Qualitative Research in Psychology* (pp. 91–108). London: Sage.

Arrol, M. & Senior, V. (2008) Individuals' experience of chronic fatigue syndrome/myalgic encephalomyelitis: an interpretative phenomenological analysis. *Psychology & Health*, 23(4), 443–458.

Ashworth, P. (2003) The origins of qualitative psychology, in J.A. Smith (ed.) *Qualitative Psychology: A Practical Guide to Research Methods*. London: Sage.

Atkinson, P., Coffey, A. & Delamont, S. (2003) *Key Themes in Qualitative Research*. Oxford: AltaMira Press.

Avdi, E. (2008) Analysing talk in the talking cure: conversation, discourse and narrative analysis of psychoanalytic psychotherapy. *European Psychotherapy*, 8(1), 69–87.

Banks, M. (2007) *Using Visual Data in Qualitative Research*. London: Sage.

Barbour, R.S. (1998) Mixing qualitative methods: quality assurance of qualitative quagmire? *Qualitative Health Research*, 8(3), 352–361.

Barker, C. & Pistrang, N. (2005) Quality criteria under methodological pluralism: implications for conducting and evaluating research. *American Journal of Community Psychology*, 35(3/4), 201–211.

Bartels, R. & Parsons, C. (2009) The social construction of a serial killer. *Feminism and Psychology*, 19(2), 267–280.

Batten, L.S. (2009) 'Lady is this civilisation?': a case study of community participation in a health programme in Aotearoa New Zealand. Unpublished Doctor of Philosophy in Development Studies, Palmerston North, New Zealand, Massey University.

Bauer, M. & Gaskell, G. (2000) *Qualitative Researching with Text, Image and Sound: A Practical Handbook for Social Research.* London: Sage.

Becker, B. (1999) Narratives of pain in later life and conventions of storytelling. *Journal of Aging Studies*, 13(1), 73–87.

Behar, R. (1993) *Translated Woman: Crossing the Border with Esperanza's Story.* Boston, MA: Beacon.

Bell, S. (2009) *DES Daughters: Embodied Knowledge and the Transformation of Women's Health Politics.* Philadelphia, PA: Temple University Press.

Benzies, K. & Allen, M. (2001) Symbolic interactionism as a theoretical perspective for multiple method research. *Journal of Advanced Nursing*, 33(4), 541–547.

Bloom, L.R. (1998) *Under the Sign of Hope: Feminist Methodology and Narrative Interpretation.* Albany, NY: State University of New York Press.

Bloor, M., McKeganey, N. & Fonkert, D. (1988) *One Foot in Eden: A Sociological Study of the Range of Therapeutic Community Practice.* London: Routledge.

Blumer, H. (1969) *Symbolic Interactionism: Perspective and Method.* Englewood Cliffs, NJ: Prentice Hall.

Bostock, J. & Freeman, J. (2003) 'No limits': doing participatory action research with young people in Northumberland. *Journal of Community & Applied Social Psychology*, 13(6), 464–474.

Bowker, G.C. & Star, S.L. (1999) *Sorting Things Out: Classification and its Consequences.* Cambridge, MA: The MIT Press.

Bradbury, M. (1999) *Representations of Death: A Social Psychological Perspective.* London: Routledge.

Branney, P. (2007) Subjectivity, not personality: combining discourse analysis and psychoanalysis. *Social and Personality Psychology Compass*, 2(2), 574–590.

Brocki, J.M. & Wearden, A.J. (2006) A critical evaluation of the use of interpretative phenomenological analysis (IPA) in health psychology. *Psychology & Health*, 21(1), 87–108.

Bronfenbrenner, U. (1979) *The Ecology of Human Development.* Cambridge, MA: Harvard University Press.

Bryant, A. & Charmaz, K. (eds) (2007) *The Sage Handbook of Grounded Theory*. London: Sage.

Bryant, A. & Charmaz, K. (2007) Introduction: grounded theory research: methods and practices, in A. Bryant & K. Charmaz (eds) *The Sage Handbook of Grounded Theory*. London: Sage.

Bryman, A. (2006) Integrating quantitative and qualitative research: how is it done? *Qualitative Research*, 6(1), 97–113.

Bryman, A. (2007) Barriers to integrating quantitative and qualitative research. *Journal of Mixed Methods Research*, 1(1), 8–22.

Burck, C. (2004) Living in several languages: implications for therapy. *Journal of Family Therapy*, 26, 314–339.

Burck, C. (2005) Comparing qualitative research methodologies for systemic research: the use of grounded theory, discourse analysis and narrative analysis. *Journal of Family Therapy*, 27, 237–262.

Burman, E. & Parker, I. (1993) *Discourse Analytic Research: Repertoires and Readings of Texts in Action*. London: Routledge.

Burr, V. (1995) *An Introduction to Social Constructionism*. London: Routledge.

Burr, V. (2003) *Social Constructionism*. London: Routledge.

Caulley, D.N. (2008) Making qualitative research reports less boring: the techniques of writing creative nonfiction. *Qualitative Inquiry*, 14(3), 424–449.

Chamberlain, K., Camic, P.M. & Yardley, L. (2004) Qualitative analysis of experience: grounded theory and case studies, in D. Marks & L. Yardley (eds) *Research Methods for Clinical and Health Psychology*. London: Sage.

Chandler, D. (2002) *Semiotics: The Basics*. London: Routledge.

Charmaz, K. (1991) *Good Days, Bad Days: The Self in Chronic Illness and Time*. New Brunswick, NJ: Rutgers University Press.

Charmaz, K. (2001) Qualitative interviewing and grounded theory analysis, in J.F. Gubrium & J.A. Holstein (eds) *Handbook of Interview Research: Context and Method*. London: Sage.

Charmaz, K. (2006) *Constructing Grounded Theory: A Practical Guide Through Qualitative Analysis*. London: Sage.

Charmaz, K. & Henwood, R. (2008) Grounded theory, in C. Willig & W. Stainton-Rogers (eds) *The Sage Handbook of Qualitative Research in Psychology* (pp. 240–259). London: Sage Publications.

Chenail, R.J. (1995) Presenting qualitative data, *The Qualitative Report*, 2(3), available online at: http://www.nova.edu/ssss/QR/QR2-3/presenting.html.

Clarke, A.E. (2005) *Situational Analysis: Grounded Theory After the Postmodern Turn*. London: Sage.

Coates, L. & Wade, A. (2004) 'Telling it like it isn't': obscuring perpetrator responsibility for violent crime. *Discourse and Society*, 15(5), 499–526.

Cohn, S. (1999) Taking time to smell the roses: accounts of people with chronic fatigue syndrome and their struggle for legitimization. *Anthropology and Medicine*, 6, 195–215.

Cole, M. (1996) *Cultural Psychology: A Once and Future Discipline*. Cambridge, MA: Belknap Press of Harvard University Press.

Colyar, J. (2009) Becoming writing, becoming writers. *Qualitative Inquiry*, 15(2), 421–436.

Connelly, F.M. & Clandinin, D.J. (1999) *Shaping Professional Identity: Stories of Educational Practice*. New York: Teacher's College Press.

Cortazzi, M. (1990) *Primary Teaching: How it is a Narrative Account*. London: David Fulton.

Covan, E.K. (2007) The discovery of grounded theory in practice: the legacy of multiple mentors, in A. Bryant & K. Charmaz (eds) *The Sage Handbook of Grounded Theory*. London: Sage.

Coyle, A. (2007) Discourse analysis, in E. Lyons & A. Coyle (eds) *Analysing Qualitative Data in Psychology* (pp. 98–116). London: Sage.

Coyle, A. (2010) Qualitative research and anomalous experience: a call for interpretative pluralism [Commentary]. *Qualitative Research in Psychology*, 7, 79–83.

Cronon, W. (1992) A place for stories: nature, history and narrative. *Journal of American History*, 78, 1347–1376.

Crossley, M. (2007) Narrative analysis, in E. Lyons & A. Coyle (eds) *Analysing Qualitative Data in Psychology* (pp. 131–144). London: Sage.

Curt, B. (1994) *Textuality and Tectonics: Troubling Social and Psychological Science*. Buckingham: Open University Press.

Davies, B. & Harre, R. (1990) Positioning: the discursive construction of selves. *Journal for the Theory of Social Behaviour*, 20, 43–63.

Deleuze, G. & Guattari, F. (1987) *A Thousand Plateaus*. London: Continuum.

Denzin, N. (2001) The reflexive interview and a performative social science. *Qualitative Research*, 1(1), 23–46.

Denzin, N.K. & Lincoln, Y.S. (eds). (2000) *Handbook of Qualitative Research* (2nd edn). Thousand Oaks, CA: Sage.

Dick, B. (2007) What can grounded theorists and action researchers learn from each other?, in A. Bryant & K. Charmaz (eds) *The Sage Handbook of Grounded Theory*. London: Sage.

Dicks, B., Soyinka, B. & Coffey, A. (2006) Multimodal ethnography. *Qualitative Research*, 6(1), 77–96.

Dilks, S., Tasker, F. & Wren, B. (2010) Managing the impact of psychosis: a grounded theory exploration of recovery processes in psychosis. *British Journal of Clinical Psychology,* 49, 87–107.

Dunne, M., Pryer, J. & Yates, P. (2005) *Becoming a Researcher.* Maidenhead: Open University Press.

Eatough, V. & Smith, J.A. (2006) 'I feel like a scrambled egg in my head': an idiographic case study of meaning making and anger using interpretative phenomenological analysis. *Psychology and Psychotherapy: Theory, Research and Practice,* 79(1), 115–135.

Eatough, V. & Smith, J.A. (2008) Interpretative phenomenological analysis, in C. Willig & W. Stainton-Rogers (eds) *The Sage Handbook of Qualitative Research in Psychology* (pp. 179–194). London: Sage Publications.

Edwards, D. (1997) *Discourse and Cognition.* London: Sage.

Elliott, J. (2005) *Using Narrative in Social Research: Qualitative and Quantitative Approaches.* London: Sage.

Elliott, R., Fischer, C.T. & Rennie, D.L. (1999) Evolving guidelines for publication of qualitative research studies in psychology and related fields. *British Journal of Clinical Psychology,* 38, 215–299.

Elliott, R., Fischer, C.T. & Rennie, D.L. (2000) Also against methodolatry: a reply to Reicher. *British Journal of Clinical Psychology,* 39, 7–10.

Emerson, P. & Frosh, S. (2004) *Critical Narrative Analysis in Psychology.* Basingstoke: Palgrave Macmillan.

Emerson, R.M., Fretz, R.I. & Shaw, L.L. (1995) *Writing Ethnographic Fieldnotes.* Chicago, IL: University of Chicago Press.

Fechner, G.T. (1966) *Elements of Psychophysics* (vol. 1) (eds: Boring, E.G. & Howes, D.H., trans: Adler, H.E.). New York: Holt, Rinehart & Winston (original work published 1860).

Finlay, L. (2003) The reflexive journey: mapping multiple routes, in L. Finlay & B. Gough (eds) *Reflexivity: A Practical Guide for Researchers in Health and Social Sciences* (pp. 3–20). London: Blackwell.

Finlay, L. & Gough, B. (eds) (2003) *Reflexivity: A Practical Guide for Researchers in Health and Social Sciences.* Oxford: Blackwell Publishing

Flowers, P., Knussen, C. & Duncan, B. (2001) Re-appraising HIV testing among Scottish gay men: the impact of new HIV treatments. *Journal of Health Psychology,* 6(6), 665–678.

Foucault, M. (1975/91) *Discipline and Punish: The Birth of the Prison.* London: Penguin.

Foucault, M. (1976/90) *The History of Sexuality. Volume 1: An Introduction.* London: Penguin.

Foucault, M. (1991) On governmentality, in G. Burchell, C. Gordon & P. Miller (eds) *'The Foucault Effect': Studies in Governmentality* (pp. 87–104). London: Harvester Wheatsheaf.

Freire, P. (1970) *Pedagogy of the Oppressed.* London: Penguin.

Freire, P. (1994) *Pedagogy of Hope: Reliving Pedagogy of the Oppressed.* New York: Continuum.

Frosh, S. & Saville Young, L. (2008) Psychoanalytic approaches to qualitative psychology, in C. Willig & W. Stainton-Rogers (eds) *The Sage Handbook of Qualitative Research in Psychology.* London: Sage Publications.

Frost, N.A. (2006) Taking the other out of mother: the transition to second-time motherhood. Unpublished thesis, Birkbeck, University of London.

Frost, N.A. (2007) The transition to second-time motherhood: an exploration of maternal narratives using a flexible narrative analysis approach, available online at: http://www.uel.ac.uk/cnr/forthcom.htm (accessed 22 July 2010).

Frost, N.A. (2008) Pluralism in qualitative research: some emerging findings. *QMiP Newsletter,* 6, 16–21.

Frost, N.A. (2009a) Pluralism in qualitative research: a report of the work of the PQR Project. *Social Psychological Review,* 11(1), 32–37.

Frost, N.A. (2009b) 'Do you know what I mean?': the use of a pluralistic narrative analysis approach in the interpretation of an interview. *Qualitative Research,* 9(1), 9–29.

Frost, N.A. & Bowen, C. (forthcoming) *Qualitative Research in Psychology: Special issue on Pluralism in Qualitative Research in Psychology.*

Frost, N.A. & Nolas, S.M. (eds) (2011) *Qualitative Research in Psychology: Special issue on Pluralism in Qualitative Research in Psychology.*

Frost, N.A., Nolas, S.-M., Brooks-Gordon, B., Esin, C., Holt, A., Shinebourne, P. & Mehdizadeh, L. (2010) Pluralism in qualitative research: the impact of different researchers and qualitative approaches on the analysis of qualitative data. *Qualitative Research,* 10(4), 399–419.

Frost, N.A., Eatough, V., Shaw, R.L., Weille, K.-L., Tzemou, E. & Baraitser, L. (in press) Pleasure, pain and procrastination: reflections on the experience of doing memory-work research. *Qualitative Research in Psychology.*

Frost, N.A., Holt, A., Shinebourne. P., Esin, C., Nolas, S.-M., Brooks-Gordon, B. & Mehdizadeh, L. (2011) Collective findings, individual interpretations: an illustration of a pluralistic approach to qualitative data analysis. *Qualitative Research in Psychology,* 8(1), 93–113.

Galtung, J. (1977) *Methodology and Ideology: Theory and Methods of Social Research: Essays in Methodology* (Vol. 1). Copenhagen: Christian Ejlers.

Gaskell, G. (2000) Individual and group interviewing, in M. Bauer & G. Gaskell (eds) *Qualitative Researching with Text, Image and Sound: A Practical Handbook for Social Research* (pp. 38–56). London: Sage.

Gee, J.P. (1991) A linguistic approach to narrative. *Journal of Narrative and Life History*, 1(1), 15–39.

Geertz, C. (1973) *The Interpretation of Cultures.* New York: Basic Books.

Georgaca, E. & Avdi, E. (2009) Evaluating the talking cure: the contribution of narrative, discourse, and conversation analysis to psychotherapy assessment. *Qualitative Research in Psychology*, 6(3), 233–247.

Giles, D. (2006) Constructing identities in cyberspace: the case of eating disorders. *British Journal of Social Psychology*, 45, 463–477.

Gilgun, J.F. (2005) 'Grab' and good science: writing up the results of qualitative research. *Qualitative Health Research*, 15(2), 256–262.

Gill, R. (2000) Discourse analysis, in M.W. Bauer & G.D. Gaskell (eds) *Qualitative Researching with Text, Image and Sound: A Practical Handbook* (pp. 172–190). London: Sage.

Gill, R. (2009) Mediated intimacy and postfeminism: a discourse analytic examination of sex and relationships advice in a women's magazine. *Discourse and Communication*, 3(4), 345–369.

Ginzburg, J. & Fernández, R. (2005) Action at a distance: the difference between dialogue and multilogue. Paper presented at the 9th Workshop on the Semantics and Pragmatics of Dialogue (Dialor' 05), Nancy, France.

Giorgi, A. (1995) Phenomenological psychology, in J.A. Smith, R. Harre & L. van Langenhove (eds) *Rethinking Psychology* (pp. 24–42). London: Sage.

Glaser, B.G. (1978) *Theoretical Sensitivity: Advances in the Methodology of Grounded Theory.* Mill Valley, CA: Sociology Press.

Glaser, B.G. (2007) Doing formal theory, in A. Bryant & K. Charmaz (eds) *The Sage Handbook of Grounded Theory.* London: Sage.

Glaser, B.G. & Strauss, A.L. (1965) *Awareness of Dying.* New Brunswick, NJ: Aldine Transaction.

Glaser, B.G. & Strauss, A.L. (1967) *The Discovery of Grounded Theory: Strategies for Qualitative Research.* Hawthorne, NY: Aldine de Gruyter.

Golden-Biddle, K. & Locke, K. (2007) *Composing Qualitative Research.* Thousand Oaks, CA: Sage Publications.

Gough, B. (2003a) Deconstructing reflexivity, in L. Finlay & B. Gough (eds) *Reflexivity: A Practical Guide for Researchers in Health and Social Sciences* (pp. 21–36). London: Blackwell.

Gough, B. (2003b) Shifting researcher positions during a group interview study: a reflexive analysis and re-view, in L. Finlay & B. Gough (eds) *Reflexivity: A Practical Guide for Researchers in Health and Social Sciences* (pp. 146–160). London: Blackwell.

Grbich, C. (2007) *Qualitative Data Analysis: An Introduction.* London: Sage Publications Ltd.

Greene, J.C., Caracelli, V.J. & Graham, W.F. (1989) Toward a conceptual framework for mixed-method evaluation designs. *Educational Policy and Evaluation Analysis*, 11, 255–274.

Gubrium, J.F. (1992) *Out of Control: Family Therapy and Domestic Disorder.* London: Sage.

Gubrium, J.F. & Holstein, J.A. (1997) *The New Language of Qualitative Method.* Oxford: Oxford University Press.

Halling, L. & Leifer, M. (1991) The theory and practice of dialogal research. *Journal of Phenomenological Psychology*, 22, 1–15. Cited in King, N., Finlay, L., Ashworth, P., Smith, J.A., Langdridge, D. & Butt, T. (2008): 'Can't really trust that so what can I trust?': a polyvocal qualitative analysis of the psychology of mistrust. *Qualitative Research in Psychology*, 5(2), 80–102.

Halling, S., Kunz, G. & Rowe, J.O. (1994) The contributions of dialogal psychology to phenomenological research. *Journal of Humanistic Psychology*, 34(1), 109–131.

Hammersley, M. (2008) On the failings of qualitative inquiry, in M. Hammersley *Questioning Qualitative Inquiry: Critical Essays*. London: Sage Publications.

Hammersley, M. & Atkinson, P. (1995) *Ethnography: Principles in Practice* (2nd edn). London/New York: Routledge.

Harper, D. (2006) Discourse analysis, in M. Slade & S. Priebe (eds) *Choosing Methods in Mental Health Research* (pp. 47–67). London: Routledge.

Harper, D., O'Connor, J., Self, P. & Stevens, P. (2008) Learning to use discourse analysis on a professional psychology training programme: accounts of supervisees and a supervisor. *Qualitative Research in Psychology*, 5(3), 192–213.

Harre, R. & van Langenhove, L. (1991) Varieties of positioning. *Journal for the Theory of Social Behaviour*, 21(4), 393–407.

Heidegger, M. (1962) *Being and Time*. Oxford: Blackwell.

Henwood, K. (1996) Qualitative inquiry: perspectives, methods and psychology, in J. Richardson (ed.) *Handbook of Research Methods for Psychology and the Social Sciences* (pp. 25–40). Leicester: BPS Books.

Henwood, K.L. & Pidgeon, N.F. (1992) Qualitative research and psychological theorising. *British Journal of Psychology*, 83, 97–111.

Hepburn, A. (2005) 'You're not takin' me seriously': ethics and asymmetry in calls to a child protection helpline. *Journal of Constructivist Psychology*, 18(3), 253–274.

Hepworth, J. (2006) The emergence of critical health psychology: can it contribute to promoting public health? *Journal of Health Psychology*, 11(3), 331–341.

Hewitt, J.P. & Stokes, R. (1975) Disclaimers. *American Sociological Review*, 40, 1–11.

Hiles, D.R. & Cermák, I. (2008) 'Narrative psychology', in C. Willig & W. Stainton-Rogers (eds) *Handbook of Qualitative Research in Psychology*. London: Sage Publications.

Hinchman, L.P. & Hinchman, S.K. (1997) Introduction, in L.P. Hinchman & S.K. Hinchman (eds) *Memory, Identity, Community: The Idea of Narrative in the Human Sciences*. New York: Sate University of New York.

Hollway, W. (1989) *Subjectivity and Method in Psychology: Gender, Meaning and Science*. London: Sage.

Holstein, J. & Gubrium, J. (2000) *The Self We Live By: Narrative Identity in a Postmodern World*. New York: Oxford University Press.

Holt, A. (2009) (En)gendering responsibilities: experiences of parenting a 'young offender'. *Howard Journal of Criminal Justice*, 48(4), 344–356.

Holt, A. (2010a) Disciplining 'problem parents' in the youth court: between regulation and resistance. *Social Policy and Society*, 10(1), 89–99.

Holt, A. (2010b) Managing 'spoiled identities': parents' experiences of compulsory parenting support programmes. *Children and Society*. Advance access published 6 August 2009, DOI: 10.1111/j.1099-0860.2009.00255.x.

Holt, A. (2010c) Using the telephone for narrative interviewing: a research note. *Qualitative Research*, 10(1), 113–121.

Holton, J.A. (2007) The coding process and its challenges, in A. Bryant & K. Charmaz (eds) *The Sage Handbook of Grounded Theory*. London: Sage.

Hook, D. (ed.) (2004) *Critical Psychology*. Cape Town: Cape Town University Press.

Hosein, I. (2002) A research note on capturing technology: towards moments of interest, in E.H. Wynn, E.A. Whitley, M. Myers & J.I. DeGross (eds) *Global and Organizational Discourse about Information Technology* (pp. 133–154). Norwell, MA: Kluwer Press.

Howard, G.S. (1983) Towards methodological pluralism. *Journal of Counseling Psychology*, 30(1), 19–21.

Humphreys, P., Nolas, S.-M. & Olmos, G. (2006) *Positive Futures Young People's Views Project Final Report: Integrated Findings on Young People's Views*. London: London Multimedia Lab, London School of Economics.

Husserl, E. (1977) *Phenomenological Psychology*. The Hague: Martinus Nijhoff (original work published 1925). Cited in King, N., Finlay, L., Ashworth, P., Smith, J.A., Langdridge, D. & Butt, T. (2008) 'Can't really trust that so what can I trust?': a polyvocal qualitative analysis of the psychology of mistrust. *Qualitative Research in Psychology*, 5(2), 80–102.

Hutchby, I. & Wooffitt, R. (1998) *Conversation Analysis*. Cambridge: Polity Press.

Jahoda, M., Lazarsfeld, P.F. & Zeisel, H. (1972) *Marienthal: The Sociography of an Unemployed Community*. London: Tavistock Publications.

Janesick, V. (2000) The choreography of qualitative research design: minuets, improvisations and crystallisation, in N. Denzin & Y. Lincoln (eds) *Handbook of Qualitative Research* (2nd edn). Thousand Oaks, CA: Sage.

Jarman, M., Walsh, S. & DeLacey, G. (2005) Keeping safe, keeping connected: a qualitative study of HIV-positive women's experiences of partner relationships. *Psychology and Health*, 20, 533–553.

Jefferson, G. (2004) Glossary of transcription symbols with an introduction, in G.H. Lerner (ed.) *Conversation Analysis: Studies from the First Generation*. Amsterdam: John Benjamins, available online at: http://www.liso.ucsb.edu/Jefferson/Transcript.pdf (accessed 24 June 2010).

Jodelet, D. (1991) *Madness and Social Representations*. Hemel Hampstead: Harvester-Wheatsheaf.

Johnson, S., Burrows, A. & Williamson, I. (2004) 'Does my bump look big in this?' The meaning of bodily changes for first-time mothers-to-be. *Journal of Health Psychology*, 9(3), 361–374.

Josselson, R. (2004) The hermeneutics of faith and the hermeneutics of suspicion. *Narrative Inquiry*, 14(1), 1–28.

Jovchelovitch, S. (2007) *Knowledge in Context: Representations, Community and Culture*. Hove, East Sussex: Routledge.

Jovchelovitch, S. & Bauer, M. (2000) Narrative interviewing, in M. Bauer & G. Gaskell (eds) *Qualitative Researching with Text, Image and Sound*. London: Sage.

Katisaficas, D., Futch, V.A., Fine, M. & Sirin, S.R. (2011) Everyday hyphens: exploring youth identities with methodological and analytical pluralism. *Qualitative Research in Psychology*, 8(2), 120–139.

Kellner, D. (1995) *Media Culture: Cultural Studies, Identity and Politics Between the Modern and the Postmodern*. London: Routledge.

Kincheloe, J. (2001) Describing the bricolage: conceptualizing a new rigor in qualitative research. *Qualitative Inquiry*, 7(6), 679–692.

Kincheloe, J. (2005) On to the next level: continuing the conceptualization of the bricolage. *Qualitative Inquiry*, 11(3), 323–350.

King, N., Finlay, L., Ashworth, P., Smith, J.A., Langdridge, D. & Butt, T. (2008) 'Can't really trust that so what can I trust?': a polyvocal qualitative analysis of the psychology of mistrust. *Qualitative Research in Psychology*, 5(2), 80–102.

Kitzinger, C. (1987) *The Social Construction of Lesbianism*. London: Sage.

Knapp, S.J. & VandeCreek, L.D. (2006) *Practical Ethics for Psychologists*. Washington, DC: American Psychological Association.

Kvale, S. (1996) *Interviews: An Introduction to Qualitative Research Interviewing*. London: Sage.

Labov, W. (1972) *Language in the Inner City: Studies in the Black English Vernacular*. Oxford: Blackwell.

Labov, W. & Waletzky, J. (1967/1997) Narrative analysis: oral versions of personal experience. Reprinted in *Journal of Narrative and Life History*, 7, 3–39.

Langdridge, D. (2004) *Introduction to Research Methods and Data Analysis in Psychology*. Harlow: Pearson Education.

Langdridge, D. (2007) *Phenomenological Psychology: Theory, Research and Method*. Harlow: Pearson.

Langellier, K.M. & Peterson, E.E. (2004) *Storytelling in Daily Life: Performing Narrative*. Philadelphia, PA: Temple University Press.

Larkin, M., Watts, S. & Clifton, E. (2006) Giving voice and making sense in interpretative phenomenological analysis. *Qualitative Research in Psychology*, 3, 102–120.

Leeming, D. & Boyle, M. (2004) Shame as a social phenomenon: a critical analysis of the concept of dispositional shame. *Psychology and Psychotherapy: Theory, Research & Practice*, 77(3), 375–396.

Lempert, L.B. (2007) Asking questions of the data: memo writing in the grounded theory tradition, in A. Bryant & K. Charmaz (eds) *The Sage Handbook of Grounded Theory*. London: Sage.

Lévi-Strauss, C. (1962) *The Savage Mind*. London: Weidenfeld & Nicolson.

Lewin, K. (1951) *Field Theory in Social Science: Selected Theoretical Papers*. New York: Harper & Brothers.

Lieblich, A., Tuval-Mashiach, R. & Zilber, T. (1998) *Narrative Research: Reading, Analysis and Interpretation*. London: Sage Publications.

Lincoln, Y.S. & Guba, E.G. (1985) *Naturalistic Inquiry*. Newbury Park, CA: Sage.

Lofland, J. (1971) *Analyzing Social Settings: A Guide to Qualitative Observation and Analysis (Sociology)*. Belmont, CA: Wadsworth.

Lofland, J. & Lofland, L. (1995) *Analyzing Social Settings: A Guide to Qualitative Observation and Analysis (Sociology)* (3rd edn). Belmont, CA: Wadsworth.

Lyons, E. (2007) Analysing qualitative data: comparative reflections, in E. Lyons & A. Coyle (eds) *Analysing Qualitative Data in Psychology* (pp. 158–173). London: Sage.

Lyotard, J.-F. (1984) *The Postmodern Condition: A Report on Knowledge*. Manchester: Manchester University Press.

Macbeth, D. (2001) On 'reflexivity' in qualitative research: two readings, and a third. *Qualitative Inquiry*, 7(1), 35–68.

Madill, A., Jordan, A. & Shirley, C. (2000) Objectivity and reliability in qualitative analysis: realist, contextualist and radical constructionist epistemologies. *British Journal of Psychology*, 91, 1–20.

Mark, A. & Snowden, D. (2006) Research practice or practicing research: innovating methods in healthcare, in A.L. Casebeer, A. Harrison & A. Mark (eds) *Innovations in Health Care*. Houndmills: Palgrave Macmillan.

Marks, D.F. (2006) The case for a pluralist health psychology. *Journal of Health Psychology*, 11(3), 367–372.

Marks, D.F., Murray, M., Evans, B., Willig, C., Sykes, C.M. & Woodall, C. (2005) *Health Psychology* (2nd edn). London: Sage.

Marshall, C. & Rossman, G.B. (1989) *Designing Qualitative Research*. London: Sage.

Mason, J. (2006) Mixing methods in a qualitatively driven way. *Qualitative Research*, 6(1), 9–25.

Mattingly, C. & Garro, L.C. (2000) *Narrative and Cultural Construction of Illness and Healing*. Berkeley, CA: University of California Press.

McHoul, A. & Grace, W. (1998) *A Foucault Primer: Discourse, Power, and the Subject*. Malaysia: Melbourne University Press.

McLeod, J. (2001) *Qualitative Research in Counselling and Psychotherapy*. London: Sage.

Mead, G.H. (1934) *Mind, Self and Society from the Standpoint of a Social Behaviourist*. Chicago, IL: University of Chicago Press.

Mello, R.A. (2002) Collocation analysis: a method for conceptualizing and understanding narrative data. *Qualitative Research*, 2, 231–243.

Miller, T. (2005) *Making Sense of Motherhood: A Narrative Approach*. Cambridge: Cambridge University Press.

Mishler, E. (1986) *Research Interviewing: Context and Narrative*. Cambridge, MA: Harvard University Press.

Mishler, E. (1991) Representing discourse: the rhetoric of transcription. *Journal of Narrative and Life History*, 1(4), 255–280.

Mishler, E. (1995) Models of narrative analysis: a typology. *Journal of Narrative and Life History*, 5(2), 87–123.

Mishler, E. (1999) *Storylines: Craftartists' Narratives of Identity*. Cambridge, MA: Harvard University Press.

Moran, D. (2000) *Introduction to Phenomenology*. London: Routledge.

Moran-Ellis, J., Alexander, V.D., Cronin, A., Dickinson, M., Fielding, J., Sleney, J. & Thomas, H., (2006) Triangulation and integration: processes, claims and implications. *Qualitative Research*, 6(1), 45–59.

Morgan, G. (1997) *Images of Organization*. London: Sage.

Morse, J. (2007) Sampling in grounded theory, in A. Bryant & K. Charmaz (eds) *The Sage Handbook of Grounded Theory*. London: Sage.

Mruck, K. & Mey, G. (2007) Grounded theory and reflexivity, in A. Bryant & K. Charmaz (eds) *The Sage Handbook of Grounded Theory*. London: Sage.

Nolas, S.-M. (2007) Disrupting the emancipatory narrative: an ethnographic study of participation in a youth inclusion programme. Unpublished PhD thesis. London School of Economics.

Nolas, S.-M. (2009) Between the ideal and the real: using ethnography as a way of extending our language of change. *Qualitative Research in Psychology*, 6(1), 105–128.

Oakley, A. (1999) Paradigm wars: some thoughts on a personal and public trajectory. *International Journal of Social Research Methodology*, 2(3), 247–254.

Onwuegbuzie, A.J. & Leech, N.L. (2005) On becoming a pragmatic researcher: the importance of combining quantitative and qualitative Research methodologies. *International Journal of Social Research Methodology*, 8(5), 375–387.

Orr, J. (1996) *Talking about Machines: An Ethnography of a Modern Job*. Ithaca, NY: Cornell University Press.

Palmer, R. (1969) *Hermeneutics*. Evanston, IL: North-Western University Press.

Parker, I. (1992) *Discourse Dynamics: Critical Analysis for Social and Individual Psychology*. London: Routledge.

Patterson, W. (2008) Narratives of events: Labovian narrative analysis and its limitations, in M. Andrews, C. Squire & M. Tamboukou (eds) *Doing Narrative Research*. London: Sage.

Phoenix, C., Smith, B. & Sparkes, A. (2010) Narrative analysis in aging studies: a typology for consideration. *Journal of Aging Studies*, 24(1), 1–11.

Phoenix, C. & Sparkes, A. (2008) Athletic bodies and aging in context: the narrative construction of experienced and anticipated selves in time. *Journal of Aging Studies*, 22, 211–221.

Pomerantz, A. (1986) Extreme case formulations: a way of legitimizing claims. *Human Studies*, 9, 219–229.

Portelli, A. (1991) *The Death of Luigi Trastulli and Other Stories: Form and Meaning in Oral History*. Albany, NY: State University of New York Press.

Potter, J. (1996) *Representing Reality*. London: Sage.

Potter, J. & Wetherell, M. (1987) *Discourse and Social Psychology: Beyond Attitudes and Behaviour*, London: Sage.

Potter, J. & Wetherell, M. (1995) Discourse analysis, in J. Smith, R. Harre & L. Van Langenhove (eds) *Rethinking Methods in Psychology* (pp. 80–92). London: Sage.

Pratt, M.G. (2009) For the lack of a boilerplate: tips on writing up (and reviewing) qualitative research. *Academy of Management Journal*, 52(5), 856–862.

Prior, L. (2003) *Using Documents in Social Research*. London: Sage.

Prus, R.C. (1996) *Symbolic Interaction and Ethnographic Research: Intersubjectivity and the Study of Human Lived Experience*. Albany, NY: SUNY.

Radley, A. (1994) *Making Sense of Illness: The Social Psychology of Health and Illness*. London: Sage.

Reason, P. & Riley, S. (2008) Co-operative inquiry: an action research practice, in J.A. Smith (ed.) *Qualitative Psychology: A Practical Guide to Research Methods* (2nd edn). London: Sage Publications.

Reicher, S. (2000) Against methodolatry: some comments on Elliott, Fischer and Rennie. *British Journal of Clinical Psychology*, 39, 1– 6.

Reichertz, J. (2007) Abduction: the logic of discovery of grounded theory, in A. Bryant & K. Charmaz (eds) *The Sage Handbook of Grounded Theory*. London: Sage.

Reid, K., Flowers, P. & Larkin, M. (2005) Interpretative phenomenological analysis: an overview and methodological review. *The Psychologist*, 18, 20–23.

Richards, G. (2009) *Putting Psychology in its Place: Critical Historical Perspectives*. London: Routledge.

Richardson, L. (2000) Writing: a method of inquiry, in N.K. Denzin & Y.S. Lincoln (eds) *Handbook of Qualitative Research* (2nd edn). Thousand Oaks, CA: Sage.

Ricoeur, P. (1970) *Freud and Philosophy: An Essay on Interpretation*. New Haven, CT: Yale University Press.

Riessman, C.K. (1988) When gender is not enough. *Gender and Society*, 1(2), 172–207.

Riessman, C.K. (1993) *Narrative Analysis*. London: Sage.

Riessman, C.K. (2002) Analysis of personal narratives, in J.F. Gubrium & J.A. Holstein (eds) *Handbook of Interview Research*. Thousand Oaks, CA: Sage Publications.

Riessman, C.K. (2004) Narrative interviewing, in M.S. Lewis-Beck, A. Bryman & T. Futing Liao (eds) *Encyclopedia of Social Science Research Methods*. London: Sage Publications.

Riessman, C.K. (2005) Narrative analysis, in N. Kelly, C. Horrocks, K. Milnes, B. Roberts & D. Robinson (eds) *Narrative, Memory and Everyday Life*. Huddersfield: University of Huddersfield Press.

Riessman, C.K. (2008) *Narrative Methods for the Human Sciences*. Thousand Oaks, CA: Sage.

Riley, S.C.E., Sims-Schouten, W. & Willig, C. (2007) The case for critical realist discourse analysis as a viable method in discursive work. *Theory and Psychology*, 17(1), 137–145.

Riley, T. & Hawe, P. (2005) Researching practice: the methodological case for narrative inquiry. *Health Education Research*, 20(2), 226–236.

Robson, C. (2002) *Real World Research* (2nd edn). Oxford: Blackwell Publishing.

Rock, P. (2001) Symbolic interactionism and ethnography, in P. Atkinson, S. Delamont, A. Coffey, J. Lofland & L.H. Lofland (eds) *Handbook of Ethnography*. London: Sage.

Rosenwald, G.C. & Ochberg, R.L. (eds) (1992) *Storied Lives: The Cultural Politics of Self-Understanding*. New Haven, CT: Yale University Press.

Roulston, K. (2010) Considering quality in qualitative interviewing. *Qualitative Research*, 10(2), 199–228.

Sandstrom, K.L., Martin, D.D. & Fine, G.A. (2003) *Symbols, Selves and Social Reality.* Los Angeles, CA: Roxbury Press.

Sarbin, T.R. (1986) *Narrative Psychology: The Storied Nature of Human Conduct.* New York: Praeger.

Schön, D.A. (1983) *The Reflective Practitioner: How Professionals Think in Action.* New York: Basic Books.

Schwandt, T.A. (2000) Three epistemological stances for qualitative inquiry: interpretivism, hermeneutics and social constructionism, in N.L. Denzin & Y. Lincoln (eds) *Handbook of Qualitative Research* (pp. 189–213). London: Sage.

Shaw, R.L. (2001) Why use interpretative phenomenological analysis in health psychology? *Health Psychology Update,* 10(4), 48–52.

Shepperd, D., Coyle, A. & Hegarty, P. (2010) Discourses of friendship between heterosexual women and gay men: mythical norms and an absence of desire. *Feminism and Psychology,* 20(2), 205–224.

Shiffrin, D. (1987) *Discourse Markers.* Cambridge: Cambridge University Press.

Shinebourne, P. & Smith, J.A. (2009) Alcohol and the self: an interpretative phenomenological analysis of the experience of addiction and its impact on the sense of self and identity. *Addiction Research & Theory,* 17, 152–167.

Singh, I. (2002a) Bad boys, good mothers, and the 'miracle' of Ritalin. *Science in Context,* 15(4), 577–603.

Singh, I. (2002b) Biology in context: social and cultural perspectives on ADHD. *Children & Society,* 16, 360–367.

Singh, I. (2003) Boys will be boys: fathers' perspectives on ADHD symptoms, diagnosis, and drug treatment. *Harvard Review of Psychiatry,* 11(6), 308–316.

Singh, I. (2004) Doing their jobs: mothering with Ritalin in a culture of mother-blame. *Social Science & Medicine,* 59, 1193–1205.

Singh, I. (2005) Will the 'real boy' please behave: dosing dilemmas for parents of boys with ADHD. *American Journal of Bioethics,* 5(3), 34–37.

Smith, B. & Sparkes, A. (2008) Contrasting perspectives on narrative selves and identities: an invitation to dialogue. *Qualitative Research,* 8(1), 213–242.

Smith, D. (1978) K is mentally ill: the anatomy of a factual account. *Sociology,* 12, 23–53.

Smith, J.A. (1996) Beyond the divide between cognition and discourse: using interpretative phenomenological analysis in health psychology. *Psychology & Health,* 11(2), 261–271.

Smith, J.A. (1999) Towards a relational self: social engagement during pregnancy and psychological preparation for motherhood. *British Journal of Social Psychology,* 38(4), 409–426.

Smith, J.A. (2004) Reflecting on the development of interpretative phenomenological analysis and its contribution to qualitative research in psychology. *Qualitative Research in Psychology,* 1(1), 39–54.

Smith, J.A. (2007) Hermeneutics, human sciences and health: linking theory and practice. *International Journal of Qualitative Studies on Health and Well-Being*, 2(1), 3–11.

Smith, J.A. & Eatough, V. (2007) Interpretative phenomenological analysis, in E. Lyons & A. Coyle (eds). *Analysing Qualitative Data in Psychology: A Practical & Comparative Guide* (pp. 35–50). London: Sage.

Smith, J.A. & Osborn, M. (2003) Interpretative phenomenological analysis, in J.A. Smith (ed.) *Qualitative Psychology: A Practical Guide to Research Methods* (pp. 51–80). London: Sage Publications.

Smith, J.A. & Osborn, M. (2007) Pain as an assault on the self: an interpretative phenomenological analysis of the psychological impact of chronic benign low back pain. *Psychology & Health*, 22(5), 517–534.

Smith, J.A., Flowers, P. & Larkin, M. (2009) *Interpretive Phenomenological Analysis: Theory, Method, and Research*. London: Sage.

Smith, J.A., Harre, R. & Van Langenhove, L. (1995) Idiography and the case study, in J. Smith, R. Harre & L. Van Langenhove (eds) *Rethinking Psychology* (pp. 59–69). London: Sage.

Smith, J.A., Jarman, M. & Osborne, M. (1999) Doing interpretative phenomenological analysis, in M. Murray & K. Chamberlain (eds) *Qualitative Health Psychology*. London: Sage.

Somers, M.R. (1994) The narrative constitution of identity: a relational and network approach. *Theory and Society*, 23, 605–649.

Squire, C. (2005) Reading narratives. *Group Analysis*, 38(1), 91–107.

Squire, C., Andrews, M. & Tamboukou, M. (2008) Introduction: what is narrative research?, in M. Andrews, C. Squire & M. Tamboukou (eds) *Doing Narrative Research*. London: Sage.

Star, S.L. (2007) Living grounded theory: cognitive and emotional forms, in A. Bryant & K. Charmaz (eds) *The Sage Handbook of Grounded Theory*. London: Sage.

Steffen, E. & Coyle, A. (2010) Can 'sense of presence' experiences in bereavement be conceptualised as spiritual phenomena? *Mental Health, Religion & Culture*, 13, 273–291.

Stenner, P. (1993) Discoursing jealousy, in E. Burman & I. Parker (eds) *Discourse Analytic Research* (pp. 114–134). London: Routledge.

Stern, P.N. (2007) On solid ground: essential properties for growing grounded theory, in A. Bryant & K. Charmaz (eds) *The Sage Handbook of Grounded Theory*. London: Sage.

Strauss, A.L. & Corbin, J. (1990) *Basics of Qualitative Research*. London: Sage.

Stryker, S. (1981) Symbolic interactionism: themes and variations, in M. Rosenberg & R.H. Turner (eds) *Social Psychology: Sociological Perspectives*. New York: Basic Books.

Tashakkori, A. & Teddlie, C. (1998) *Mixed Methodology: Combining Qualitative and Quantitative Approaches.* Thousands Oaks, CA: Sage.

Tashakkori, A. & Teddlie, C. (2003) Issues and dilemmas in teaching research methods courses in social and behavioural sciences: US perspective. *International Journal of Social Research Methodology*, 6, 61–77.

Tedlock, B. (2003) Ethnography and ethnographic representation, in N.K. Denzin & Y.S. Lincoln (eds) *Strategies for Qualitative Research* (2nd edn). Thousand Oaks, CA: Sage.

Teram, E., Schachter, C.L. & Stalker, C.A. (2005) The case for integrating grounded theory and participatory action research: empowering clients to inform professional practice. *Qualitative Health Research*, 15(8), 1129–1140.

Thomas, W.I. & Znaniecki, F. (1927) *The Polish Peasant in Europe and America (Vols 1 and 2).* New York: Knopf.

Thomas, W.I. & Znaniecki, F. (1996) *The Polish Peasant in Europe and America: A Classic Work in Immigration.* Urbana, IL: University of Illinois Press.

Timmermans, S. & Tavory, I. (2007) Advancing ethnographic research through grounded theory practice, in A. Bryant & K. Charmaz (eds) *The Sage Handbook of Grounded Theory.* London: Sage.

Todd, Z., Nerlich, B., McKeown, S. & Clarke, D.D. (2004) *Mixing Methods in Psychology: The Integration of Qualitative and Quantitative Methods in Theory and Practice.* Hove: Psychology Press.

Turner, A., Barlow, J. & Ilbery, B. (2002) Play hurt, live hurt: living with and managing osteoarthritis from the perspective of ex-professional footballers. *Journal of Health Psychology*, 7(3), 285–301.

Turner, A.J. & Coyle, A. (2000) What does it mean to be a donor offspring? The identity experiences of adults conceived by donor insemination and the implications for counselling and therapy. *Human Reproduction*, 15, 2041–2051.

Ussher, J.M. (2003) The role of premenstrual dysphoric disorder in the subjectification of women. *Journal of Medical Humanities*, 24(1/2), 131–146.

Van Maanen, J. (1988) *Tales of the Field: On Writing Ethnography.* Chicago, IL: University of Chicago Press.

Van Manen, M. (1990) *Researching Lived Experience: Human Science for an Action Sensitive Pedagogy.* Albany, NY: State University of New York Press.

Walton, C. (2007) Doing discourse analysis, in E. Lyons & A. Coyle (eds) *Analysing Qualitative Data in Psychology* (pp. 117–130). London: Sage.

Ware, N.C. (1999) Toward a model of social discourse in chronic illness: the example of chronic fatigue syndrome. *Culture, Medicine and Psychiatry*, 23, 303–331.

Warner, S. & Spandler, H. (forthcoming) *Qualitative Research in Psychology: Special issue on Pluralism in Qualitative Research in Psychology.*

Wetherell, M. (1998) Positioning and interpretative repertoires: conversation analysis and post-structuralism in dialogue. *Discourse and Society*, 9(3), 387–412.

Wetherell, M. (2008) Subjectivity or psycho-discursive practices? Investigating complex intersectional identities. *Subjectivity*, 22, 73–81.

Wetherell, M. & Potter, J. (1992) *Mapping the Language of Racism*. London: Harvester-Wheatsheaf.

Wilkinson, S. (1988) The role of reflexivity in feminist psychology. *Women's Studies International Forum*, 11, 493–502.

Willig, C. (1999) Beyond appearances: a critical realist approach to social constructionist work in psychology, in D. Nightingale & J. Cromby (eds) *Social Constructionist Psychology: A Critical Analysis of Theory and Practice* (pp. 37–51). Buckingham: Open University Press.

Willig, C. (2000) *Introducing Qualitative Research in Psychology: Adventures in Theory and Method*. Milton Keynes: Open University Press.

Willig, C. (2008) *Introducing Qualitative Research in Psychology*. Maidenhead: McGraw-Hill, Open University Press.

Willig, C. & Stainton-Rogers, W. (eds) (2008) *Handbook of Qualitative Research in Psychology*. London: Sage Publications.

Wilson, D. (2009) *A History of British Serial Killing*. London: Sphere.

Wolcott, H. (2009) *Writing Up Qualitative Research* (3rd edn). Thousand Oaks, CA: Sage Publications.

Wood, L. & Kroger, R. (2000) *Doing Discourse Analysis*. London: Sage.

Wood, L.A. & Rennie, H. (1994) Formulating rape: the discursive construction of victims and villains. *Discourse & Society*, 5, 125–148.

Yardley, L. (2007) Demonstrating validity in qualitative psychology, in J.A. Smith (ed.) *A Practical Guide to Research Methods* (2nd edn). London: Sage Publications.

Yardley, L. & Bishop, F. (2008) Mixing qualitative and quantitative methods: a pragmatic approach, in C. Willig & W. Stainton-Rogers (eds) *The Sage Handbook of Qualitative Research in Psychology* (pp. 240–259). London: Sage Publications.

Zahavi, D. (2008) Phenomenology, in D. Moran (ed.) *Routledge Companion to Twentieth-Century Philosophy*. London: Routledge.

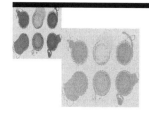

Index

Locators shown in *italics* refer to figures, tables, case studies and boxes.

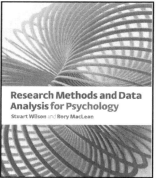

RESEARCH METHODS AND DATA ANALYSIS FOR PSYCHOLOGY

Stuart Wilson and Rory MacLean

9780077121655 (Paperback)
2011

eBook also available

This book has been written to show students that research methods and data analysis can be interesting and to help students understand why the subject is important.

Key features:

- Provides a comprehensive coverage of research methods and statistics with an introduction to SPSS all in one accessible volume
- Uses clearly illustrated links between research methods and statistics to help students understand how their choice of analysis is informed by research design and vice versa
- Covers qualitative and quantitative research methods

www.openup.co.uk

OPEN UNIVERSITY PRESS
McGraw - Hill Education

INTRODUCING PSYCHOLOGY THROUGH RESEARCH

Amanda Albon

9780335221349 (Paperback)
2007

eBook also available

This student-friendly textbook clearly outlines the subject matter and research methods used in psychology for those who are new to the subject. A brief overview of the history of psychology is followed by chapters covering the core research areas defined by the British Psychological Society.

Key features:

- Provides an overview of major sub-disciplines in psychology and introduces the key concepts in that area of research
- Presents a summary of an original research paper for each topic discussed
- Includes an overview of the ethics of psychological research

www.openup.co.uk

 OPEN UNIVERSITY PRESS
McGraw · Hill Education

QUALITATIVE METHODS IN PSYCHOLOGY
A Research Guide
Second Edition

Peter Banister

9780335243051 (Paperback)
October 2011

eBook also available

Qualitative Methods in Psychology: A Research Guide, the *Second Edition,* provides advanced undergraduate and postgraduate psychology students with an accessible introduction to qualitative methods. It combines a solid grounding in the theory behind research methods, as well as serving as a practical guide to conducting qualitative investigations and a critical assessment of these methods.

Key features:

- Covers the BPS syllabus for Qualitative Methods
- Shows readers how to evaluate methods critically
- Includes new chapters on phenomenology, psychosocial analysis, narrative inquiry, future directions for qualitative research, emerging forms of representation, and problems in qualitative research

www.openup.co.uk

LEARNING TO USE STATISTICAL TESTS IN PSYCHOLOGY
Third Edition

Judith Greene and Manuela D'Oliveira
9780335216802 (Paperback)
2005

eBook also available

Learning to Use Statistical Tests in Psychology Third Edition has been updated throughout. It continues to be a key text in helping students to understand and conduct statistical tests in psychology without panic! It takes students from the most basic elements of statistics.

Key features:

- Provides students with a step-by-step guide to the simplest non-parametric tests
- Includes a section on the principles of psychological research and psychological statistics
- Incorporates statistical tests based on ANOVA (Analysis of Variance) conditions as well as tests for multiple comparisons between individual conditions

OPEN UNIVERSITY PRESS
McGraw - Hill Education

www.openup.co.uk

INTRODUCING QUALITATIVE RESEARCH IN PSYCHOLOGY
Second Edition

Carla Willig

9780335221158 (Paperback)
2008

eBook also available

Introducing Qualitative Research in Psychology is a vital resource for students new to qualitative psychology. It offers a clear introduction to the topic by taking six different approaches to qualitative methods and explaining when each one should be used, the procedures and techniques involved, and any limitations associated with such research.

Key features:

- Contains more interactive exercises and tasks
- Includes three qualitative research reports with annotations highlighting key issues for novice researchers
- Examines appropriate ways of writing up research

www.openup.co.uk

OPEN UNIVERSITY PRESS
McGraw - Hill Education

DESIGNING AND REPORTING
EXPERIMENTS IN PSYCHOLOGY
Third Edition

Peter Harris

9780335221783 (Paperback)
2008

eBook also available

This book will help undergraduate psychology students to write practical reports
of experimental and other quantitative studies in psychology. It is designed to
help with every stage of the report writing process including what to put in each
section and recommendations for formatting and style. It also discusses how to
design a study, including how to use and report relevant statistics. As such, the
book acts both as an introduction and reference source to be used throughout an
undergraduate course.

Key features:

- Provides new pedagogy website icons
- Includes a completely revised section on how to find and cite references
- Gives advice on the ethics of conducting research on the Internet

www.openup.co.uk

SPSS SURVIVAL MANUAL
Fourth Edition

Julie Pallant

9780335242399 (Paperback)
2010

eBook also available

In this thoroughly revised edition of her bestselling text, now covering up to version 18 of the SPSS software, Julie Pallant guides you through the entire research process, helping you choose the right data analysis technique for your project.

Key features:

- Outlines each technique used clearly
- Provides easy to follow step-by-step procedures for performing the analysis
- Supported by a website with sample data and guidelines on report writing.

www.openup.co.uk

OPEN UNIVERSITY PRESS
McGraw - Hill Education